PLAY, SHAPE, CREATE

Play, Shape, Create: The Joyful Art of Songwriting

This book is set in the typeface Myriad Pro designed by Carol Twombly, Robert Slimbach at Adobe Fonts.

Paperback ISBN: 978-1-967262-22-9

A Publication of *Tall Pine Books*
PO Box 42 Warsaw | Indiana 46581
www.tallpinebooks.com

| 1 26 26 20 16 02 |

Published in the United States of America

PLAY, SHAPE, CREATE

The Joyful Art of Songwriting

Aryn Michelle Calhoun

Table of Contents

INTRODUCTION

Red Rover, Red Rover

"It is impossible to look good and get better at the same time."
Julia Cameron

Red rover, red rover, songwriters come over! I'm inviting you to run full speed into a songwriting experience all about *play*. I don't want you to worry about what you know or don't know, or how many songs you have or haven't written. I've set out to write a book on songwriting that is accessible for almost any songwriter ready to take their craft to the next level. If you don't know the technical difference between a verse and a chorus, come on over—there's something for you. Even if you've been penning lyrics and recording songs for years, I still think you'll find new ideas and inspiration through these exercises and content. You might get jostled around a little bit, but we're having fun, so lean into it! The game wouldn't be much fun if we didn't stumble and spin and fall down a bit along the way.

But before you "run over," let me introduce myself. My name is Aryn Michelle Calhoun, a songwriter and recording artist with hundreds of songs and many albums under my belt. Sure, I've learned a lot through my experience, but I've also found that songwriting is not about resting on your past accomplishments; it's about noticing and discovering what's next to create. I may not be famous, and I've definitely never had a Top 40 hit, but that doesn't matter. Why? Because I'm a good songwriter and I care deeply about helping others find joy in the process of writing songs. If you're only reading this book to find a fast track to fame, I'd suggest you turn back now. This book is about joyful play, not a road map to a record deal. But it's not completely reckless play—we're gonna learn a lot of technical tricks as we go.

So, who am I? Ultimately, I'm a student, a teacher, and a lover of songs.

A Lover of Songs

As a lover of songs, I'm writing a book that I hope will help you fall in love with the characteristics of songs that make them connect and last. There's so much to love about songs. They can accomplish so much in just a short time. They can transport us through time and space. They meet us in life-altering moments and sustain us in the doldrums of the everyday.

I spent most of my childhood with an FM radio by my side. I was, and still am, obsessed with the era of music from 1960 to 1975. Born in the 1980s, my parents thought the oldies station was pretty innocuous, so I was allowed to soak it in morning, noon, and night. Stevie Wonder, Elton John, Three Dog Night…these were my musical heroes. I once called in on a landline telephone to the oldies station to request "Classical Gas" from the night DJ. I think I was 11 years old. What a weird kid, right?

As a teenager in the 90s, I embraced alternative rock and female singer/songwriters as my sonic role models. Alanis Morissette, Sarah McLachlan, Jewel, and Gwen Stefani (from the No Doubt era) sang me through high school. And the intrigue with different genres didn't stop there! I studied classical music in undergrad and added jazz when I took even more college. The main problem I face, and still do, is that there's just too much music to love. I'll never be able to listen to it all.

The thing I love most about music is *the* song—the one that sticks with me, the one that can be reinterpreted by many artists, and the one that can change my attitude, my mindset, and pierce down to my soul. So, I set out to discover how songs can make me love them so much.

A Student of Songs

My passion for music and songwriting inspired me to study songs. Now, I'm writing the book I wish I had when I was 18. I didn't have a good textbook or songwriting teacher at that moment when songwriting shifted from a hobby to a full-fledged passion. I was just a singer who stumbled blindly into songwriting.

I always wanted to be a singer. In fact, I spent most of my childhood convinced that being a famous singer was my destiny. When I was 15, I cajoled my mom into taking me to a talent competition hosted by a small record label in Oklahoma City. I sang a CeCe Winans song that was *way* too hard for me, performed terribly and was immediately cut from the competition. Do not pass go, do not collect a record deal. However, what happened next changed my life. I watched as the young woman who had won the competition accompanied herself on the piano while singing an *original* song she had written. I had never considered accompanying myself, let alone writing my own songs!

As they say, you learn much more from defeat than from victory. And as fast and brilliant as a lightning strike, I knew that writing my own songs was what I truly wanted to do. So, I spent years experimenting with songwriting on my own. Like a child finger painting, I clumsily taught myself to play chords on the piano while trying to sing at the same time. I created primitive charts and labeled so many chords incorrectly that my early songs are barely coherent. I was writing blobs of song sections. Was that part a verse? A chorus? Who knew! All I knew was that I was discovering myself through every word and melody I tried to string together.

By the time I headed to college, I realized I needed more guidance and wisdom from the masters to turn my hobby into a craft. If that's where you find yourself as you read these words, you're in the right place. Or maybe you've kept songwriting on the back burner for a long time, but now you're ready to start cooking with more nuanced flavors. I believe you'll find what you're seeking in these pages as well.

A Teacher of Songs

I started as a lover of songs, then became a student of songs, and now I am a teacher of songs. To be completely honest with you, I never wanted to be a teacher. I thought music teachers were people who couldn't make it as performers. Years ago, I reluctantly tried teaching piano lessons to elementary-aged kids, but it wasn't my passion. Later, I taught voice lessons to college students, and I liked that a bit more, but it still wasn't my sweet spot. But when I had the chance to teach a songwriting class, there was that lightning strike again. I had finally found something I could do all day that didn't feel like "work."

Teaching songwriting is a thrill because it's an ever-evolving art form. No two writers or songs are ever exactly the same. Since I started teaching songwriting seriously, I've been searching for that one book that could carry me through a single class with students of almost any experience level. Many great songwriting books exist, but I'm a little high-maintenance, and I still haven't found *the one*. I wanted a book that covers melody, lyrics, and harmony, each with appropriate weight. I wanted a book that addresses the dozen or so topics I believe are most important and includes practical exercises, games, and play. So I tried to create it for you.

I'd like to take a moment to acknowledge my teaching assistant, colleague, and friend, Hallie Mares Jewett, who spent many months helping me craft the "playtime" activities, as well as proofreading and suggesting edits to this book to make it more thoughtful, practical, and inspiring. I couldn't have written it without her. We've both learned a great deal from other writers and teachers, so there will be plenty of content in the bibliography to give credit to those we've learned from and provide references for further reading. If you've ever thought, *I'd love to try teaching a songwriting class at my school*, or *I'd love to have a book my songwriting friends and I could work through together*, or even *I'm ready to take a songwriting class on my own terms*, then you're in good company.

A Soapbox

We titled this book *Play, Shape, Create: The Joyful Art of Songwriting* because we want to encourage you to play and explore. I'm going to step onto my soapbox from the beginning because how you think about your creations before, during, and after you make them has massive implications on how you experience freedom in songwriting. I'm going to ask you to set aside the restrictions of "industry standards" and the voices of gatekeepers who would tell you "things *must* be this way" to write a hit or secure a publishing or record deal. We are focused on joyful artmaking here, not being slaves to what sells. Consider that authentic songwriting is a discipline with no rules. There are guidelines, best practices, and preferences, but no hard-and-fast rules. Why? Because it's morally "bad" to break rules. We're not here to create or break rules. We're here to *play*—to make weird and wonderful things and connect with what we *want* to say, do, and experience in each moment.

Of course, there are tried and true songwriting techniques worth mastering, and we're going to talk about many of them. However, the more you write, the more you realize these guidelines can be veered away from in many situations. Your songs may begin to cry out to tell you when they need an exception, not some "rule."

Every song and songwriter is unique. We all have different passions and paces. Before we dig in too deep, I want to offer a few words of advice for those who like to read/write/work quickly and those who prefer to do so more slowly. Neither disposition is wrong, but both come with inherent strengths and challenges.

How to Use This Book

For those of you who are "fast writers"—list checker-offers and goal keepers—I would encourage you to take the time to slow down while reading through this book. Look up the lyrics I ask you to look up. Do all the solo exercises at the end of each chapter. Then do them again. Don't rush to the finish. The good work *and* fun are in the journey. Songwriting is not about assembly line efficiency; it's about eccentricities and exploration.

If you consider yourself to be more of a "slow writer"—prone to overthinking, overworking, and not quite ever finishing a song—I encourage you to let go of perfection and play around. Try adding words and sounds that don't make sense, but *feel* right. Try to finish a song even if you know it might be better one day. Take chances. You can't do songwriting "wrong." Remember that songs are subjective; there are no rules, just guidelines that are frequently ignored.

You may be tempted to give up and stop going through this book when it gets hard. But I want to encourage you to push past the difficult parts and keep going. You may be tempted not to finish a solo exercise or a song assignment because your idea doesn't seem clever enough. Keep digging and write it anyway. Pat Pattison has famously said that sometimes you need to write some "fertilizer" songs—the stinky ones that provide fertile ground for the hearty song growing beneath them. It's ok to get your hands dirty.

Each chapter will explore a different songwriting concept and conclude with solo activities, group activities, homework, and song assignments to keep you engaged in playing. Use this book on your own, with a friend, with a songwriting cohort, or to teach a class. Do the activities and challenges as they are, or adapt them to make them work for you. Read them and then throw them out the window if you're inspired to create better activities. Whatever you do, just don't forget to play.

QR Codes: You'll find a QR code next to the title of most chapters. Scan the code for a playlist of the song examples discussed within the chapter.

Solo Activities: These are songwriting "games" you can do alone to explore the concepts. There is no way to do them wrong. If you are a junkie for solo activities, I'd highly recommend getting a copy of *The Art of Noticing* by Rob Walker and *Songwriters Playground* by Barbara L. Jordan.

Group Activities: Do these in a class or with a group of friends or co-writers. Some activities may not be a good fit for every group, so you'll want to modify them accordingly. For additional group activities beyond this book, check out Chapter 8 of Andrea Stolpe's *Beginning Songwriting*.

Homework Challenges: Homework challenges are included for those who desire a more formal songwriting course or for those using this book that way. But even if you're just reading this book for fun (I promise you won't be graded), you can still do the homework. It's only going to make you a better songwriter, so why not?

Song Challenges: Each chapter concludes with two songwriting prompts that encourage you to use the concepts covered as you create a new song. If you commit to writing a song from all of the prompts in this book, then you'll walk away with 30 new songs. Not too shabby!

No matter how many songs you've written, I think you'll find something new in the pages that follow. I've read *a lot* of books on songwriting, so I'm not here to tell you that all of these ideas are uniquely mine. This book is an amalgamation of my original ideas and the most important concepts I've gleaned from other teachers of songwriting. I've tried my best to give credit to these teachers, books, and resources, so you will find a bibliography and references for further reading at the end of the book.

Let the Games Begin

This is going to be fun, but it won't be easy. When faced with "creativity for creativity's sake," everyone quickly starts pushing their own agendas. It's difficult to dance in the middle of the day for no reason. I know because I tried it once! I put on my favorite dance songs, turned them up extra loud, and started twirling in the living room. My husband, my 5-year-old, and my phone all immediately tried to stop me in my tracks, demanding that I attend to "more pressing matters."

Couldn't everyone see I was dancing?

As you embark on this adventure in songwriting, be prepared to resist the forces that will try to demand your attention or tell you that your search for creativity is something to put on the back burner once again. Other voices—even the one in your own head—may tell you what you're doing is silly or unimportant. But please don't view your songwriting as an easily dismissible, low-priority activity. Commit yourself to the process and play for real.

Lastly, try not to get distracted by the accessories to songwriting. You don't need a lot of fancy instruments or gear. Don't worry about the publishing deal just yet. All you need is some melody and lyrics. It's not always bad to consider producers and recording timelines or social media and streams, but that's not the game we're playing here. Keep your eye on the ball. Keep your hands in the clay. Dance a little. Run full speed ahead. And red rover, red rover...songwriters come over.

CHAPTER 1

Playdough Monster

A Songwriting Philosophy

"Becoming a successful writer in any field…is a process of learning to let go of the mediocre, with the implicit belief that you will replace it with something much better." Sheila Davis

Imagine with me that you have a best friend who has just had a baby, and they've invited you over to meet the child for the first time. This precious baby is the love of their life, the apple of their eye. They are perfect in every way to your friend, and Mom and Dad are hopelessly in love—as they should be.

They greet you at the front door and slowly walk you back to the nursery, telling you how much they can't wait for you to meet the baby. You're ushered past mountains of diaper boxes as they tell you how their world has turned upside down. They gingerly open the nursery door, and you tiptoe in to peer over the bassinet at the slumbering babe. The moment has arrived for you to react, and you instinctively know just the right words to say. You whisper, "She's so precious—absolutely perfect," and you've done your duty as a loving and loyal friend. You've gazed intently at a precious baby and proclaimed it perfect. As you should!

But songwriters, we are not gathered here, reading this book, to gaze at precious babies. Babies are coddled and protected. Babies are to be handled with soft voices and care. And if we treat our songs like precious babies, there's only one type of feedback we can hear. Anything less than "perfect" feels offensive. Remember, we're not here to fawn over precious babies. We are here to *play*. And when you play, things can't be perfect. Paint must be splattered. Knees may be skinned. You might even use a little too much glue and glitter, so to speak.

I would like to introduce you to the songwriting philosophy I call the "Playdough Monster." We are going to start thinking about our songs (especially while we are creating and editing them) as playdough monsters instead of precious babies. With that in mind, let's revisit the opening scene and see if it feels any different.

Playdough Monsters

Think back to when you were 8 years old and imagine this with me. Your best friend just invited you over to open a new jar of playdough for the first time. This new playdough is instantly the most interesting thing in the room, and you can't wait to dig into the colorful blob with infinite potential. It's soft and smells fresh, and it feels nice between your fingers. After a few minutes, your friend shouts, "Look at my monster!" They show you their creation and explain that their monster has stripes, can fly, has eight arms, and only eats candy. Your friend parades their playdough monster around the table and gives it an otherworldly roar.

Now, the moment has arrived: It's your turn to play. "It's so cool! But what if it had eight *eyes* too? What if it were taller and had polka dots instead? What if he also ate garbage?!" You've done your duty as a fun playmate—you've kept the game and the creativity going.

This chapter is meant to encourage you to stop seeing your songs as precious babies and instead start seeing them as playdough monsters: creations that are moldable, flexible, and flourishing in their potential. The songwriters who struggle to grow are the ones who think of their songs as precious babies they couldn't possibly be asked to change. But if you're reading this book, then I believe you are somewhat open to this playdough monster philosophy. However, I acknowledge that a transition from a precious baby to a playdough monster songwriting style can be quite extreme. So, let's outline some steps to work toward it.

The first step in this process is choosing your playmates wisely. We are *not* asking you to subject your songs, your new creations, to anyone and everyone for overly critical or ill-informed feedback. You don't want to show your playdough monster to someone who only wants to smash it to bits. And maybe don't show your new playdough monster to someone who has never played with playdough before. Writer and teacher Julia Cameron advises that it can "create embarrassment and discomfort to show a project too early to too many people." If we open ourselves up to too much creative abuse, especially in the early stages of a particular creation, then we may be tempted to shelve our song or our dream to be a songwriter before we really even get started.

Seek out songwriting peers, teachers, and trusted creative friends who are willing to engage your creations with encouragement, empathy, and nuance. If you encounter playmates who only point out what's wrong with your playdough monster because they know how they would do it better, it's okay not to schedule any more playdates with them. However, playmates who never challenge you to grow, change, and dream bigger can also hold you back. My thoughtful and empathetic teaching assistant, Hallie, became one of these people in my life as I continue to learn to be a better teacher. She has played a huge role in helping me write this book with you in mind. The best collaborators care about discovering the heart of what you're doing, enabling you to take steps to the next level by offering critique from a place of understanding.

Now, I know exposing something we've created to critique is hard. It requires humility, vulnerability, and bravery. Thankfully, there are gradual stages in our songwriting journey that help us go from being a parent of precious song babies to becoming a crafter of playdough monsters. For most songwriters, it's a step-by-step process, not an overnight shift.

So, what does that process look like?

What Stage are You In? (All Answers Valid)

I asked Hallie to describe how she experienced the different "stages" of growth as a songwriter, and she broke it down into four categories. She first resonated with the **"Precious Baby"** stage of the beginning songwriter who struggled to receive feedback without taking offense. We've all been there—it takes time and courage to build the confidence to be vulnerable.

Next, she entered what she called her **"Lego Building"** stage, where there was more room to fall in love with the craft of songwriting through willingness to analyze, shift pieces, and rebuild. This stage was a realization that songwriting isn't just about pouring out raw emotions, but it's also a dynamic and interactive building process.

After this, Hallie entered her **"Sandboxing"** stage, where instinct and experimentation became more comfortable, leading to greater openness in meeting others in the sandbox to play. Going into the songwriting experience with flexible expectations and an open mind led to new ways of writing songs, including cowriting.

Eventually, Hallie felt comfortable with the full-on **"Playdough Monstering"** stage, where collaboration and feedback are no longer discouraging or offensive, but rather desired and treasured. She felt the freedom to create, twist, squish, and reimagine her way toward art. No longer intimidated by the process, she was instead finding joy in the discovery.

My hope for you is to reach this stage where you anticipate that you can uncover something special and bring forth songs that possess beauty, depth, and the ability to connect with others. Songwriting can become more than just a cathartic diary entry. It can be a symphony of artistic expression that marries music and words in a way that reaches beyond ourselves, our years, and our spheres of influence.

It has been my joy as a teacher to work with students like Hallie who continue to challenge themselves to break new boundaries with their songwriting. She is fiercely talented, yet also thoughtful and empathetic. I have learned and continue to learn about songwriting through interacting with my students. You will read about many of my interactions with them throughout the book.

One of the first lessons I learned from teaching songwriting is that you can't push too hard too soon. I used to jump straight into playdough monster songwriting with my first-year students. I probably overwhelmed a few of them by giving them too much feedback too soon, and for that, I apologize and strive to make amends! Hallie helped me realize that playdough monster songwriting is not a philosophy that can be applied with the flip of a switch. For most writers, its application takes time and experience, a little bit of faith and courage. So, whatever stage you find yourself at, you are welcome here.

Red Cabbages and Onions

There is a Van Gogh painting entitled *Red Cabbages and Onions*. The title of this painting was not selected by Van Gogh himself; rather, it was assigned to the painting by his estate after his death. *Red Cabbages and Onions* lived in several museums and was prominently displayed for decades, treasured because of the fame and genius of Van Gogh.

But despite its popularity, there was one big problem with the title... Van Gogh didn't actually paint red cabbages and onions.

To clarify, Van Gogh did create this painting with his own two hands, but what Van Gogh had painted was red cabbages and *garlic* (not onions). Over 100 years after it was labeled *Red Cabbages and Onions* (in 1928), a chef named Ernest De Witt, a 38-year-old art lover, finally took notice of the mislabeled vegetables and questioned the title of the piece. Sarah Cascone for ArtNet reported that "Scholars and experts had studied the painting for nearly a century without anyone questioning what kind of vegetable was pictured in the work."[1]

1 "A Museum Has Renamed a Vegetable Still Life by Van Gogh After a Chef Spotted Something Was Off About the Onions." *ArtNet News*, October 24, 2023. https://news.artnet.com/art-world/chef-spots-misidentified-vegetable-in-van-gogh-still-life-2287691.

A title for this painting was quickly assigned before fully understanding each element of the work. Once that title was linked to the piece, no one challenged it. Similarly, we can be tempted to fall into red-cabbage-and-onion songwriting. (I'm talking specifically to you, fast writers!) We jot something down, choose an opening chord, and sing the first melody that comes to mind. Then, it becomes cemented as a definitive part of our song without coming back to question it.

In his book *Art and Faith,* artist and writer Makoto Fujimura shared, "Most of the time, we are trained not to see, but to categorize and move on. It's our basic survival mode." But we don't want to create in survival mode. To be a playdough monster songwriter, we've got to start re-training our brains to go beyond just being sufficient. We need to tolerate, in a sense, the perceived inefficiency of play. So, we must refuse to settle. Don't settle for the same kind of song you've always written. Don't settle for having writer's block. We'll begin by resisting fixed labels as we write new songs—resisting the urge to label anything as "my chorus," "my first line," or "my title"—and instead keeping the process open-ended.

Red-cabbage-and-onion songwriting can hold back more than just our songs. It can seep into our mindset about who we are as songwriters. We can be tempted to think we can only write one genre of song. Or that we're only considered a "successful" songwriter if we hear our songs on the radio, or make the editorial playlist, or win a songwriting contest. That's red-cabbages-and-onions, my friends. Don't label the song or the songwriter until the creations are more fully known, and until we've had some time and space to reflect.

Practical Playdough Monstering

Let's get practical. What does playdough monster songwriting mean, and how can you apply it to your own writing? It's a philosophy you can embrace during editing, and hopefully (eventually) while you are creating songs. I encourage students toward playdough monstering when I ask questions like:

"I wonder what would happen if your chorus becomes your pre-chorus?"
"Can we consider taking line 4 of your verse and swapping it with line 1?"
"Can we try the song 20 bpm faster, and give it a different underlying groove?"
"We've got two big ideas here. Can we separate them and find which one is at the heart of the song?"

Playdough monstering can have cascading effects. If you really get your hands dirty and play with one thing, it might compel you to start playing with another element of your song. (Spoiler: It probably will.) It's fun if you trust the process, but it's maddening if you're dead set on tightly clutching that Polaroid of your precious baby.

Letting Go of "Good" and "Bad"

I've been harping on the precious baby for a while now, but it's crucial to acknowledge that songwriters have big feelings, as we should. It's okay to wrestle with how our emotions get tangled up with our art. We are embodied artists with histories, wounds, and fears, *yet* we are still looking for beauty and truth in broken places. What I'm asking you to do isn't simple, and I still don't think it is. Untangling my identity from my artistic creations is a challenging task, and I continue to work on it.

Is my newest song a little reflection of myself? Maybe yes. Is it a true representation of all of me? Absolutely not. If someone judges your precious baby, they're basically insulting you. If someone disses your playdough monster, you don't have to take it personally. They just didn't get it, or it wasn't really meant for them anyway. In an episode of the TV series *This Is Pop*, T-Pain said, "I just want to make music that makes me feel good, and if you don't like it, I didn't make it for you. If you do like it, welcome to the club."

First, we've got to stop thinking about other people's songs—from Taylor Swift's latest hit to your Aunt Linda's song she wrote for bible study—as "good" or "bad." Start to take "good" and "bad" out of your song vocabulary and replace them with "I like it" or "I don't like it," then provide specific reasons why. This will help you not just as a music listener, but as a songwriter. Let's practice:

If you tend to say things like "That new Beyoncé song was so bad!"

(It wasn't necessarily bad, you just didn't like it.)

Instead, try "I had a difficult time emotionally connecting to that new Beyoncé song because of the subject matter."

(This is a more honest and specific assessment.)

Or try "I didn't prefer the new Beyoncé song to her previous record because the genre shift took it to a place that's not my favorite."

(By taking ownership over your preferences, you can leave "good" and "bad" out of it.)

Why are we practicing on Beyoncé? Because I want you to start practicing for when you interact with your *own* songs. Letting go of "good" and "bad" is one of the steps along the journey toward playdough monster songwriting. We're gonna talk a lot more about this in a later chapter, but for now, remember that embracing "I like it" or "I don't like it" opens up a world of possibilities that leads us to the important question of "why." When we ask ourselves why we like or dislike something, we begin to understand what works and what doesn't for us as songwriters and artists. It enables us to learn from others and keep the conversation going.

Monster Mantra

I'm going to leave you with a little mantra to help you keep playdough monstering as we move forward. This is not a list of rules, but rather a collection of aspirational values for songwriting. Feel free to print it out or add to the list. We've been heavy on the philosophical up to this point, but I promise the practical is right at the doorstep. Say this quick mantra with me, and then let's get down to some serious songwriting play.

Playdough Monster Songwriting Mantra:

1. I am willing to reimagine almost everything as something else.
2. I won't settle for the first thing I make or try.

3. I will say "I like it" or "I don't like it" and allow it to help me move forward.
4. My playdough monster is unique, and I want to discover what it's really all about.
5. I will engage with my creation and let it tell me what it wants to be.
6. **Add your own mantra, like "it's okay to write songs just for fun" or "I'm willing to try something in my songwriting that seems risky or weird."**

Enough talk. Let's make some playdough monsters.

PLAYTIME

Solo Activities:

Lyric Remix: Choose a song written by someone else and remix it. You can change the point of view, add or swap out imagery, alter the rhyme scheme, or make any other rewrites you like. You might rearrange song sections, cut them, or add to them. The goal is to explore how songs can be continually reimagined. (If you're stuck, do your lyric remix to "I Want It That Way" by the Backstreet Boys.)

Genre Swap: Take a song that you admire, preferably in a genre you don't tend to write in, and reimagine it in your own style. How would you say the lyric differently? How would you modify the melody to make it singable for you? Change the chords to suit your style. This exercise encourages you to acknowledge your own artistic voice while studying a song you respect. (If you're stuck, try a genre swap for a jazz standard like "Fly Me to the Moon" or Blue Skies.")

Group Activities:

Instrument Jamboree: Ditch the keyboard and/or acoustic guitar and provide your group with a variety of instruments that aren't typically used for songwriting. Let students pick an instrument and work on writing a song or song section using their unconventional instruments in groups of two or three. Preschool-style musical instruments are perfect for this activity, including spoons, tambourine, small xylophone, castanets, triangle, egg shaker, and handbells. Or be creative and make your own unconventional instruments!

Cafe Marc: (solo or group activity) Print out the text for the song "Cafe Marc" (on the last page of this chapter) for each group and have them "playdough monster" the lyrics. The lyrics can be manipulated by removing the labels from the song sections, reordering the sections, breaking the sections into individual lines, or reordering the lines. You can also take it a step further and swap lines between sections, cut lines into smaller pieces of words, or delete lines and words. Heck, you could even cut some additional blank strips to write new lines and change the rhyme scheme. Add melody to your playdough monster-ed lyrics if you wish! You can quite literally do whatever you want in Cafe Marc.

Homework Challenge:

Monster Mash-Up: Take a song you've written and identify your favorite part, whether it's the chorus, verse, or another section. Try to write a new version of the song that uses only your favorite part as a starting point. Be intentional about taking a new direction. Could the story be different? Could your melody go to a brand-new place? Perhaps stripping everything else away has helped you realize that the tempo, key, or groove should be modified. Submit both the original song and your reimagined version side by side. (If you're stuck, try to do a monster mash-up starting with the chorus of "Heat Waves" by Glass Animals.)

Feedback Findings: Select a completed song that you are open to rewriting. Reach out to a fellow songwriter and ask for honest, constructive feedback. Afterward, take a moment to document your thoughts and feelings in a 200–300-word reflection. Explore how you emotionally responded to the feedback. In your reflection, affirm your willingness to make changes where the feedback rang true. Talk about the elements of the song you are open to altering and those you are committed to keeping. Ask yourself: Did vulnerability in seeking feedback help you take steps toward playdough monster songwriting?

Song Challenge:

The Fun Song: Recall a memory of a specific time you really had fun. Like the most fun you've ever had. Take a few minutes to write down as many specific sights, smells, sounds, and details about that memory of fun. Then, write a song about it. The song itself doesn't have to be fun, but it has to be inspired by the fun memory. Make sure the music matches the tone of the lyrics.

Don't Settle Song: Think of a time you've settled. Did you stay in a terrible job for too long, or keep on dating someone you really shouldn't have? Write a song about refusing to settle and use your memory as fuel for your lyrics. Choose a strong emotion related to this memory (rage, regret, disgust, liberation) and make sure to emphasize it through your musical choices. For an additional musical challenge, force yourself to write three versions of the chorus melody before picking the best one.

CAFE MARC

(use these lyrics for the Cafe Marc activity)

Verse 1
There are too many clouds here
I need some clear skies
Life is buzzing in my ears
I'm begging for silence
Pre-Chorus
When the music just won't stop
It's blocking every thought
When my whole world is getting loud
It makes me want to shout
Chorus
I need some peace and quiet
Sweet relief from the riot
It's too loud and I can't find it
Honey you know I've tried
Post-Chorus
Peace and quiet is all I need
Peace and quiet will set me free
Verse 2
This cafe is too full of conversation
Espresso machines and clinking spoons
I just dropped in to hear myself think
But I think I will be leaving soon
Bridge
Maybe the problem ain't the outside
Maybe the noise is in my mind
Maybe I need to still my soul
Maybe I need to give up control
Maybe I need to be real and see
Admit that the uproar is within me

CHAPTER 2

Rock Collection

Gathering & Storing Ideas

"I'm more likely to come up with great insights while writing about a coffee mug or a cereal packet than if I contemplate la condition humaine." Steve Turner

My son loves rocks. Oftentimes, he comes home from school with his pockets full of them. Usually, his favorite "rocks" are not rocks at all, but brightly painted chunks of concrete that have broken off the curb at the school parking lot. Though I tire of the ever-growing pile of pebbles on my laundry room windowsill, I try not to discourage his rock hoarding because I love that he's taking the time to notice small things. I admire that he wants to treasure and hold onto the simple things he finds beautiful and interesting. When I ask him what he is going to do with all these rocks, the answer is simple: He doesn't know! All he knows is that he really wants to keep them.

Living life as a songwriter means that you start to feel the same way about words, melodies, and chord changes that you just can't get out of your head. What will you do with all those small, beautiful ideas? You don't know! You just know that you want to keep them. Sadly, for my son, I only allow him to keep a small portion of his rock collection in his room. The rest must stay in the yard. Fortunately, for you, you don't have a mom who won't let you keep all of your song rocks. You're responsible for discovering all the ideas and cataloging, organizing, and saving them for easy retrieval. In this chapter, we're going to learn how to grow our rock collection. Then we will discuss how to manage it so that each idea can be properly valued.

Mark Simos was a formative teacher of mine. He called song ideas "song seeds." To him, song seeds were little fragments of songs that contained the spark of creativity from which a song could grow. Mark's approach to song seeds was helpful for me as a beginning songwriter because it is much like my own way of engaging with songwriting. People often ask me, "Which comes first, the music or the lyrics?" And after taking classes with Mark, I finally had an answer that felt right: "Neither comes first; I gather song seeds!" For me, a song seed is a tiny bit of melody and lyric that go together. I have no idea what they're all about, or where they'll go; I just know I need to keep them.

Mark taught me about song seeds, but in this book, we're going to refer to small song ideas as rocks for our rock collection. We'll start by building our rock collection through a practice called object writing. I first encountered object writing at the Berklee College of Music. I learned many of the following ideas from Pat Pattison, Mark Simos, and other teachers at Berklee and beyond, and I'm so thankful for those who have shaped the way I think about songwriting.

Object Writing

Object writing is a way to creatively engage with the physical world. Engaging with our surroundings and senses can help us generate songwriting ideas right where we are. I'm going to outline the quick and easy steps to object writing, and I want you to actually do it while you read!

Step 1: Get something to write with.

Purists will tell you it must be pen and paper, but if you prefer to type on a blank Google doc, more power to you. Writing anything is better than writing nothing!

Step 2: Get a timer.

We are going to object write for either three, five, or ten minutes. Three or five minutes is usually the best starting point for beginners. (But don't start the timer just yet.)

Step 3: Select any physical object.

Examples: scissors, window, bulldozer, oyster, planet, etc. If you're not feeling super creative, scroll through an online news article or pick up a book and look for a "thing" noun.

Step 4: Prepare to engage with the object.

What we're about to do is free association journaling that leans into sense-based language. You should be writing in an *unfiltered* and *unedited* way that allows your mind to wander wherever it will go. Try to write in bursts of short phrases or sentences, and don't just make a list of individual words. But you're also not trying to write formatted lyrics. Lastly, you do not have to keep writing about your chosen object if your mind leads you elsewhere. Your object is simply a starting point. Whatever you do, don't stop writing.

If you're still unsure of what to write about, or you get stuck, take a look at this list of questions below and come back to it so that you can keep writing:

1. What does the object feel like? (Think textures or composition.)
2. What kind of sounds does it make? (Imagine how it would sound if you touched, dropped, or used the object.)
3. What does the object do, and how does it do it?
4. What does it smell like?
5. What does it taste like? (Even if it's not something edible.)
6. Where would you usually find this object?
7. What memories does this object bring to mind?
8. If you were the object, what would you say?
9. Does the object remind you of any other objects? (It's like a ____.)

Step 5: Start your timer and write.

Set your timer for five minutes, choose an object, and write about it now!

Step 6: At the sound of the timer, stop writing and process your object write.

There are a lot of different things you can do as you process your writing:

- Go back and underline interesting words or phrases. These could become titles, song ideas, lyrics, metaphors, or simply something you like and want to keep.
- Reflect on how you used your senses. Did you only talk about things you could see and touch? Did you mention your sense of smell, taste, or hearing anywhere?
- Consider whether any of your words or phrases stand out as a melody. If so, make sure you record a voice memo right now of how you would sing that combination of words.

Object writing is a primary entry point into the greater discipline of establishing a regular writing habit. Maybe object writing isn't your favorite activity. I'd argue you still need to do it, but I'd also like to give you some alternatives. Any sort of journaling is going to benefit you as a songwriter. If you don't believe me, I'll take a moment here to give a personal testimony.

I used to hate journaling. I always imagined journaling was for bored teenage girls pouring out their hormone-induced drama and recounting what they had for breakfast. As someone who values efficiency, journaling seemed like an elaborate waste of time. So, I resisted. For years, I didn't have a daily writing habit of any kind. Daily writing wasn't a priority because it felt unfocused. How could I give precious minutes every day to something that was aimless and overly emotional?

I finally learned my lesson at the tail end of my 30s. I signed up for a commitment of 30 minutes of journaling every morning for 12 weeks to prove that daily journaling was a waste of time. However, after only three days, I discovered that the writer within me had been suppressed and squandered for *years*.

Magician's Interlude

Below is an entry from my notebook, written August 17, 2023. I did a long object write on the topic "magician." This object write led me to a specific memory of seeing a magician when I was on an anniversary trip with my husband in Cancun. The night ended badly, so reflecting on that memory led me to the word *sabotage*. That word then gave me an idea for a lyric and melody, which I immediately recorded into a voice memo. A simple object write led me to a concrete song idea. Amazing! After all that, I wrote this in my journal:

"It's really interesting to me how this process of object writing reveals song ideas pretty effortlessly but also pretty randomly. I am glad for this new discipline and I need to remind myself right now that this is

important. I need to keep making time for it, especially when things get a lot busier. "

Really, Journaling?

Am I asking you to start a 30-minute journaling habit every morning? No. That's probably a bit extreme for a starting point. But I *am* asking you to go buy an empty journal, one that you like the look and feel of, and try adding one new entry *most* days. It could be as simple as doing a three-minute object write once a day when you have a few minutes, or just adding an idea for a song title. Little pebbles, day by day.

Here are a few journaling prompts to get you started, but this is by no means an exhaustive list. You can utilize these prompts as many or as few times as you want:

1. Journal about a significant person in your life and a specific memory with them. Include details, but stay focused on one memory—just one moment in time—and be honest.
2. Journal about a memorable family holiday, making sure to paint the scene using all five senses.
3. Journal about a specific place you liked to hang out as a kid. Describe that place in detail, including how you felt in your body. What were you doing, feeling, and thinking?
4. Journal about a specific historical event, whether you were alive to experience it or not. Remember to lean into the physical details. Paint a vivid scene with your words.
5. Journal while looking at a painting or an interesting photograph. Not just "pretty" ones. Find visual art that evokes all the emotions. Or look at a bunch of paintings and then journal about which one you'd buy and which one you'd burn and why.
6. Journal after listening to a piece of music, or watching a film or TV show that stirs your emotions. Make sure to start writing while it's still fresh in your mind.

7. Journal after scanning a news article for interesting titles, words, and word combinations. Browsing news articles for interesting words is my favorite thing to do when I'm bored with object writing and feeling uninspired. Science articles are my favorites.
8. Journal about whatever it is that you can't get off your mind right now. You're supposed to be focused on reading this book on songwriting, but you can't stop thinking about that other thing. Write about whatever is keeping you up at night or preventing you from focusing on anything else. That conversation you keep playing over and over in your head? That's what you journal about.

Playbreak

Now that you've read through all those potential journal prompts, I want you to choose one right now and write about it. Set a timer for five minutes and go! Timers are important because if you don't use one, you might write for too long today and burn out, which means you won't write tomorrow. Our practice is about getting a pebble or two every day, not a boulder once a month. Seriously, though, do a journal entry before you read anything else on this page!

We must give ourselves space to let our minds wander through words on the page. When you approach journaling, you are not setting out to write song lyrics, although you may. You're trying to get at the heart of the songwriter, the maker of things, that is within you. If you don't make space to let that part of you dream, confess, and explore, your songwriter will remain fairly dormant.

In his book *How to Write One Song*, written in 2020, Jeff Tweedy said, "Most of the time, inspiration has to be invited." Forty years earlier, in her book *Walking on Water*, Madeleine L'Engle said, "If the artist works only when he feels like it, he's not apt to build up much of a body of work. Inspiration far more often comes during the work than before it, because the largest part of the job of the artist is to listen to the work and to go where it tells him to go." This is the advice passed down from generation to generation by the craft masters: You can't wait for inspiration to strike.

Well, you can, but you'll lose years of ideas.

Once I made a daily habit of journaling, I have never been without new song ideas. In fact, I have so many rocks in my collection right now, I don't think I'll ever be able to write them all into full songs. If you want to be a writer who is consistently inspired, you have to make consistent space for inspiration. Keeping up a healthy songwriting habit simply means choosing to show up even if you don't think you have a lot to say.

But I Don't Wanna

I hear you. You don't wanna have a daily writing habit. I know wandering and dreaming through journaling can be difficult to prioritize. It *is* "romantic" and has a reckless disregard for using time "efficiently." Our Westernized, consumer-driven brains see productivity and progress as linear. We are often discouraged from prioritizing adventure, romance, or a playful journey because they might take us nowhere. But prioritizing creative habits like journaling is not a luxury. For the artist, they are creative priorities. For the artist, this is food for our creative soul.

Sometimes—well, many times—object writing or journaling will seem to go nowhere. You'll feel uninspired and run out of steam halfway through your timer. This is normal. It's like exercise that doesn't always feel rewarding in the moment. In fact, sometimes it's quite exhausting. But you are building songwriting muscles that *notice* things. These muscles can quickly create metaphors by seeing connections between physical objects and memories. You will begin to connect details, even mundane and ordinary ones, to access deeper emotional meaning. You are building habits that acknowledge that there's a lot within you that needs space and time to process. There's also a lot swirling outside of you that requires space and time to untangle.

I know a commitment to regular journaling can be hard for some people because it's hard for *me*. But even if you don't wanna, please give it a try. It might just change your life.

Cloud Candy

We've mainly been discussing lyrical ideas for our rock collection, but what about melody ideas we discover and need to store? Where do these singable snippets come from? If you're like me, you don't usually sit down with a pen and paper and craft a melody. Most melodies just pop into my head while I'm driving or when I'm in the shower (usually the places that are most inconvenient).

Sometimes it feels like these melodies float in on thin air, and we just get lucky enough to pluck one out of the sky. Succulent little melodic bites I like to call "cloud candy." Cloud candy melodies can be singable and fun. Emotive and explosive. They're like a feeling personified in pitches and rhythm. If we catch melody cloud candy, what do we do with it? Our melody ideas can become a part of our rock collection via voice memo (like rock...candy?), but that's only the start. We'll talk more about storing our rock candy melodies in a bit. But first, I want to talk about what to do if melody or lyric ideas aren't appearing out of thin air.

Can I Just Force Rocks to Appear?

Maybe you've been here before: Guitar in hand, empty page in front of you, and you're not feeling the magic. You sit down and say, "I'm gonna write a song about this topic right now!" but the ideas just aren't flowing. You think to yourself, *Do I have writer's block?* You've given yourself a limited amount of time to be creative on command, and it's not working. Well, that's because forcing yourself to write a song with no pre-existing idea collection to draw from is usually unpleasant. It feels like conjuring—trying really hard to be creative. You don't need to force it. You *are* creative.

When I find myself flailing over the page like a cartoon witch trying to summon something from her cauldron, I'm pretty sure I'm conjuring in my songwriting. You can definitely write songs from that place, but there won't be much joy in it. These songs will probably feel uninspired and inauthentic, and they usually struggle to emotionally connect. But I'm not just talking about writing songs here; I'm talking about journaling as well. Trying to force ourselves to "be" creative means we're trying to make rocks appear instead of discovering them. This looks like making yourself journal about something deep and earth-shattering instead of just writing about what happened yesterday or what's really on your mind. Musically, we can arrive at a place of conjuring if we're trying to write a melody in a vacuum. This happens when we sit in the quiet room and say to ourselves, "Sing something! Play something! Be brilliant!" and all we hear are crickets. In her book *The Artist's Way*, I think Julia Cameron said it best:

Art is not about thinking something up. It is about the opposite, getting something down. The directions are important here. If we are trying to "think something up" we are straining to reach for something that's just beyond our grasp, "up there, in the stratosphere, where art lives on high..." When we get something down, there is no strain. We're not doing, we're getting...Instead of reaching for inventions, we are engaged in listening.

So, how do we get away from conjuring? By getting in touch with what's really going on inside of us. We remove the pressure to be brilliant and get honest about where we're at right now. Perhaps you could open your mouth and try to sing how you feel in the moment, instead of trying to sing something "cool." Is it a shout of joy? A weeping descent? Maybe there's a rhythm bouncing on your lips because you just want to dance. Create notes to express how you feel.

Make Space & Rotate the Crops

No matter what you set out to create, keep in mind that you can't pour from an empty bucket. "What do I write about?" my student, Clay, asked me one day in class. "I've got nothing to pull from but dorm room walls, classes, and homework, and I don't really want to write any more songs about that!"

Maybe you feel that way too. Maybe you're stuck in the daily grind, lacking variety and wide-open spaces. The first step to filling your creative bucket is to refuse to be a slave to the priorities of what you "have" to do and choose to play instead. There are plenty of small things we can do to create just enough space and variety in our lives to open the door for inspiration. It doesn't require tons of money or major lifestyle changes. Stop using the excuses of "I'll write more when I have more free time," or "I'll write more when I have more ideas." The truth is, you won't.

I told Clay to do two things: make space and rotate the crops. Making space is all about prioritizing time to fill your creative bucket. Perhaps you have a pile of homework—or any type of work, for that matter. Instead of always caving to the work you *have* to do, you choose to take a walk first, because space is important. You could answer emails, but instead you listen to music while doing something "unproductive" because your brain, heart, and soul need space to be fed.

Again, most of us tend to get great melodic ideas when we're washing the dishes or walking the dog because we're doing something that gives our brain space. We collect the best ideas when we take the time to slow down and see those rocks next to the roses that we're smelling. We notice them when we take the time to wander and decide that looking for rocks is worth our time. Beyond temporarily putting off the things we *have* to do for the things we *want* to do, we can also begin to reclaim lost minutes.

Personally, I know I waste time every day scrolling on my phone. If you find yourself nodding in solidarity, I want to challenge you: The next time you're tempted to scroll to fill those five minutes before your next thing starts, do a five-minute object write instead. If you're scrolling the news at the breakfast table, you could be noticing cool words and phrases that might be titles or song ideas. What are you doing as you drive? Are you listening to another opinion podcast, or could you choose to listen to a great album all the way through from start to finish? Pick the art film over *The Office* reruns this time. There's nothing wrong with comfort shows, but you've seen them before. You *need* variety. Reclaiming space is all about prioritizing things that will fill and fuel the songwriter inside of you.

If you're successfully beginning to add space and variety to your life, you're ready for the next challenge. In an interview, Joni Mitchell said she was never afraid of being uninspired because she "rotates the crops." She doesn't just write songs; she also paints. In agriculture, crop rotation refers to the practice of planting a different crop on the same piece of land each growing season, which helps prevent disease, pests, and soil stagnation. It builds healthy soil. In the same way, we can keep our songwriting soil healthy by engaging in other artistic activities. It doesn't matter if you feel gifted in these other mediums; it's healthy to try to engage with them anyway.

Since you engage your brain so much in songwriting, try some form of art with your hands. Try drawing, painting, or modeling with clay. Do you think you're too untalented at these things? Don't worry, I'm worse. The point is not to be good; the point is to explore something different. You can also engage with visual art by visiting a gallery or noticing the details of nature by dabbling in photography. Go and see a live play or listen to live music.

Can't leave the house? Write a poem, write anything. If you're really daring, dance. Dancing at home doesn't cost you anything except setting aside your pride. Whatever you do, make space to fill your bucket and rotate the crops. It is essential for those of us who can't focus on songwriting full-time, which is most of us, to be intentional about finding inspiration.

Organizing Our Rock Collection

Prioritizing object writing, journaling, making space, and engaging with nature and other art forms opens up our songwriter self all day long. And when this happens, we will start to collect words, phrases, song titles, melodies, chord progressions, and more. Organizing this collection can be challenging. For years, my method of organizing ideas was a haphazard mess. I kept a paper journal for lyric ideas and a note on my phone for titles, along with hundreds of untitled voice memos and chord charts saved in Word documents on my computer… somewhere? Then, when I had a few spare minutes to work on a song, I could never find what I needed. My collection was a big, jumbled pile, and I wasted a lot of songwriting time trying to sift through my unorganized ideas.

I could never find the voice memo I was really excited about last month. I couldn't locate that journal entry with the killer song idea. I started getting invitations to cowrites, but couldn't find my best song starts. I decided to make a change because I know I am a real songwriter, and a real songwriter needs to steward their ideas wisely. And you need to find a method for storing and organizing your rock collection that works for *you*. The most important things to consider are the convenience of capturing, organizing, and sharing ideas, as well as ensuring that your ideas won't be easily lost. The pieces we will be saving include titles, lyrics, melodies, chord charts, worktapes, and demos. Here are a few terms to keep in mind as we're talking about workflow.

Songwriter's Stuff Lingo

Chord Chart: A doc containing your written-out lyrics with chord symbols.
Worktape: A rough version of a song from start to finish with lyrics sung over basic chord changes (usually the quality of a voice memo).
Demo: A more polished version of the song with more carefully recorded vocal and instrument takes. (This is a cleaner recording than a worktape, usually to a click track, but just the basic instruments.)

What follows is the system that I use to store and organize my ideas. I'm not claiming it's the best system, but it works for me. Perhaps it will inspire you to adjust a few things you're currently doing so that you'll have a more functional rock collection.

Most of my lyric ideas come from journaling; however, keeping them in a paper journal isn't enough because I can never find them again.

Whenever I capture a lyric worth saving, I immediately add it to a Google Doc with a memorable title at the end of my journaling session. If I have a lyric focused on sabotage, I'd title the doc "Sabotage." I use Google Drive to organize most of my rock collection. All of my documents related to potential songs are stored in a folder called "Song Projects."

When it comes to storing melodic ideas, I use the Voice Memos app, much like the majority of songwriters. It's convenient because my phone is always with me, and I can quickly capture ideas wherever they may strike. But there is a crucial step in using Voice Memos that some people overlook: You want to make sure you title the voice memo and immediately transfer it to a more organized and secure location. Again, I use Google Drive for this. As soon as I record a voice memo of a melody idea, I give it a memorable title and save it to my Google Drive in the Song Projects folder. (TIP: If you have the Google Drive app on your phone, you can send a recording straight to Google Drive from within the Voice Memos app!)

Some items in my Song Projects folder are just docs with lyrics, while others are just voice memos of melodies. Whenever I have free time to write, I go straight to my Song Projects folder. If I have both a Google Doc and a voice memo for the *same* song idea, this is usually where I look first because I have a lot of rocks in my collection that I can begin to explore. I start by listening through a few of the voice memos and looking at the docs to see if anything sparks my interest.

If a particular song idea is clicking with me, I create a subfolder to pair the two items together (lyric doc and voice memo recording) as I start working on the song. The initial Google Doc turns into my chord chart as I build the song. At the end of my writing session, I will record a new voice memo, which will become my worktape (that I also save in the same folder). I may eventually include a more polished demo of the song in the folder if I anticipate sending the song to a producer. This is what it looks like:

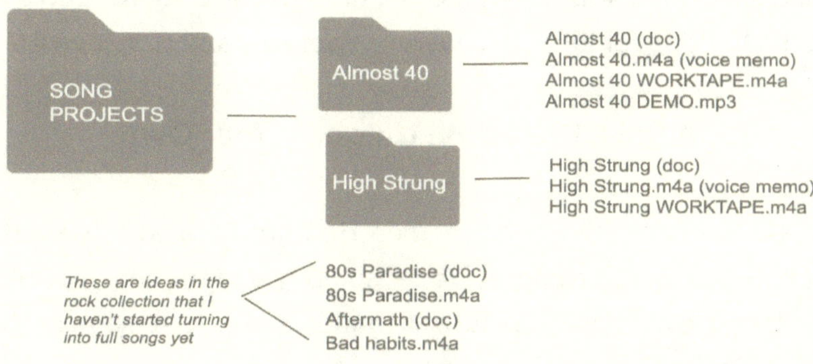

Digital folders are important because saving my lyrics, melodies, chord charts, and worktapes together allows me to find all my song pieces in one place. I can see which ideas I've started and which ones I can play with further in the future. Before a co-writing session, I often create new folders and share them with my co-writers so they can check out what I've been working on. The same system works if I'm sharing ideas to get feedback from a producer—I'm sending my collaborators a link to a shareable folder containing everything. This system saves time and space because I'm not texting voice memos that people might lose or emailing large attachments that my producers don't want.

My friend Steph, a phenomenally talented singer and songwriter, lost years' worth of melody ideas stored only in voice memos on her phone during an iPhone update. Please write like Steph, but don't store like Steph! It's devastating to lose such a large part of your rock collection. These melodies might never come back to you. The same problem can happen if you're using the "notes" app on your phone exclusively. Digital notes are far too easy to accidentally delete, and we can't afford to lose our treasures! Lastly, physical journals are great for journaling, but they aren't ideal if they're the *only* way you record and store ideas. Please find a digital backup method, at the very least.

Managing your rock collection is essential to ensuring you have ideas to work with when you have precious time to write songs. Don't waste your time hunting for ideas that weren't captured and stored well.

A Rock Collection Uniquely Your Own

There is a German philosopher named Hartmut Rosa who has a theory about how our increased access to technology and the speed at which it allows us to live ultimately leads to alienation and a decrease in perceived free time. Basically, we're never satisfied because we constantly feel the pressure to do more. His response to this modern problem is through practicing what he calls "resonance." Rosa encourages us to consider living in resonance with the world around us by connecting and being on the same "wavelength" as whoever or whatever is right in front of us. It's not about finding some zen or equilibrium. It's about allowing the people and objects around us to enter into conversation with us, allowing them to affect us in the moment.

Kind of sounds like object writing, doesn't it? It's slowing down and resonating with the cup of coffee in front of you. Notice it. How does it smell? What does it look like? What does it remind you of? No one else in the world has your exact same combination of history, experiences, and physical surroundings. You are a unique expression of one soul in one space at one time. You have the opportunity to build a rock collection of song ideas that is uniquely your own. Allow the world around you to speak to you. Give it the time and space to speak to you, and then listen. Soon you will watch your rock collection grow into something interesting, distinct, and beautiful.

PLAYTIME

Solo Activities:

Personification Journaling: Do a five-minute journaling session personifying one of the following objects: push pin, coffee mug, pair of scissors, duct tape, bucket, flower, ladder, or table. Consider the question, "If I was a _____, what would I say?" You can write anything about the object that comes to mind. If your mind wanders away from the object, that's okay, too.

Scene Setting Journaling: Spend ten minutes journaling a scene starting with a specific place. Dig into tactile details using all your senses. It may be easier if you select a real place you've been. If your scene is fully developed, try introducing a character. Describe them in detail, and then write about what the character is feeling in this place. Finally, ask yourself: What could a song based on this scene be about?

The Melody Emerges: Read the following lyric lines, separately, five times in a row:

"The best is yet to come"

"Everybody needs a Friday-night friend"

"Freedom is at your fingertips"

"Happy days have burned away"

After you read them all, ask yourself if any of these lyric lines make you think of a melody. Try singing one. If a melody for one of them emerges, record it. After you record your melody, consider editing the lyric to make it feel more personal to you. If you change the lyrics, re-record your melody with the new words. If the melody really inspires you, keep going!

Group Activities:

Mystery Box: Have the group leader place a variety of random items inside a box before the group gathers. Items can include anything from a spoon to a small porcelain doll. Cut a large hole in the box so people can reach in without seeing the items. Then, each member of the group pulls an item out of the mystery box and performs a timed object write on their chosen item. After doing the object write, members can continue pulling out more items from the box or swap items with each other for additional object writing.

Magazine Pitch Lines: Pick up several magazines. (If you're on a budget, check your local library.) You'll need at least one per person. Have group members focus on the advertisements, taglines, and titles of articles found in their magazine. Ask, "Do any of the words you've come across sound like a song title?" Have each person write down all the potential song titles they can find in their magazine in three minutes. Then, have each person review their list to craft a big idea about one of those titles. (A "big idea" is one phrase or short sentence defining what the song would be about.) Trade magazines to repeat the activity.

Fishbowl Narrative: Using individual strips of paper, have every group member write down one "setting," one "character," and one "big idea" for a song.

Example:

Setting: outer space

Character: a farmer

Big Idea: a song about star-crossed lovers

Have each group member put their strips in three corresponding bowls labeled "setting," "character," and "big Idea." Then have each person draw one strip of paper from each bowl. Have each person try to write a four-line lyric pulling together the setting, character, and big idea they drew out of the bowls.

Example:

Setting: the kitchen

Character: a doctor

Big Idea: a song about a big life change

Sample Lyric:

The doctor hangs his head over the kitchen sink

He never saw this one coming

Been saving lives for so many years

He couldn't see the ones in front of him he'd lost

Homework Challenge:

Journaling Sampler: Select three different entries from the sample list of "journaling ideas" in this chapter and complete them. Then, gather a list of your best ideas from each entry (including titles, words, phrases, and song concepts) to submit. Also, include a brief written reflection on which journaling experience was the most rewarding or the most challenging.

Fishbowl Ballad: Write a limerick or narrative short story with a setting, character, and big idea that wouldn't normally go together. (Example: A post-apocalyptic world, a ballerina, and a big idea dealing with "boredom.") Create a song section called "The Ballad of _____" featuring the character from your narrative.

Voice Memo Wrestling: Find a voice memo (or wherever you have stored melody ideas), and commit to developing the melody into a complete song section with lyrics. It can turn into a chorus or verse; doesn't matter. Just take the melody idea to a place of completion in a song section. Submit your completed song section (written and sung).

Song Challenge:

Personification Song: Write a song featuring a central metaphor that is an animal or an inanimate object. The object can be named in the song, or it can simply be the voice you have taken as you write the lyrics. Start with the question "If I were this object, what would I say, think, and feel?"

Sample song: "Pilot Light" by Aryn Michelle

Rooms of the House Song: Write a song with three verses where each verse mentions or places you in a different room in a house or living space. The chorus needs to tie your song together with a central emotion and theme. For an additional challenge, limit the chorus of your song to no more than 15 words.

Sample song: "Can't Really Be Gone" recorded by Tim McGraw

CHAPTER 3

Show & Tell

Scene Setting & Sensory Language

"Colors drip down, not up. Show first, and watch everything else gain impact." Pat Pattison

One of the first "rules" you learn from creative writing teachers is that it's better to "show" rather than just "tell." As you work through this book, you may notice that I begin each chapter with a personal story or thought picture to set up the topic. This is because I also believe in the concept of "show before you tell." However, I'm not opening *this* chapter with a story or a thought picture quite yet because I think Pat Pattison probably gave the best example in the chapter "Rusty's Collar" in his book *Writing Better Lyrics.* (Hopefully, this truncated intro will tempt you to buy that book and read it. It will improve your lyric writing by 1000%.) The lesson Pattison teaches is that "showing makes the telling more powerful because your senses and your mind are both engaged."

Showing before telling basically means you *earn* the right to tell your listener big things by inviting them into your big feelings through a story or reference point. But why? Isn't it more efficient to just say what you mean? Perhaps. But good songwriting isn't about getting your point across quickly; it's about making your point hit *deeply*. We cannot feel things deeply when we have no context.

Let me explain.

Spill the Tea

I had a student who wrote a song about how her heart felt hardened. The first draft of her lyric was pretty much all tell. She plainly stated that she was initially excited about a budding relationship but then started struggling with feelings of bitterness and loneliness after it all fell apart. As real as her feelings were, I found it hard to emotionally connect with her song. I could tell she was upset from her lyrics, but I couldn't quite understand why. She left out all the details and context.

When we start songwriting, we are tempted to think that exposing our raw emotions, being vulnerable, and owning up to them will do the bulk of the work in connecting with our listeners. This unfiltered display of honest feelings might be effective in fostering deep connections in real life, but it only works with people who already know us and know our story. You can go straight to your best friend and tell them honestly that they hurt you. That's real and raw. But it's only effective because they know everything that led up to that moment. They remember the text they left unanswered when you really needed them. They can picture you sitting alone in your apartment, watching reruns because they forgot to invite you to the party. They understand the context of how they let you down, so when you share your honest feelings, it can make a real impact.

And that's the point. If you want your listeners to feel your big feelings, you've got to show them everything that's swirling around those emotions. Our listeners benefit from getting a glimpse of the room, the smell in the air, and the noise you can't drown out. If your audience is going to be angry with you, they need to know the details of how someone has wronged you. You gotta spill *all* the tea.

Show the Big Idea

My students have a shorthand for labeling lyric lines as "showy" or "telly." This usually comes up for discussion when we're being too telly in our lyrics, meaning the lyric is laying it all out there too soon. I want you to stop reading right now and look up the lyrics to "Before He Cheats," made popular by Carrie Underwood. This song is a great example of a lyric that holds off as long as possible on the tell, and fills up most of the lyric space with rich amounts of show. As you read over the lyrics, I want you to observe how the scene is shown line by line.

Like, seriously, go read the lyrics right now, even if you're already familiar with the song. Read them slowly and really soak in the action. Pay attention to the nouns and verbs.

If I were to sum up the verses of this song, it would boil down to this tell: *Right now, he's probably cheating on me.* But aren't you much more likely to be angry along with the singer when you see *how* her man is cheating on her? She detailed and demonstrated his behavior, and it's downright despicable!

As with all elements of songwriting, show more than tell is a guideline. To prove to you that you don't always have to be 90% show and 10% tell, I'll point to a song by revered artist, songwriter, and producer Charlie Puth. Again, I want you to stop reading and look up the lyrics to his song "Attention."

As you look over them, ask yourself: Do they feel different from "Before He Cheats?"

The lyric for "Attention" isn't very showy, which is a little more common for pop songs. We get a bit of context but not a whole lot of details. However, there is one line that anchors the "show" for this song. It's the first line of the pre-chorus that says, "I know that dress is karma, perfume regret." This one line gives us a sight, a smell, and maybe even a sound if we can infer the music of the club in the background. Not only that, but it also perfectly supports the title and big idea of the song. She, the woman, wants his attention to make him regret leaving her. That one lyric is more poetic and interesting than everything else around it. It's just enough to paint the scene needed to understand the emotion. As Dar Williams would say, "A precise, beautiful, and interesting word can wake up a whole stanza or even a song."

Vivid Specificity

We can take our "showing" a step further by doubling down through vivid specificity. Pull up the chorus to "Before He Cheats" one more time.

I rewrote a version of the same chorus where all the nouns have been watered down, and the verbs substituted for more passive ones:

I put my key into the side of his nice little car
I wrote my name on the car seats
I used a bat to hit out the headlights
I put a hole in all the tires

This is still a show lyric because we're still painting the scene instead of plainly telling you, "I'm super mad!" It's still a violent scene, but we've lost a lot of the drama. We can't picture it in our mind's eye as clearly as the original version. Why? Vivid specificity chooses "Louisville Slugger" over "bat" and "slashed a hole" instead of "put a hole."

Let's try adding some vivid specificity to some lyrics. You can add to, take away, or rewrite these lyrics however you like. Aim to make each line show the same idea more vividly, with more drama and detail. It might help to have a specific emotion in mind as you work to elevate this lyric—any emotion will do. And don't worry about syllable count or rhyme scheme. I'll underline some words, and you can replace them with more interesting alternatives.

Add some vivid specificity by rewriting these four lines:

I walked to the park this morning (Example rewrite for line 1**:** Skipping to Dove Park with the early sun)

The sun was rising over the trees

I could hear the birds singing

There were leaves crunching beneath my feet

Did you decide to shuffle, retreat, or drift to the park instead? Perhaps you heard bluejays chatting instead of birds singing. Or if you went to a more negative emotional space, perhaps there were crows shouting at you. If you opted for a more positive emotional space on the first rewrite, try the exercise again and go towards a more negative emotional space.

Show Better: Scene Setting

Now that we've laid some groundwork, let's cover three go-to strategies we can use as we attempt to show more than tell:

1. Set the scene
2. Elevate nouns and verbs
3. Create metaphors

Setting the scene through showing is where we started. By grounding the listener in the physical context, we help them connect with big feelings. If you are struggling to set the scene, try placing the singer of your song wherever you were when inspiration struck for writing this song. Did you have a memorable experience at a wedding? A funeral? A vacation? A hospital? Put your singer (and your listener) where you were when the song idea came to you. Have you ever had a conversation or interaction that changed your life? Where were you, when was it, and what were you doing? Scene setting doesn't have to be exact, but our real experiences can be a good starting point to ground our ideas.

We are embodied creatures, and physical spaces are important. We are creatures of memory, and we find significance in particular smells, tastes, sounds, and sensations. **Take a mid-chapter break and write for**

three minutes about the best trip or vacation you've ever had. Don't write about how you felt about it, just describe everything your senses (sight, touch, taste, smell, and sound) remember. Get specific because no detail is too small to be neglected. If you can't think of the best vacation, then think of the worst one. Good songwriters are good storytellers, and good storytellers are good scene setters. And good scene setters think about nouns and verbs.

Show Better: Nouns & Verbs

Nouns and verbs are the building blocks of strong lyric writing. Chuck Berry is famously quoted for saying, "When you're writing a song, nouns and verbs will carry you right through." You might have noticed this in our "vivid specificity" rewrite. The lyrics improved significantly when we focused on strengthening the nouns and verbs. You might be tempted to dress up your writing by adding superfluous adjectives, but nouns and verbs hold the true power.

Here is a sample lyric with a basic noun and verb:

We danced at sunset

Here is the sample lyric with the addition of a superfluous adjective:

We danced at the majestic sunset

Here are versions of the sample lyric with elevated nouns and verbs:

We twirled at twilight / We swayed 'til day's end

Can you see how substituting the nouns and verbs added more "punch" than simply adding an adjective? You might also notice that I took the opportunity to elevate the nouns and verbs to include more poetic choices. "We twirled at twilight" uses alliteration of the "twi" for creative emphasis, and "We swayed 'til day's end" makes use of the internal rhyme found in *swayed* and *days.* Trying on elevated nouns and verbs allows you the opportunity to dig deeper and avoid settling for the first words that come to mind.

For another exercise, I want you to look up the lyrics for "Title and Registration" by Death Cab for Cutie and make special note of all the nouns and verbs. Have they painted a scene you can visualize?

Can you see how the use of interesting nouns and strong verbs places us right there in the car with the singer, bringing this lyric to life? Finding interesting nouns to use in your songwriting starts by paying attention to the objects you interact with, such as taking the time to really consider a glove compartment. Quality nouns also favor specificity, like using Louisville Slugger instead of baseball bat. Take another break and see how quickly you can write down an A-Z list of nouns, one for each letter. If you're up for a challenge, try to use only out-of-the-ordinary nouns—go for alfalfa over apple.

Make your A-Z noun list now. You don't have to limit yourself to only things you can see, and you can use a person, place, thing, or idea, as these are all nouns. Example: Alfalfa, Bulldog, Covenant, Disease.

Did your noun list give you any song or lyric ideas? Sometimes the simple process of considering a thing leads us to a fresh perspective.

Now that we've talked about nouns, let's dive into verbs. Discovering strong verbs can be as easy as grabbing a thesaurus. So, let's do that now. Let's pretend you've written the lyric "and he walked away." Now we're going to take the verb from this lyric and elevate it.

Look up the word *walk* or *walked* in a thesaurus and find 10 other verbs that mean roughly the same thing as *walked*. Write down your 10 synonyms on a piece of paper. Now read the lyric "and he walked away" out loud and substitute your new words for *walked* one at a time.

The lyric instantly becomes more interesting and nuanced if we try "he ambled away" or "he trudged away." You might try on lots of different verbs before discovering the one with the perfect nuance, rhythm, and feel that you're looking for. However, "this does not mean that while you are writing, you should stop and contemplate a new verb for an hour," says writing guru Natalie Goldberg in her bok *Writing Down the Bones*. "Only be aware of your verbs and the power they have and use them in fresh ways." So, remember, we're elevating our words to have fun exploring possibilities, not to drive ourselves crazy.

Show Better: Metaphor Making

The last thing to consider as you're trying to show better is your intentionality in creating metaphors. In a later chapter, we will discuss avoiding and undoing cliché metaphors, but for now, we will start by making some metaphors from scratch.

The Oxford Dictionary defines a metaphor as a figure of speech in which a word or phrase is applied to an object or action to which it is not *literally* applicable (my paraphrase). Basically, a metaphor is created when you say something *is* something else (the sun is a lamp) or is *doing* something that it actually cannot do (the sun is sneezing). A metaphor involves smashing together two things that don't typically go together, at least on the surface level. Combinations that are literally true, such as a "warm sun," "bright sun," or "yellow sun," are not metaphors. "Depressed sun" is a metaphor, while "depressed son" is not. We also need to remember the difference between a simile and a metaphor, which you probably learned in elementary school. Similes say "is like," and metaphors do not. "The sun is like a smile in the sky" is a simile. "The sun is smiling at me" is a metaphor.

Metaphors can come in big or small packages within a song lyric. You might have a metaphor that enhances just one line and then doesn't come back. For example, you could have a line that says, "Drink up some drama," which is a metaphor because you can't literally drink drama. Alternatively, you can have a central metaphor that the whole song revolves around. You can check out my song "Pilot Light" as an example of this. I'll share the opening lines here, but the rest of the song continues to support the central metaphor "I'm a pilot light," which literally can't be true because I cannot, in fact, transform into a pilot light.

I'm a little pilot light
Gentle fire inside
And I'll keep on burning
Waiting for my time

Let's try to create a metaphor and then build a chorus around it. We'll call this game "That Girl is on Fire!" We're using "Girl on Fire," a song made popular by Alicia Keys, as a reference for a song that has a chorus featuring a title metaphor. Instead of saying "This girl is on fire," we're going to say "This ____ is ______." You can pick two nouns or a noun/verb combo, or you could change the opening "this" to a pronoun like he/she/my if you'd like.

Here are a few examples:

This dog is an elephant
My soul is an earthquake
His heart is a hurricane (I think the alliteration makes this one the coolest.)

This sandwich is talking
Your party is bursting
My future is shining (Feels a little cliché to me.)

Keep creating combinations until you find one you really like. Then, follow the lyrical pattern of the chorus of "Girl on Fire" to write your own chorus. Here's the original, followed by my example version.

Original:
This girl is on fire
This girl is on fire
She's walking on fire (something slightly different in line 3)
This girl is on fire

My Version:
His heart is a hurricane
His heart is a hurricane
I find him in the hurricane (something slightly different in line 3)
His heart is a hurricane

This lyric feels pretty dramatic and yearning. I can almost hear a melody based on this lyric structure. I also already have a clear central metaphor and a title, which is a pretty solid start to a song.

Playbreak

Write your own "Girl on Fire" chorus right now. We're doing: _____ is a _______ with the following pattern:
Line 1
Line 2 (same as line 1 lyrically)
Line 3 (slightly different lyric)
Line 4 (same as line 1 lyrically)
Once you have your lyric, try to sing it! Even though the lyrics for lines 1, 2, and 4 are the same, the melody does not have to be the same.

You can play games like this anytime you find a song that inspires you. Observe the patterns the song establishes and try to play within that framework. Not just to craft metaphors but to develop your own songwriting challenges to sharpen your skills. Scene setting, vivid specificity, and metaphor making are a great place to start. However, thinking about your lyrics is only part of showing rather than telling. We can also show through melodies.

Show Through Melody

Showing what's important, rather than just telling it, is also essential when considering the crafting of a melody. The choices you make in melody signal to your listener what they should really focus on. Identify key lyrical moments, such as your title or emotionally charged lines, and then ask yourself: How are you emphasizing these melodically? We want to keep the pieces of our growing song in alignment so that both lyrics and melodies are bringing the same energy. Let's talk about some tools you can use to encourage people to pay attention melodically. We'll quickly cover rhythm, rests, repetition, and contour.

Firstly, don't overlook the importance of melodic rhythm. I'd dare say that some of your favorite songs are your favorites because of their catchy and distinctive melodic rhythm. A great melodic rhythm can express emotion and help you feel it in your body. Jeff Tweedy states that "All words have their own music." Can you hear the rhythm of these lyrics in your head? *Speak* them, don't sing them.

I-I-I-I- stayin' alive, stayin' alive
(from "Stayin' Alive" by the Bee Gees)

How about…
Pink Po-ny Club…I'm gonna keep on dancing at the Pink Po-ny Club
(from "Pink Pony Club" by Chappell Roan)

Or one more for good measure…
Put your __pink-y__rings up__to the__MOON!
(from "24K Magic" by Bruno Mars)

While melodic rhythm can reveal emotions in our bodies, strategic rests can also help your listener focus on what's important. Rests allow us to chew on what came before or pay attention to what's to come:

You gotta fight (REST) for your right (REST) to paaaaaarty!
(from "Fight for Your Right" by The Beastie Boys)

Don't neglect the show power of a rest.

We can also show melodically through notes that some people call "money notes." Personally, I like to call them "sparkle notes." Sparkle notes are melody notes that demand our attention because of their unexpected shine. Interval jumps often generate sparkle. "SomeWHERE over the rainbow" is a melody that begins with an octave jump that causes us to take notice. Sparkle notes melodically show us the words to pay attention to, so we don't want to squander a sparkle note on an unimportant word. Bejewel your jean jacket, not your undershirt. (We'll talk more about sparkle notes in a later chapter.)

Productive repetition of your melody can also help show your listener what to focus on. For example, we can highlight the song's title by pairing it with a hooky melody. We might also emphasize a prominent melody from the lead vocal by having other instruments repeat it in the arrangement. Melodic productive repetition is all about reusing and reinventing strong melody ideas throughout your song.

Take a moment to consider the melody of the chorus of "Dancing Queen" by ABBA. The bulk of this chorus melody is built around the repetition of the notes of the scale from 7-1-1 (or "ti-do-do" if you prefer solfege). If you look up the sheet music, you will see this melody pattern occurs eight times in the chorus, three of those times on the title lyrics. These are the pitches on this rhythm that you're listening for (that first occur on the line "dancing queen").

I'll help you get started counting this melody pattern as you sing through the chorus. (1) dan-cing queen, (2) young and sweet, (3) se-venteen. Keep looking for those notes and you'll see them EIGHT times in one chorus! Now that's some productive repetition!

Melody can also show through its shape. Shapes matter because shapes mean things to us. Ascending shapes climb and reach upward, while descending shapes land and settle downward. Flat-ish shapes feel like they're walking or marching. Melodies built on lots of interval jumps might sound like bouncing with joy or, in a different context, feel emotionally volatile. So, what is your lyric line saying? Does your melodic shape (contour) communicate this message? Or is the shape you've chosen working against the meaning of your words? Your shapes can help tell the story. Make sure to use distinctive melodic shapes to your advantage as you show through melody.

A Toast

Leah is a talented songwriter who brought me a Christmas song that needed editing. When we considered her song from top to bottom, we realized that her bridge melody was too similar to her chorus melody. It had the same starting note and a similar melodic shape. If she didn't change something about the bridge melody, it would be stealing the thunder from the chorus. A too-similar bridge melody could have left the listener with the sense that they weren't really in a different song section, which could cause the song to start to feel boring.

The lyrics that needed the new melody began with the words "toast to the past." When I suggested a new melody idea to Leah, she tried it on and didn't like it. So, she came up with a new melody idea and sang it for me. Her new melody started pretty high, then the pitches ran up even higher in an ascending line all the way to a D above high C. I balked at her new melody idea.

"It's too high!" I said. "No one can sing that!"

"But it's a toast!" she said. "It's the same shape as the motion you make with your arm when you're quickly raising up your glass."

The brilliance! I was floored by her insight. The melody she sang *showed* the lyric "toast to the past" through its shape, its rhythm, and even its stretched and "shouty" range. Needless to say, we went with her new melody. I encourage you to be brilliant like Leah and consider whether your melody is showing what your lyric is saying. This isn't always quantifiable, but it's always worth pursuing.

Just Say No to Disclaimers

I've included this final paragraph about disclaimers because it's important to encourage you not to tell your listeners what your song is about before you play it for them. If you need to preface your song with an extended introduction or disclaimer before sharing it, then you probably still have writing and editing to do. Your goal should be to show us what your song is about as you play it. Your song should be able to stand on its own two feet as a complete work, without needing excuses or explanation, in order to communicate effectively with your listeners. As Mike Errico would say in *Music, Lyrics, and Life*, "Disclaimers don't work. They don't absolve us from what we've created." I recognize there is a time and place for hearing the "story behind the song." However, if we *need* to hear the backstory before your song has any hope of making a connection, then songwriter, back to the playdough you go.

PLAYTIME

Solo Activities:

Grounding & Writing: Be present in the moment you find yourself in right now. Then, without overthinking it, jot down five things you see in your surroundings, four things you hear, three things you feel, two things you smell, and one thing you (could) taste.

Example:

5 things I see: lamp, computer, a pencil, window, bottle

4 things I hear: clicking of typing words, breathing, sizzle of lightbulb, closing door

3 things I feel: sweat, smooth metal buttons, cotton clothes

2 things I smell: sourdough bread, perfume

1 thing I taste: mustard

Did any of these sensory experiences evoke memories or feelings? Take a few minutes to journal about it or record new ideas.

Crafting "Show" Melodies: Create short melodies, one at a time, that show the following themes: victory, failure, jealousy, contentment, and childlike joy. Keep the melodies short (two bars or less). Record these "show" melodies without worrying about adding lyrics. Use nonsense words like "nah nah nah" and let the melody speak for itself. If a particular melody inspires you, save it for a song.

Group Activities:

Descriptive Word Bank

Working together as a group, create nouns and verbs that would correlate with words in the following word bank. I've written out a few examples.

Word Bank: enchanting, energetic, cozy, radiant, mysterious, melancholic, majestic, frightening

Examples:
Enchanting nouns: magic, trance, fairies
Enchanting verbs: casting (a spell), capturing
Energetic nouns: puppy, extrovert, light blue
Energetic verbs: running, explode
Cozy nouns: cabin, tea, fire
Cozy verbs: drinking, wrapped, resting

Choose one word from the word bank and use the nouns and verbs to start a journaling prompt (as individuals). You could also gather three categories from the word bank, include all the verbs and nouns you've added, and craft a story using as many of these words as you can (as a group).

Musical Mad Libs*: Break into groups of two or three. Use the Mad Libs-style template at the end of this chapter for song lyrics. Have each group fill in the blanks before they see the lyrics, leading to funny and surprising combinations. Then, have each group read their Mad Lib song lyrics aloud. After you have a good laugh, let the groups try again to fill in the blanks with more legitimate alternatives.

Homework Challenge:

Vivid Specificity: Take the following list of ten plain words, and reimagine each one with vivid specificity:

Flower, Car, Dog, House, Guitar, Computer, Shoes, Book, Necklace, Bag

Example:
Flower: a wilting white orchid
Car: a rusting Toyota Sienna

Then use as many of your "vivid" items and work them into an eight-line verse lyric.

Motif & Repeat:

Create a very short melody (one bar or so). Try to repeat this melody as many times as possible within one chorus, similar to the "Dancing Queen" melody piece. You can reimagine it by adding notes, transposing, or making other small adjustments. See how many times you can work your melody piece into a chorus before it becomes too repetitive. Record your full chorus melody using nonsense words or try adding lyrics.

Song Challenge:

90% Show Song with Senses: Write a song that is 90% *show* and 10% or less *tell* lyrically. Try to cover all five of your senses somewhere within the lyric. Make sure to use scene setting, nouns & verbs, and metaphors!

A "Victory" Song: Start with an object write on "victory." Reflect on a time you or someone else experienced a victory, whether it was winning the peewee tournament, excelling in a spelling bee, or getting a big promotion. Write a victory song, making sure your title or refrain line truly captures the emotion you felt through the lyrics *and* melody.

***Musical Mad Libs**

Fill out this form FIRST:

Noun:	
Verb:	
Plural Noun:	
Verb:	
Adverb:	
Person in Room:	
Past Tense Verb:	
Adjective:	
Adjective:	
A Number:	
Noun:	
Verb:	

Then plug into these lyrics in order:

I gave my heart to a ____(noun)____
I ____(verb)____ and I might never stop
The ____(plural noun)____ in the trees are ____(verb)____ ____(adverb)____ at me
Saying ____(person in the room)____ you've ____(past tense verb)____ all along

Love isn't ____(adjective)____
And heartbreak is ____(adjective)____
I could live for ____(a number)____ years
My ____(noun)____ would ____(verb)____ and disappear

CHAPTER 4

Miss Mary Mack

Rhyming

"As artists, we seek to restore our childlike perception, a more innocent state of wonder and appreciation not tethered to utility or survival." Rick Rubin

Words. Words can be used as weapons, and words can create worlds. From words, we make blessings and curses. As songwriters, we put a lot of pressure on ourselves to write the words in songs that "make the whole world sing." Words can sometimes feel very heavy, and often we forget that in the beginning, words were mostly fun. Babies learn *mama* and *dada* (and *no*), and toddlers pick up animal sounds. (My son Cohen had spot-on cat and donkey noises.) Some of the earliest words we memorize are nursery rhymes, and for most of us, rhyming begins with the first songs we learn.

Up above the world so high, like a diamond in the sky, are all those twinkling little stars.

In the preschool years, rhyming becomes a fun tool to help us learn how to recognize sounds for reading and writing. We learn how to spell by filling in the blanks and matching pictures to short words that have the same endings. Can you see that worksheet with the picture of the pig, above the wig, above the twig? Let's have some fun getting back to the basics by thinking about how to make a rhyme and how to use rhyming words to create rhyme schemes.

Basic Rhyme & Rhyme Scheme

Imagine yourself on the blacktop during your elementary school recess. Maybe you and your BFF are seated criss-cross applesauce across from each other, clapping and rhyming away.

Miss Mary Mack Mack Mack
All dressed in black, black, black
With silver buttons, buttons, buttons
All down her back, back, back

This verse is anchored on the ends of lines 1, 3, and 4 by the rhyming words *Mack*, *black*, and *back*. These three words are what we call "perfect rhymes" with each other. The most basic elements two words need to rhyme are (1) a shared internal vowel sound, and (2) the same ending consonant sound. Mack and black both share the same internal vowel sound ("ae") and the same ending consonant sound ("ck"). We can note that rhyming has little to do with how the words are spelled, but rather how they sound. You could also rhyme these words with *plaque* because the vowel and consonant sounds match. Similarly, *rough* and *buff* are perfect rhymes because of their sounds, not their spelling. I'm confident most of you understand how perfect rhymes work. Later in the chapter, I will show you ways to generate other types of rhymes, but for now, we'll move on to discuss how to manipulate them in different orders to create rhyme schemes.

Crafting a rhyme scheme is all about selecting how our ears experience space and time within a lyric. Rhyme scheme is another element of songwriting where there are no rules, but lots of helpful best practices. Mastering the use of rhyme scheme is all about establishing and then sometimes selectively breaking expectations. We're going to walk through some basic rhyme schemes while demonstrating the standard shorthand for labeling them. Rhyme schemes are determined by the final word (or stressed syllable of the final word) in the lyric line. The following two lines rhyme because the last words rhyme with each other:

Bluebird in the sky
How'd you get so high

We will label the first pair of rhyming lines that appear in a song section with the letter "A." The second pair of rhyming lines in that same section will be labeled "B," and so on until the end of the section. If the last word of a lyric line doesn't rhyme with any other end words, it is labeled with an "X" to show there's no rhyming pair. Since the rhyme scheme labels only retain their label within a song section, the label "A" for a rhyming pair in the verse doesn't carry over into the chorus. Here's a quick example of a four-line verse and a four-line chorus to show a basic rhyme scheme.

Verse:

Bluebird in the **sky**	A
Beauty in its wings	B
How'd you get so **high**	A
And find new songs to sing	B

Chorus:

I wanna fly like **you**	A
I got nothing to **prove**	A
I wanna soar high **too**	A
Little bird	X

The verse above had rhyming words at the end of lines 1 and 3, so we labeled those lines "A," and the rhyming words on lines 2 and 4 were labeled as "B." Then, the labeling of the rhyme scheme started fresh when we entered the chorus. The ending word *bird* in the chorus does not share an end rhyme with any other line in the chorus, so we labeled it "X."

Here's another example from our recess rhyme above:

Miss Mary Mack Mack **Mack**	A
All dressed in black, black, **black**	A
With silver buttons, buttons, buttons	X
All down her back, back, **back**	A

Labeling is a tool that allows us to easily visualize the sound patterns we are establishing for listening ears. However, paying attention to your rhyme scheme is just the beginning. Opening yourself up to new possibilities will help you choose the rhyme scheme that best fits the mood and pacing of your song. Here's a quick rundown of some of the most common rhyme schemes:

"Couple of Cute Couplets" AABB

We can sing a **song**	A
Won't you sing **along**	A
Just lift up your voice	B
Make a little noise	B

"The Matching Set" ABAB

We can sing a **song**	A
Make a little noise	B
Won't you sing **along**	A
Just lift up your voice	B

"The Long Game" XAXA

We can sing a song	X
Make a little **noise**	A
Confident and loud	X
Just lift up your **voice**	A

"The Bob Dylan" AAAA

We can sing a summertime **song**	A
Won't you join and just sing **along**	A
'Cause everybody here **belongs**	A
It feels so right it can't be **wrong**	A

"One Harmonica Short of a Bob Dylan" AXAA

We can sing a summertime **song**	A
Won't you come and lift up your voice	X
'Cause everybody here **belongs**	A
It feels so right it can't be **wrong**	A

These examples represent just a narrow slice of the rhyme schemes open to you. For starters, the lyrics above only have four lines. There's nothing stopping you from creating a two or eight-line section, or anything in between. More lines just lead to more combinations and possibilities. Whatever rhyme scheme you choose, it's helpful to be aware of the choices you're making and the patterns you're establishing.

Listeners usually enjoy rhyming patterns that stay consistent within song sections. If verse 1 follows an ABAB pattern, your listeners' ears will expect an ABAB pattern in verse 2. It doesn't mean you *have* to give it to them, but they might latch on to your lyrics better if you satisfy their desire for the pattern you've established. People love patterns, but they also enjoy variety beyond established patterns. This balancing act is fundamental not only in rhyme schemes but in all aspects of songwriting—both music and lyrics. Creative use of rhyming and rhyme scheme means wrestling with language to your playful advantage. This is fun work that is intentional, not something to be done on autopilot. As you experiment with rhyme schemes, consider another easy way to "level up" your songwriting by being aware of and avoiding cliché rhymes.

Cliché Rhymes

In Chapter 13, we will cover all kinds of clichés you will inevitably wrestle with as you write songs, but the first and most obvious clichés you will have to negotiate are cliché rhymes. Picture this: You're writing a lyric, and you get to the end of a line. Here's the setup:

We've spent so many nights apart
I'm here alone with my broken _______

You need a rhyme to finish your thought, and now you've got a choice to make. The word *heart* screams out to you as the obvious "fill in the blank." But you realize that if this word is the first rhyme you thought of, then it's also the first rhyme most people will think of. Your listeners will probably hear it coming from a mile away. And if they know it's coming, they won't be excited; they'll be bored when it arrives. It's difficult for a listener to feel an emotional connection to a story they find dull.

So why do *apart* and *heart* make for a cliché rhyme? Typically, cliché rhymes are perfect rhymes. Again, perfect rhymes are the kind you learn in kindergarten, where the central vowel sound and the ending consonant sound are both exactly the same.

Heart and apart both feature an "aR" sounding vowel followed by the consonant "t."

Try going through the alphabet, swapping out the first letter to find a few perfect rhymes for the word *bake*. You just need an "A" sounding vowel in the middle with a "K" consonant on the end. Cake, fake, lake, rake, shake, take... you get the idea. You can also add more than one consonant sound to the front of the word and still have a perfect rhyme, so *bake* to *break* is still perfect.

Now, please don't hear me say that all perfect rhymes are boring. Perfect rhymes can still be interesting if they're not overused. *Heart* and *apart* have become cliché rhymes because of their overused connection in love songs. But perfect rhymes can easily be utilized for fresh rhymes when their connection to each other is not obvious. Take, for example:

Her buttercream smile was sweeter than cake
But underneath the sweet was a layer of snake

Cakes and snakes usually don't go together, so this perfect rhyme doesn't feel cliché. You might have to play around to find interesting rhyming pairs because there are already a lot of predictable pairs out there. Songwriting teacher Mike Errico once noted that "As great as the rhymed word is, its sonic predictability can drain some of its power. The puzzle's too easy." We need some tools to branch out from perfect and predictable rhymes when we want to.

An easy way to stretch perfect rhyme is to stay perfect, but to switch from a one-syllable word to a two-syllable word. Using this trick helps us go from *cake* to *mi-stake* or *for-sake*. Take care with two-syllable words to make sure you're lining up the emphasized syllable. These pairs are still basically perfect rhymes because the vowel sound is on the emphasized syllable: *mis-TAKE, for-SAKE*. Conversely, if your two-syllable word emphasizes the first syllable, like *PILL-ow*, then a perfect match would be a word like *still*. (Or ultra-perfect, musical theater-level rhyming if you rhymed *PILL-ow* with a two-word combo like *still though*.)

Taking another step further away from perfect rhymes are several categories of rhyming pairs that are looser in their sonic connection. These categories include family rhyme, additive/subtractive rhyme, assonance, and consonance rhyme. If you'd like to look up a detailed chart explaining all the intricacies of how to differentiate perfect rhyme from the other types, I've included one at the end of this chapter. We're not going to get bogged down in the categories; we're just going to cover three basic ways to go beyond perfect rhyme.

Beyond Perfect Trick #1

To generate our first "beyond perfect" rhyme, we will change the ending consonant sound and keep the middle vowel sound the same. So for a word like *cake*, we're going to keep the long "A" sound in the middle, but choose an ending consonant sound that is NOT a "k" sound:

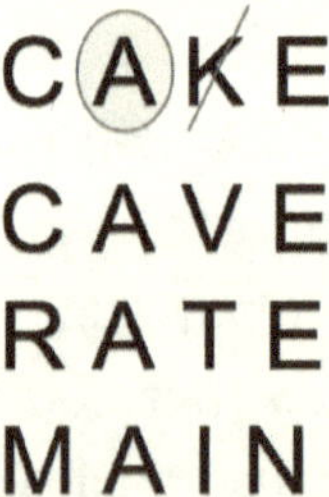

This leads us to words like *cave*, *rate*, *shame*, or *change*. Also, words like *main* because, remember, it's not how the word is spelled, but how it *sounds*. Try to come up with some beyond perfect rhymes for the word *smoke* right now using this technique. Keep the "O" sounding vowel of *smoke* and swap out the "K" at the end for a different consonant. In the end, you will have created either family or assonance rhymes with this trick (by choosing words like *boat*, *own*, *hose*, and *cove*).

Beyond Perfect Trick #2

The next step beyond perfect rhyme is to take away the ending consonant sound completely (or add one if there wasn't a consonant initially). Using this trick, if our word is *cake*, we are going to keep the long "A" sound and remove the final "K" sound entirely. We are looking for words that end with a long "A" sound, and that's it.

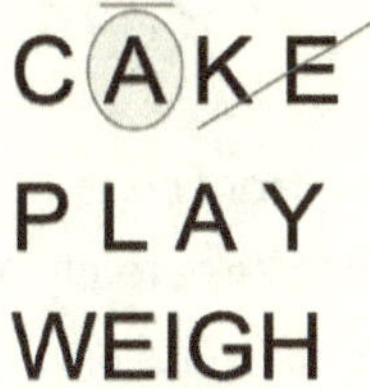

Rhyming words found with this trick include *play*, *stray*, and *weigh*. These are considered subtractive rhymes because they subtract the ending consonant. This trick can also be used in reverse. If you start with a word that ends on a vowel sound (a word like *play*), then you can add a consonant sound to the end to get a fresh rhyme:

PLĀY
GAME
WAVE
BAIT

Using this trick, we get words like *game*, *wave*, *bait*, and *lake*. This is an additive rhyme because it adds a consonant after the original vowel sound.

Beyond Perfect Trick #3

Lastly, we come to the stretchiest of rhymes, those that don't share the central vowel sound. To you, these rhymes might not sound like rhymes at all, but we're expanding our horizons. With this trick, we're going to use the ending consonant in the word to establish the sonic connection and sub in a new central vowel sound. If we begin with the word *cake*, we will keep the ending "K" sound, then pick a new central vowel that is NOT an "A" sound:

CAKE
COOK
POKE
LIKE

In this instance, you're going from *cake* to words that have a "K" sounding consonant, like *cook*, *poke*, or *like*. We're really pushing the boundaries of what people hear as a rhyme when we're relying only on the ending consonant to create the connection. If you choose to keep *both* the opening and the closing consonant the same (as in *cake* to *cook*), it can help the words to feel more closely related. The jump from *cake* to *poke* and *like* is the most extreme rhyme because it has the loosest relationship in our ears. But sometimes that's the kind of rhyme you need. Some emotional lyric moments don't call for a perfect rhyme; they need a subtle connection instead.

There are no rhymes that are inherently better or worse; we just need to know how to keep our options open. Sometimes, end-of-line rhyming isn't what you need at all. Maybe you need a sonic connection that isn't wrapped up with a perfectly rhyming "bow." Or maybe your go-to rhyme schemes don't suit the emotion of your song, and you'd rather let go of strict end-of-line patterns altogether.

Internal Rhymes

If you want to be really adventurous, try playing with internal rhymes. Internal rhymes let you keep sonic connections within your lyrics without needing to rhyme the ends of lines. This can be an effective way to break you out of a cliché rhyme or rhyme scheme funk. Let's look at this Paul Simon lyric to see how internal rhyme moves the verse forward.

Let us be lovers, we'll marry our fortunes together
I've got some real estate here in my bag
So we bought a pack of cigarettes and Mrs. Wagner pies
And walked off to look for America

First, observe that none of the words at the ends of these lines rhyme with each other. However, there's still a lot of rhyming going on. In line 1, the words *lovers* and *together* sonically connect through the "er" endings. In line 2, *real* and *here* are the loose rhyming pair. The ending word of line 2, *bag*, has a connection with the internal rhymes of *pack* and *Wagner*, which help carry the listener through line 3. The forward motion in this lyric has been established through internal rhymes and has paved the way toward a completely *unrhymed* refrain line: "and walked off to look for America."

The following sample is a lyric I wrote one morning while looking out the window and watching a little green lizard crawl up the brick on our house. I wanted to write something that felt cute, but not in an obviously or oppressively cute way. I wanted a lot of rhymes, but I didn't want any that would occur at the end of the lines. I've noted the sonic connections (the internal rhymes) with bolding, underlining, and shapes to make them more obvious.

Little green **li**zard on the b**ri**ck outside
How do you climb like th**is**
Your hands so **sti**cky like Spiderman
Gravity doesn't mean a thing to you

Do these lines feel like they flow and work together even though there is no end line rhyming? Being aware of the sonic connections between the vowels and consonants of your lyrics can free you from exclusively end-line rhyming. It can also invite you to less commonly used rhyme schemes. Take, for example, this verse from Alanis Morissette's hit "One Hand in My Pocket." First, read through the lyric and notice the abundant amount of "R's" found throughout, causing the non-rhyming words to feel related. Next, note the underlined internal rhymes that carry the lyric forward, despite not having end-of-line matches.

I feel drunk, but I'm sober
I'm young, and I'm underpaid
I'm tired, but I'm working, yeah
I care, but I'm restless
I'm here, but I'm really gone
I'm wrong, and I'm sorry, baby

If you want to gain more experience with crafting internal rhymes, I'd suggest you start to listen to and study quality rap music. I assign my level 4 students to study the structure of Eminem's "Lose Yourself." I have them do exactly what I did for you in the above example, line by line, taking note of every sonic connection they can find. Then they observe how the patterns repeat and when they change to something new. A little bit of quality rap in your life will do your lyric writing a lot of good.

Observing the patterns and practices of any genre outside of your norm will help you craft beyond clichés. There's also a lot we can learn about the movement of words through other artistic mediums besides songwriting. It took me a long time to realize that lyric writing is a *writing* practice, and many lessons can be learned from other types of writing. We're going to play around with a few literary devices before we wrap up this chapter on word games.

Alliteration

Alliteration is when the same letter or sound shows up at the beginning of two words that appear close to each other. What kind of writer are you? Are you bad to the bone, or the subtle and sweet type? It doesn't matter if you're cool as a cucumber or busy as a bee; you can use alliteration to your advantage because listening ears like it. Not only do people like to hear it, but it also makes the content of the language feel more believable. Etymologist Mark

Forsyth asserts that, "Any phrase, so long as it alliterates, is memorable and will be believed even if it's a bunch of nonsense. Curiosity, for example, did not kill the cat" (*Elements of Eloquence*). We're not setting out in our songwriting to assert nonsense, but we are using every tool and trick at our disposal to make a connection to listeners. If alliteration makes words memorable and believable, we should be on the lookout for opportunities to use its power.

"The mundane can be beautiful" could be rewritten to "the boring can be beautiful." Perhaps "I'm free like the wind" could be enhanced to "I'm wild like the wind." Notice how a simple word swap adds more punch and magic to the phrase. Some of the greatest literary writers from Shakespeare to Dickens understood the power of alliteration and used it to their advantage. Even politicians and ad men understand its strength in short phrases to win campaigns and sell cars. Let's experiment with some short lyrics to make them more memorable.

Take these lyric lines and see if you can rewrite them, substituting the noun and/or verb to create alliteration:

All my troubles are piling up (Example: All my troubles are towering)
I'm pulling all my dreams
He loves like a tiger
She sparkles like a diamond and I'm a rock

When people talk about "hooks" in songwriting, they're often referring to the melody, but we should also strive to hook listeners with our words. Playing with alliteration is only the beginning. There are many ways we can play with words to make each word in a lyric line have impact. Often, strategic repetition of words can be a way to capture our listeners' attention (just like Miss Mary Mack Mack Mack did). To illustrate, let's take a look at a repetition trick sometimes utilized by songwriters called diacope.

Diacope

You've heard it said that "less is more," and this aphorism is often true in lyric writing. Sometimes we have nothing of substance left to say, and yet there's still a line or two in a song section to fill. Instead of writing something new, the most elegant solution may be to double down on the best thing that we have already said. Exact repeats of strong lyric lines often give our lyrics more power. We can even use this principle of repetition amongst key words within a single lyric line. I want to introduce you to diacope and show you how you can use it to your advantage.

Diacope is a fancy term that simply means "word repetition with a small buffer in between the repeats." You say an important word like *Sunday* and then buffer it with the word *bloody* before returning to the repeat of *Sunday*. This one lyric line, "Sunday Bloody Sunday" makes up almost the entire chorus of the U2 song by the same name:

Sunday, Bloody Sunday
Sunday, Bloody Sunday
Sunday, Bloody Sunday
Sunday, Bloody Sunday
Alright, let's go

But using diacope doesn't limit you to single words. You can use groups of words to form the repeated pattern. Consider the song "Lovefool" by The Cardigans, where the first half of the chorus is built around a diacope structure. I have underlined the "buffer" phrase.

Love me, love me <u>say that you</u> *love me*
Fool me, fool me <u>go on and</u> *fool me*
Love me, love me <u>pretend that you</u> *love me*

The point is to use repetition to your advantage. Double down. Give your listeners the one-two punch. If you enjoy playing with devices like alliteration and diacope, I would highly recommend books like *The Elements of Eloquence* by Mark Forsyth as inspirational reading for further lyric play. If you want to grow as a lyric writer, you've got to be willing to mess around. Most of the time, our best ideas aren't the first ones that come to us. Mature writers are willing to try something silly because it may lead them somewhere compelling. This is true about lyric writing and equally, if not more so, when we consider melody crafting. In our next chapter, we will learn how resolving not to settle in melody writing can be hugely transformative for our growth as songwriters. But before you rush over there, please slow down and take the time to play with rhyme, rhyme scheme, alliteration, and diacope in the "Playtime" activities!

Rhyme Types Chart:

Perfect Rhyme: Same vowel sound, same ending consonant: *tap - nap*
Family Rhyme*: Same vowel sound, ending consonant in the same family* of consonants: *tap - dab* (In this example, both are in the "plosive" family.)
Additive Rhyme: Same vowel sound, add an ending consonant: *day - mate*
Subtractive Rhyme: Same vowel sound, remove the ending consonant: *same - play*
Assonance Rhyme: Same vowel sound, ending consonant from a different family* of consonants: *tap - snack* (In this example, plosive-fricative.)
Consonance Rhyme: Different vowel sound, same ending consonant: *tap - top* or *blip - top*

***Consonant Families** (Words ending in the letter/sound)

Plosives:

b	d	g	p	t	k
ri<u>b</u>	ri<u>d</u>	ri<u>g</u>	ri<u>p</u>	wri<u>t</u>	tric<u>k</u>

Fricatives:

v	Th	z	zh	j	f	th	s	sh	ch
co<u>v</u>e	clo<u>th</u>e	do<u>z</u>e	colla<u>g</u>e	bud<u>g</u>e	of<u>f</u>	mo<u>th</u>	mos<u>s</u>	po<u>sh</u>	bot<u>ch</u>

Nasal:

m	n	ng
sa<u>m</u>e	sa<u>n</u>e	sa<u>ng</u>

PLAYTIME

Solo Activities

Do a Diacope: Play around, creating lyrics for two separate choruses. The first chorus will be based on a single-word diacope, like "Sunday, bloody Sunday." Remember that the repeated word is the most important, so consider a strong noun or verb.

Examples: "Runaway, my runaway," "Love, foolish love," or "Dream, baby dream."

The second chorus will be built of phrases using a diacope like the one we see in "Lovefool." Feel free to do direct repeats or change the diacope with each line.

Example: "break free I'm gonna break free" and/or "get lost I'm gonna get lost."

Rhyme Scheme Remix:

1. Create a two-line couplet using a perfect rhyme, but try to avoid a cliché rhyme.
   Example: basking in the <u>sun</u>, feeling like I've <u>won</u>
2. Create an additional couplet that has a different vowel rhyming pair than the first two lines. Try to keep the content of the lyric related to the first couplet.
   Example: wind combing my <u>hair</u>, losing all my <u>cares</u>
3. Take the two couplets you've created and manipulate them in the following ways. You are free to change the order and change words at the end of lines.

- AABB: *Basking in the sun, Feeling like I've won, Wind combing my hair, Losing all my cares*
- ABAB: *Basking in the sun, Wind combing my hair, Feeling like I've won, Losing all my cares*
- XAXA: *Basking in the sun, Wind combing my hair, Feeling like I'm free, Losing all my cares*
- ABBB: *Basking in the sun, Wind combing my hair, Losing all my cares, Summer like a prayer*

Group Activities

Super Food Verse: Break into groups and have each group write an eight-line lyric focused on the topic "food." Challenge the groups to use an unconventional rhyme scheme. With long verses, there may be more than two rhyming pairs. Groups are welcome to extend their rhyme schemes to include "C" and "D" pairs. After the groups share, have them rewrite their verse to a new rhyme scheme.

The Odd Couple: Break into partners. Have each pair agree on a central vowel sound and ending consonant such as -AKE, -OTE, or -ooN. Each partner will pick a one-syllable word using their chosen vowel-consonant combo, but not working together. Once each partner selects their word separately, they will work together to combine the words in a two-line couplet linking the ideas together.

Example: Pair chooses "-OTE". Partner 1 selects the word boat. *Partner 2 selects the word* throat. *They work together to write the lyric "I got a lump in my throat, she's a battleship and I'm a boat."*

Repeat the activity to use different combinations in different rhyme schemes.

Homework Challenge

Internal Rhyme Lyric: Write a four-line verse using only internal rhymes (no end-of-line rhyming). See how many sonic connections you can make within the lyric without going overboard into "too much rhyme" territory. If you are on a roll, try to write a verse 2 using the same sonic patterns you've established, or write a chorus to go with your internal rhyme verse.

Rhyme Rewrite: Create a mini-song of just one verse and a chorus (both melody and lyric). Call this version 1. Now, do a rewrite of the lyric, intentionally changing the rhyme scheme in both song sections. Now do a second rewrite, intentionally changing the rhyme scheme again. Lastly, compare all three mini-song lyrics side by side and choose your favorite of the three versions. (It might not be the one that makes the most sense, but it might *sound* the best.)

Song Challenge:

Alliteration Title: Start your songwriting process by first writing an alliteration title.

Example: "Free Fallin'" by Tom Petty or "Lay Lady Lay" by Bob Dylan (which is also a diacope!)

If you'd like more of a challenge for this prompt, see if you can include a diacope somewhere in the lyric.

Playground Games: Write a song rooted in a playground memory. Immerse yourself in the details of a vivid memory from the blacktop, trampoline, or kickball field. The song doesn't have to stay on the playground; just let this be the jumping-off point. For an additional challenge, attempt to use a rhyme scheme in the verses you wouldn't normally gravitate to.

CHAPTER 5

King of the Mountain

Melody Writing

"Melody is a form of remembrance. It must have a quality of inevitability in our ears." Gian Carlo Menotti

My friend Jonathan once said, "Melody is king." I think he's right. Melody is king, lyrics are queen, and harmony is the kingdom that they live in. Everybody's got to work together to keep the land in peace and prosperity. (I know some kingdoms are ruled by queens—girl power—but just pause reality on that for this metaphor.)

In the more formal analogy, the king is the face and figurehead of the nation. If the story of that nation is briefly mentioned in a history book, it is the monarch's name we see listed there. Everything else exists within the context of that king and his era. What does this have to do with songs?

When everything about a memorable song is stripped back, it is the melody that we hum. It's the one song element to rule them all.

But this songwriting book is all about fun and games, so let's talk about a more playful kind of king. Have you ever played King of the Mountain? I can only remember one time in my childhood when I engaged in an authentic king of the mountain battle. My parents competed in church league softball in the early 90s—look it up, I promise it was a thing. My brother and I spent hours entertaining ourselves on those long evenings at the ballpark, eating countless grape snow cones and goofing around with the other kids whose parents also played softball all night.

There was a small hill in one corner of the softball complex where we would congregate. The hill had a gentle slope that was perfect for rolling down, and now that I'm thinking about it, I guess the grass must have been extra fluffy. We'd play King of the Mountain, with one kid standing at the top of the hill and throwing challengers down. The roughness was tolerated because when you lost the fight to be king, you weren't so sad. The best part was rolling down the fluffy grass anyway.

But I digress. The point is, in the battle of melody, lyrics, and harmony, melody wins. Everything else can roll down the hill and be okay if you've got a melody that's truly worthy to be king.

So, what makes up a melody? At its most basic definition, melody is just pitch and rhythm (and magic). Why is it so challenging to create melodies that achieve kingly status if it seems like it should be so simple? Because the components of pitch and rhythm contain a lot of variables. We've got moving parts like melodic rhythm, melodic contour, starting pitch, rests, non-chord tones, non-diatonic pitches, repetition, variation, note lengths, intervals, phrasing… and probably even more important than any of these is the intangible quality of "magic" found in a melody that feels good to sing. We want to create melodies that get stuck in our heads and stay on our lips.

We're going to contemplate each of these melody parts and manipulate them as we go. We will work in small melody pieces called "melodic motifs." These are musical phrases that are most often about two bars long. I'm going to give you some tricks I've learned along the way and also show you some pitfalls where melody writers often get stuck. Ultimately, we're playing around to try to create a melody worthy of leading a song (and improve melodies that are holding our songs back).

The Crown

If melody is king, then rhythm is the crown. I'm not talking about the drum part, the "groove" type of rhythm. I'm talking about melodic rhythm, or the rhythm of the notes you sing. Melodic rhythm is the crown because it's the *symbolic* thing giving the king his authority. It represents the king's power. It's the thing that makes everything else fall in line, so to speak.

As a songwriter, do you listen to rap music? Again, you should. The rhythm within words is where the magic happens. We can be abundantly inspired by soaking in these songs, not just by hearing the words, but by noticing how other people play with the rhythm of the words. I want you to start a playlist right now of rap songs that have a gripping spoken rhythm. Choose songs that make you think, "I want to find that same energy and flow in my songwriting."

Do it right now. Add at least five songs to your melodic rhythm rap playlist for further study.

Generational songwriting tendencies are shaped by melodic rhythm. In his book *The Elements of Song Craft,* Billy Seidman argues that "Rhythm and syncopation seem to represent the roots of each generation's musical originality." Each generation prefers different rhythmic flows. If a song feels outdated to you, it might not just be the production; it could be the rhythm of the melody. If *your* songs seem out of touch or outdated, you might want to experiment with new melodic rhythms. Hooks aren't just made with pretty notes. Hooks live or die based on their melodic rhythm. How much do you care about the rhythm of your melody? Whatever your answer, you should care about it *more.*

So let's play with the rhythm of words. We're gonna think of a short string of words that could be interpreted and emphasized in a lot of different ways. Let's use the phrase:

"Give me all your money"

In the same way that actors in a theater troupe might warm up by delivering this line with different emphasis choices, we will do the same thing with rhythm. The following examples are all on the same pitch because we're not worrying about pitches right now. Clap and speak each of the following examples to observe how the rhythmic choices change the feel of the line.

First, let's try the lyric with a marching feel, where almost every syllable gets equal weight starting right on the downbeat:

Ex: 5.01

Now let's try an emphasis on a couple of different words. This first one really emphasizes the word *give* because of the length of the note and its placement on the downbeat:

Ex: 5.02

This next interpretation brings our focus to the word *money*, because that word gets the most rhythmic length and lands on the downbeat:

Ex: 5.03

We could literally do this all day, but you will start to notice that certain rhythms serve these words to your ears better than others. Here's one that utilizes a rest space to mix it up:

Ex: 5.04

There are always more rhythmic choices available if we decide not to settle on our first idea. Next time you get an idea for one line of lyric, challenge yourself to see how many different ways you can rhythmically interpret it.

It's important to consider how lyrics can guide the rhythm of a melody. However, some melodies free us to sing in a way we probably wouldn't speak. Dolly and Whitney can make these words work when they're singing them, but no one's probably going around speaking like this:

"and I---ee--I--will al–ways love you---oo---oo----"

(from "I Will Always Love You" by Dolly Parton)

You don't *have* to start with the lyrics when you're creating a melody. I encourage you to experiment with crafting melodies you love before committing to some or all of the lyrics. It's okay to find a melody that you love that doesn't have words yet. I'll have more to say on "which comes first, melody or the lyrics?" in a later chapter.

The Cloak

If melody is king, then the melody shape, also known as contour, is the cloak. It is the beauty that enwraps our melody king, giving him distinctive character. There are five basic shapes we will start with. Obviously, there are more variations and combinations of these shapes, but we're just looking at the simplest structures.

The most basic of the melody shapes is "flat." Melody master Jack Perricone would call this shape "stationary." Flat shapes are basically hanging around a central pitch, possibly moving up or down by a half step here or there, but they mostly form a flat-looking line. (Look up the verse to the song "On the Floor" by Jennifer Lopez for an example of a melody built exclusively on a flat shape.) Let's take a rhythm for our sure-to-be-hit "give me all your money" and attach it to some melodic contour. We will start with the mostly flat shape.

Ex: 5.05 #1 Flat:

Basic melody shapes #2 and #3 are just "going up" and "going down." If you are into more technical terms, you can call these "ascending" and "descending." Here's our lyric on these two shapes. Notice that not all the notes are in perfectly stepwise motion. We're just looking at the general shape.

Ex: 5.06 #2 Going Up:

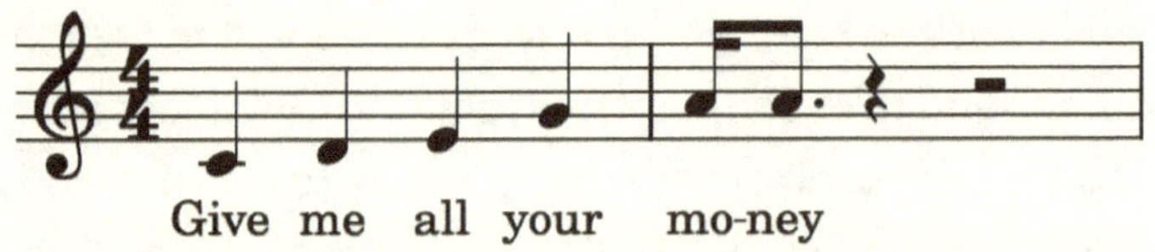

Ex: 5.07 #3 Going Down:

The last two basic shapes have fancy names like "arch" and "inverted arch," but that sounds like math to me. Let's go with "hill" and "ditch" (since we're playing King of the Mountain, after all).

Ex: 5.08 #4 Hill:

Ex: 5.09 #5 Ditch:

Every once in a while, you'll see a bouncing melody that's built around large interval jumps and doesn't easily fit into one of these five shape categories. You can look up the verse to the Miley Cyrus song "Wrecking Ball" for an example. We'll call this outlier shape the "yo-yo."

Ex: 5.10 #6 Yo-yo:

Most melodic motifs (short melodies) can be simplified to one of these shapes or a combination of them. Here's an example of a longer motif, which is a combination of "flat" and "going down."

Ex: 5.11 Flat then Going Down:

So why the brief tour of basic shapes? Because we've got a lot of different cloaks to try on. As we build little pieces of melody into larger melodies across the expanse of our song, it helps to be aware of the shapes we're making. We can work toward more repetition of shapes if our melody seems too random, or more variation in shapes if everything starts to sound the same. So what shape is your melody wearing? Is it elegant and unique, or is it that same old thing you've been putting on all season? If your shape is feeling a little tired, maybe it's time to try on something new.

The Jewels

In Chapter 3, we covered how sparkle notes are pitches within a melody that catch our attention. They stand out in a good way. They are the crown jewels within our melody that make it precious. Let's take a basic melody and see if we can sub in some sparkle.

Ex: 5.12 This one's about as sparkly as a dull rock:

Our first trick will be to encourage our listeners to pay attention with an unexpected melody jump. Let's raise a note from the first example to cause some interval jumps for sparkle. Notice how raising one note creates two interesting interval jumps.

Ex: 5.13 Add interval jump(s):

That's feeling a little shinier. Let's go back to the dull rock melody, but this time let's add a non-diatonic pitch (a note that doesn't occur naturally in the key).

Ex: 5.14 Add non-diatonic pitch:

If we already have harmony underneath our melody, we can also try suspended tones where our ear might normally expect a resolution.
Ex: 5.15 Add suspension:

We could also establish a melody pattern and then slightly modify it to add a jewel.
Ex: 5.16 Repeat and change the pattern:

If you feel like your melody is lacking luster, here's the main question to ask yourself: What notes can I adjust to add some sparkle? Try on lots of jewels until you find the one that suits your melody best. Ultimately, these kingly vestments (the crown, the cloak, and the jewels) are just ways to play with a melody to make it intentional and beautiful. There are still more pieces to consider, but for now, we're going to do a quick case study on a famous "melody king" found in many hit pop songs.

A Famous King: Front-Heavy Fa

When we become writers who love to play with melody, we start noticing patterns that consistently work in other songs. An essential part of your journey and growth as a songwriter is listening for what makes melodies shine in other people's songs. A melody king that draws my attention from time to time is one I call "front-heavy fa."

Front-heavy fa is a melodic trick that can provide maximum tension and resolution as the singer goes into a new song section, usually a chorus. The "front-heavy" part indicates that the melody starts *before* the downbeat. The "fa" part indicates that the melody hangs on the 4th scale degree of the key (the "fa" in solfege). I know that's a lot of technical language. Hang on, and I'll break it down.

Notable examples of front-heavy fa include the beginning of the chorus for Kelly Clarkson's "Since U Been Gone," Miley Cyrus's "Wrecking Ball," Tina Turner's "The Best," and the verse of "La Bamba" by Ritchie Valens. All of these melodies start before the downbeat and feature a repetitive melodic rhythm on the fourth scale degree. Additionally, they all resolve to a chord tone within the one chord (when the chorus lands harmonically).

Listen to the portions of each of these songs indicated above to see if you can hear the similarities. You're listening for:

- The distinctive scale degree 4 pitch "fa"
- On a repetitive rhythm
- That starts before the downbeat
- And resolves melodically and harmonically to the 1 chord.*
  **Since U Been Gone is a small variation to our "trick" because it lands on the 6 minor chord, but it eventually resolves to the 1 chord at the end of the first line.*

Ex: 5.17 Front-Heavy Fa:

This king is powerful because of its resolution. The melody can resolve down to scale degree 3 (an E in the key of C Major), which is what both "Wrecking Ball" and "The Best" do. Alternatively, it can continue to wind down and resolve to scale degree 1 (a C in the key of C Major), as seen in "La Bamba." The front-heavy fa provides a payoff to the listener's ears when it resolves.

Ex: 5.18 Front-Heavy Fa Resolution:

And that's just one famous melody king. Isn't he divine? This is just one piece of melodic royalty that I've learned to recognize in the wild. There are plenty more if you start looking for them, and you can learn to utilize them in your own melody writing.

Pitfalls & Challenges: The King Is Dead

We learned in Chapter 2 that simply capturing a melody idea is just the beginning. We also need to have the discipline not to settle for the first idea that comes to mind. Sometimes our initial melody idea could benefit from some "adornment" in the form of more compelling rhythm, bigger interval jumps, or more productive repetition. So much of intuitive melody composition comes from finding something you love, then building upon it.

One of the most prevalent melody problems songwriters tend to have is something I call "same/same/same." This happens when we find a melody shape or pattern that we prefer, but then we never attempt to rework it. Our sweet tooth takes over, and we use that same-ish melody for most of the song. No, I'm not talking about creative ways to reinvent that melody through intentional manipulation; I'm talking about the exact same melody essence—such as the same range, starting pitch, phrasing, rhythm, or shape—being overused. A same/same/same king has limited power to lead people because he's a one-trick pony. He can't grow and adapt.

It's easy to drift into same/same/same when our original melody doesn't have much character to begin with. We morph from one song section to another, and our listener can't really tell that we're somewhere new because, well, it all sounds the same! It is easier to avoid the same/same/same problem when your melody demands attention. A melody that *feels* like a chorus will probably not feel like a verse. Writers who tend to be lyric-forward and care more about their words sometimes find this to be the real issue. They never really found a unique melody in the first place, so they just kind of sang something that seemed "sufficient" to carry their words. Let me tell you, songwriter, sufficient is not delicious.

On the other end of the spectrum from the same/same/same problem is an even worse alternative: The king is dead. This melody issue is the other side of the coin; it's "different/different/different." Here, we find a melody with a lack of intention among the elements. Not enough repetition, disconnected and wandering shapes, and "jewels" out of place. This is a melody bereft of memorability. In *Great Songwriting Techniques*, Jack Perricone says, "The most obvious and important element in making anything memorable in a song is repetition." A melody king without intentional patterns at its core is a king with no beating heart.

This prognosis seems harsh. Most of the time, we don't have dead kings; we just have kings on life support, wandering through their kingdoms, looking disheveled and missing their crowns. The easiest way to diagnose a king on life support is to ask someone to sing a piece of your song back to you—any piece of it. Can they do it? Or take a few days' break from your own song. Can you remember how it goes? I often use this tool when revisiting a song I wrote a few days ago. I note what melodies I *can't* remember. This is valuable information.

While we remain vigilant to keep our kings off life support, we've also got to watch out for challengers to the throne. I'll spend most of the next chapter arguing why I think the melody king needs to reign supreme, but let's talk about what can happen when someone else tries to take the throne.

Pitfalls & Challenges: Chords Usurping the Throne

Crafting a singable melody can be tricky if you're working with just pen and paper. This is where noodling on an instrument can sometimes help us find new musical ideas. But if you're noodling, beware of letting chord changes be the sole driving force behind your melody choices. When I was a beginner songwriter, I fell in love with interesting chord changes. However, crafting an interesting chord progression *before* writing anything else in my song became my default way to create. I'd sit down at the piano and start playing the same chord changes that I naturally gravitated towards. Familiar tempo, familiar keys, same chords changing at the same time. I couldn't even conceive of a melody without my hands roaming the keyboard, playing chords. And this worked...for a while. Then two things kept happening:

1. My songs all started sounding very similar to one another.
2. I'd craft a very long and intricate chord progression that was so busy that the melody I was singing became an afterthought.

Am I saying it's wrong to start writing songs by playing chords first? Absolutely not. But if your melody is always dictated by chord changes, you might be sacrificing the beauty and memorability of the melody for the sake of your chord progressions. Over time, you could fall into tired and predictable melodic patterns because your chords have taken the throne. So if you're one of those people who *need* to touch an instrument, try not to do it every once in a while. Or try holding instruments you're *not* very good at. Or, if you must play chords first, then immediately try to reharmonize the melody once you've created it. Make sure the melody holds up when you replace the chords.

You want people to walk away from your song humming your melody, not contemplating your brilliant chord changes. (Because, let's be real, most people outside of musicians won't notice those chord changes.) I am not arguing that you shouldn't use harmony or production elements to help you get inspired. However, I encourage you to be mindful when your chord changes are taking over. Ultimately, strive to care more about your melody than your harmony. As we continue to guard the king, there is another usurper in the wings, and she's dangerous if she's an inflexible tyrant.

Pitfalls & Challenges: The Queen is Taking Over

Our next challenger to the throne is the lyric queen. She stomps her royal foot, declaring, "It's my way or the highway!" and the king starts to buckle and loses his power. Before you get offended and throw this book in the trash, let me be clear:

1. Girl power, still about it.
2. Chill, this is just a metaphor.
3. Starting with lyrics is *not* a bad place to start!

Many songwriters are lyric-forward writers, and there's nothing wrong with that. Starting with lyrics can be a great beginning if you're mindful to craft a melody that brings their meaning alive.

So what's the problem? We've already talked about how we shouldn't settle for the first melody that comes to mind. Oftentimes, the first thing that comes to us is not compelling or unique. Sufficient ≠ delicious. But the real power struggle is when we decide that our lyrics will *win,* and the melody has to bow to them. If we force our melodies to wrap around words that don't naturally lend themselves to catchy melody patterns, we have a problem. Instead of adjusting the lyrics to make the line singable and memorable, we start modifying the melody by adding or removing notes. Compromising the melody for the sake of the lyrics may have a negative effect on the melodic rhythm, line length, and patterns we are building.

What does this power struggle look like? Let's take a song you probably know and compromise the melody to fit new lyrics. First, sing this song in your head the way you know it:

Amazing grace how sweet the sound
That saved a wretch like me
I once was lost but now I'm found
Was blind but now I see

Now, try to sing the song again, with lyrics that try to wrestle control away from the melody:

Amazing grace how sweet the sound
That saved a wretch like me
I once was lost alone but now I'm found
Was blind to my sin but now I see

This melody bows to a dominating lyric queen when you decide that the exact words are more important than the melody's rhythm and shape. On the other hand, if you decide your melody is the priority, you won't entertain a queen attempting to overthrow it. If there are lyrics making the melody harder to sing and remember, those words are probably not adding value to the song.

Pitfalls & Challenges: Unrest in the Kingdom

If you're still learning an instrument, you may struggle with time. I'm talking about musical time here, not about being habitually late to church. Managing musical time may come intuitively for some, but for others, it might take practice and intentional awareness. When we are managing musical time, we are:

- Aware of how long (how many beats) we're holding a chord
- Aware of where the melody and the chords are interacting with the beats within the measure
- Aware of how many bars are contained in each song section
- Aware of how much rest space we want between melody lines

I mention this challenge of time because writers who are still learning an instrument or recording their melody ideas a cappella may struggle to get others to understand how (or rather *when*) they want their melody to land. If people have trouble latching onto your idea rhythmically and you're not sure, I'd encourage you to start recording your ideas to a metronome, even if that "metronome" is just you snapping your fingers while singing into a voice memo. Rhythmic alignment problems can happen when we are writing while unaware of the downbeat, the time signature, or how many bars should occur between melodic lines. As you use your metronome, try to feel where the potential chord changes will land, even if you can't play them yet.

If it's difficult for you to sing and play at the same time, try recording your chords first, thinking only about how long each chord should be held. Then go back and sing your melody, paying attention to when your sung lines feel too short, too long, or misaligned with the chord changes.

It's easier to unwind musical timing problems when you can separate the harmony from the melody and focus on one thing at a time.

Kingmakers

There's a lot to consider when crafting a melody, but in the end, I want to remind you not to overthink it. Melodies need magic, and you should enjoy singing them. Don't tweak them to death. Sometimes I get bogged down on a melody and rewrite it so many times that I begin to fall out of love with it.

So what can you do if your melody king isn't taking the throne like he should? Start playing with other song elements to get unstuck. Take away all the lyrics and focus on the melody again. Or eliminate the harmony. Or try playing your melody on guitar instead of piano, or vice versa. I often find that when I change instruments, I will change inherent grooves, which impacts the rhythm of my melody.

Or, consider the kingmakers. At the beginning of this chapter, I mentioned my friend Jonathan. He's an amazing producer, songwriter, and overall music aficionado. I showed him a song with a great chorus melody, except for the very last line. Something about it just didn't land quite right. It resolved too neatly and made the ending feel overly happy when we wanted it to be bittersweet. I rewrote the melody several times, but it still didn't work. Jonathan suggested we try a little "WWTD"—What Would Taylor (Swift) Do. We thought about how this chorus might end if it were a Taylor Swift song, and it worked! Often, when we put ourselves in the headspace of another songwriter who has the musical and emotional sounds we're going for, it can help unlock new melody paths forward. So think of some kingmakers you admire the next time your melody gets stuck. Ask yourself: What would they do? Then play pretend.

PLAYTIME

Solo Activities

The Blinding Lights Verse: Create a short piece of melody no longer than two measures. Just sing "nah nah nah" for this one, no lyrics needed. The short melody you create will be line 1 of your verse. Call it Melody A. Next, create a second melody line that sounds good after Melody A but is somewhat different. Call this Melody B, which will be verse line 2. Then repeat Melody B exactly for line 3. Finally, create one last melody that "lands the plane" (Melody C), which will be verse line 4. You now have a verse melody structure based entirely on an ABBC pattern.

The verse melody structure should look like this:

Line 1: Melody A

Line 2: Melody B

Line 3: Melody B

Line 4: Melody C

We call this activity the "The Blinding Lights Verse*" because it mirrors the melodic pattern of the verse of that song, but there are lots of other examples of this melody king in the wild.

**We took the inspiration for this activity from a video by Logan Grime, who goes by the name ViB3 MACHiNE.*[2]

Borrow from a Bird: Borrow a melody from a bird. Or the washing machine. Or an iPhone ringtone. Find the beginning of a melody in an unusual place and then build it out to make it your own.

Group Activities

Time After Time (in pairs): First, find a partner. One person will create a short melody idea around two bars long. The other person will then compose a different short melody to complement the first. Sing the motifs back and forth as you figure out how they will fit together, then switch roles so the other person creates the first motif. If you need a model for

---

2 "ViB3 MACHiNE." *YouTube.* Accessed January 9, 2025. http://www.youtube.com/@vib3machine.

trading motifs, look up the chorus to "Time After Time." In this chorus, the first motif is "if you're lost you can look and you will find me," and the second is "time after time." Have partners add lyrics once they finalize their paired melody pieces.

Melody Ladder: Break into groups of four or fewer, and set a metronome to a medium tempo (around 80 bpm). Have one group member create a short, two-bar melody without lyrics. The next group member sings the original motif and then adds to it. They can repeat the motif exactly, modify it, or create something completely new. Keep adding on to the growing melody one member at a time. Remind participants that they can repeat or manipulate previous motifs at any time. For example, person three might repeat what person two created. Try to limit exact repetitions to no more than three times in a row. After the fourth person finishes, have the group sing all the melodies in a row.

Homework Challenge

Adding Sparkle Notes: Explore the concept of sparkle notes and understand how they enhance a melody. Write three short, basic melodies and then experiment with adding sparkle notes. Try introducing unexpected interval jumps, non-diatonic pitches, or suspended non-chord tones to make the melody more interesting. Use the examples in the chapter as a guide. Submit your original melodies and the sparkle versions side by side, both on staff paper and recorded.

Rhythmic Emphasis: Write a short sentence and experiment with different melodic rhythms (don't worry about the pitches). Create variations by placing rhythmic emphasis on different words or syllables, and remember to place the emphasized syllable of important words on beats 1 & 3 of the measure. If you're unsure what to do here, reference "The Crown" section of this chapter. Record all versions spoken to a metronome, then add pitches to your favorite rhythm.

Example: (Record all lines on different rhythms)

1. *Equal Rhythmic Emphasis: take me to the moon tonight*
2. *Emphasis on* Take*:* *TAKE me to the moon tonight*
3. *Emphasis on* Moon*: take me to the* *MOON tonight*
4. *Emphasis on* Tonight*: take me to the moon TONIGHT*
5. *Varied Emphasis:* *TAKE me to the MOON to-NIGHT*

Song Challenge

The "Ryan Tedder:" Write what you would consider to be a strong chorus melody, but don't add lyrics just yet. After you've settled on the chorus melody, turn it into your verse melody. Working from this verse melody, create a new chorus melody. We call this the "Ryan Tedder" because he famously composes verses by creating a chorus first and then creating another chorus that feels like even *more* of a chorus.

A King with No Queen: Try to write a complete song melody before you add any lyrics. You are welcome to experiment with vowel sounds, but don't try to write cohesive lyrics. Once you have arrived at a complete song melody that you like, start adding lyrics. DO NOT compromise the melody for the lyrics. It's okay if your lyrics don't make much sense, just choose words that feel right more than words that "make sense." If you think this is ridiculous, go listen to "Come Together" by the Beatles, and then you'll get what we're going for.

CHAPTER 6

Finger Painting Part 1

Chords & Harmony

"Creativity is intelligence having fun." Albert Einstein

I started taking piano lessons when I was around 6 or 7 years old. I learned from a very nice lady who attended our church, Sherlene, who I'm sure was doing my parents a favor. They knew I loved music and enjoyed singing, so they thought piano lessons were the next logical step. I would go over to Sherlene's house and sit at her scratched, black upright piano and work out of the dinky kid's piano books that everyone learns on. It was torture. These songs didn't sound like the music that I loved—they were short and strange, and I wasn't sure I wanted to play piano if this was what it was all about.

I remember sitting at the piano in my own house one afternoon, dramatically "practicing" (more like crying and throwing my hands around the keyboard). I was raging through a little song about a knight on a horse. I hated the song, but more than that, I couldn't even play it right, which made things even worse. The last straw of my first formal piano lesson experience was when my sweet piano teacher insisted that I practice in front of her with a paper cutout draped over my head to cover my hands. I was already having enough trouble when I *could* see my fingers. I felt like an idiot, even at my young age, to be sitting in front of her with a giant paper laid over me like a ridiculous cloak. I quit soon after.

I'm sure my piano teacher meant well, but this method of learning piano wasn't fun for me. I couldn't find the wonder and play in it. I didn't lose track of time playing; instead, I was desperately counting down the minutes until I was done. Add embarrassment on top of that, and I was pushed over the edge. (I never make my own kids perform recitals for their music lessons. Perhaps I still have unresolved wounds!)

Several years later, I approached the piano again on my own terms. My grandmother's upright Baldwin, dinged up but still beautiful, was a staple in my parents' living room. There was a big brass-rimmed mirror hanging right above it, so you never felt like you were playing to a wall. It was the same instrument I had "raged" at when I was 7, but I had a new approach this time. I sat at the piano not to "accomplish" anything or to log lessons from a workbook, but just to goof around.

In high school choir, I began to piece together some basic music theory on my own. I started to notice how the different notes of voices coming together at the same time made chords. I reasoned that if I could begin to understand how major and minor chords are formed and come together, then perhaps I could learn to play the piano that way.

Finger Painting

When I interacted with the piano by just playing around, I stuck with it. I realize now that it was like "finger painting" for piano. At first, I could only play in primary colors. I started with major triads, all in root position and all in my right hand. Then I became more adventurous and learned how to make some minor chords. I had no idea which chords belonged to which keys; I just built what I could figure out by counting the half steps. More adventurous finger painting happened when I began adding the root of each chord into my left hand.

But things got real messy when I tried to figure out 7th chords. Any time I added a note on top of a triad, I added the number "7" to the chord. I had no reference for the difference between major, minor, or dominant 7ths. All 7s, or any extra note above the triad, for that matter, were a 7 to me!

It was a beautiful mess. I spent countless hours, weeks, and months finger painting on the piano. The real joy of this process was that I was in control of the play, and I was having fun. Now I could write my own songs, and the music would follow me. I may have been painting in big blobs of mismatched hues, but I was the one who did the painting. I told the colors where to go, how much, and how bright. I look back at some of the old chord charts I wrote in my finger painting era, and I can hardly make sense of them. I seldom stayed in one identifiable key. I used sharps, flats, and minor symbols interchangeably. I put an asterisk on chords if I couldn't figure out what I was playing. And that's okay. It's awesome, actually, because I didn't let my lack of knowledge hinder my creativity.

Eventually, I learned a lot of music theory in college. I can now paint in many more colors. I use finer strokes and paint with detail, vision, and precision. But I could never have arrived where I am now without my piano finger painting days. (Let's be honest: They were more like finger painting years.) Wherever you are in your music theory knowledge, I want to encourage you to reconsider your relationship with accompanying instruments. For today, I'd like you to think of interacting with them like finger painting.

I am *not* going to try to cover or review all there is to know about basic music theory in this chapter. That is a job for another textbook. What I am going to give you are some basic theory starting points, just to make sure we've all got access to the primary colors. **You need to sit in front of a keyboard while you read through this chapter; otherwise, it's not going to**

be much fun. If you don't have a piano or keyboard, that's okay—there are a million free piano apps you can download on your phone that will suffice. There's a lot of "play" written into this chapter, so please don't rush through it. If you need to work through it in several sittings, please take your time.

For those of you who already have a comprehensive working knowledge of music theory, feel free to jump to the "playbreak" boxes at the end of each section.

Triads

Building major and minor triads (three-note chords) in root position on the piano is where I started, so we'll begin there. Hang with us even if the guitar is your go-to instrument. It's important to understand how basic triads are built, so you can translate the principles to the guitar. It's only going to benefit you to learn a little bit of piano along the way. Going forward, I'm going to use capital letters to represent chords (such as C) and lowercase letters to represent individual notes (such as c).

Piano 101

If you're brand new to the keyboard, here's the super condensed version of how the piano works. The *smallest* distance between any keys, white or black, is called a half step. A whole step is two half steps in a row. To go higher in pitch, you move on the keyboard to the right. To go lower in pitch, you move to the left. Any time I tell you to take a half step up (higher), you will go to the next closest key, whether it's white or black, moving to the right.

Higher pitch = right. Lower pitch = left.

You will also see notes labeled with sharps (#) or flats (♭). These are usually black keys. A sharp indicates a black key that is a half step **up** from the named note, and a flat is a half step **down** from the named note. In this way, both c# and d♭ are the *same* black key, but they are labeled differently depending on the context.

To build a major triad chord, pick any note and call that the root (or 1) of your chord. For our example, we will make a C Major chord and start with the note c. To make a triad chord, we will call the starting note the 1, then go up *four* half steps, and then go up another *three* half steps to find the last note in the chord. Remember, a half step is the smallest distance you can move from one key to the next on the keyboard. To build a C Major triad, we start on c, go up four half steps to find the next note, which is e, and then another three half steps to find the last note, which is g. We've built a C Major triad, which is made of the notes c, e, and g.

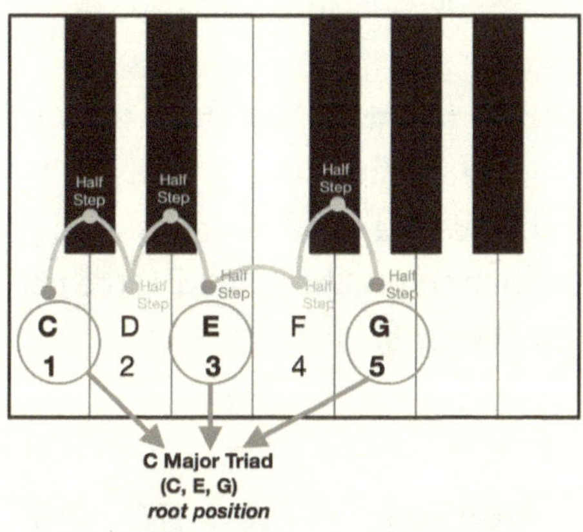

Anytime you see a chord symbol that has just the letter name (as in C), you will assume this is a major triad chord. C = C Major, G = G Major, F = F Major.

Now let's build a minor triad. A minor triad is similar to a major triad; the only thing that changes is the order of the half steps we're counting. Start with the root of the chord, but this time go up three half steps and then four half steps. You will observe that the only difference between C Major and C minor (in root position) is the middle note. This is the e in the C Major chord and the e♭ in the C minor chord. All we did was flip the order of the half steps. It is important to remember that minor chords *must* be indicated by adding the word "minor" or an "m" to the chord symbol. C minor = Cm.

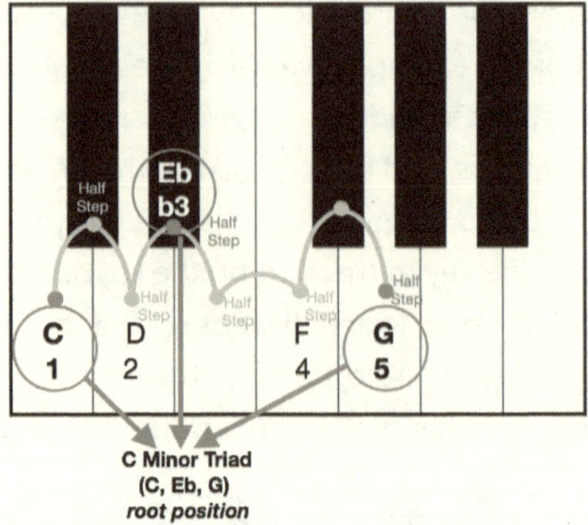

This combination of counting half steps from the root note is how you build EVERY major and minor triad in root position, regardless of the starting note. Let's observe the same pattern starting on the note d. Major triad: four half steps then three. Minor triad: three half steps then four. So D Major is d, f#, a. D minor is d, f, a.

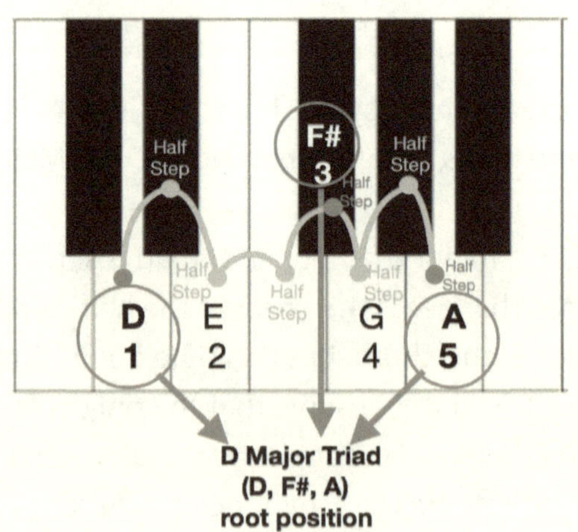

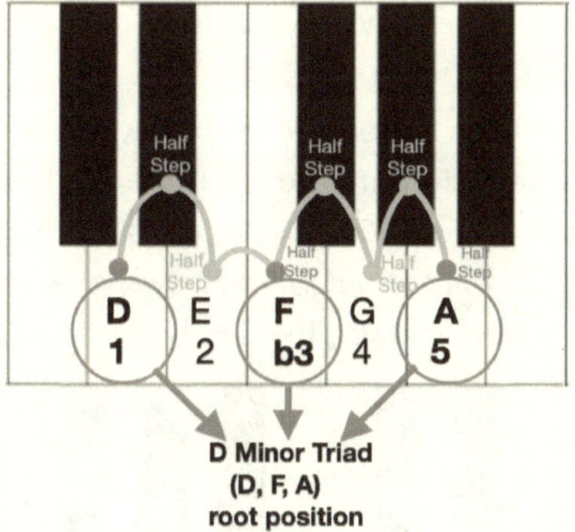

Playbreak 1

There are two exercises in every playbreak in this chapter. "Finger Painting" is for theory beginners, and "More Advanced" provides a challenge for those more comfortable with basic theory.

Finger Painting: On the keyboard, build the triads for this chord progression in root position:

C Major - G Major - A minor - F Major

Go to the end of the chapter to check your notes, then get comfortable playing the progression over and over. Afterward, try to sing a melody while you play.

More Advanced: Build an unusual progression of triads that are linked together by one common pitch. If you need some structure, try this chord progression:

Example: E Major - A Major - C# minor - C Major

Sing a melody on top of your unusual progression that ONLY uses the common pitch that all the chords share (e natural for the above progression.) Utilize an interesting rhythm for your melody, but only sing that one common pitch.

Wild Triads

There are two other kinds of triads we can build with the half-step patterns. Diminished triads are built with a root followed by three half steps, and then *another* three half steps. (Cdim = c e♭ g♭) Diminished chords feel a bit "squished" and sound a little crunchy. You may also see a diminished chord indicated with a ° symbol following the chord letter name, such as: c° or vii°.

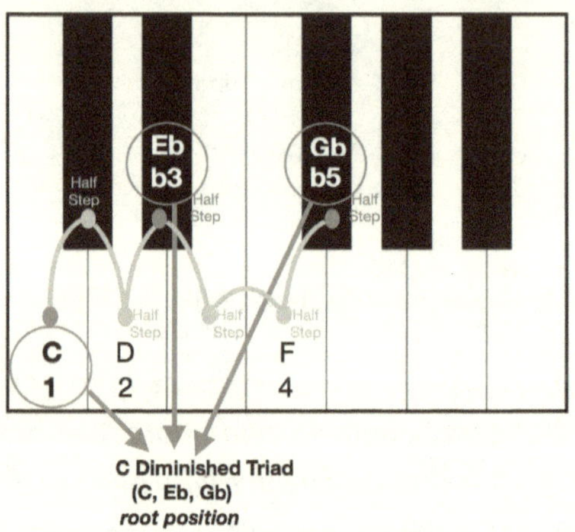

C Diminished Triad
(C, Eb, Gb)
root position

On the other end of the spectrum, we have an augmented triad. This chord is built from the root followed by four half steps, and then another four half steps. We abbreviate these chords with "aug" (Caug = c e g#), or you may see a "+" in jazz notation. Augmented chords sound a little dreamy.

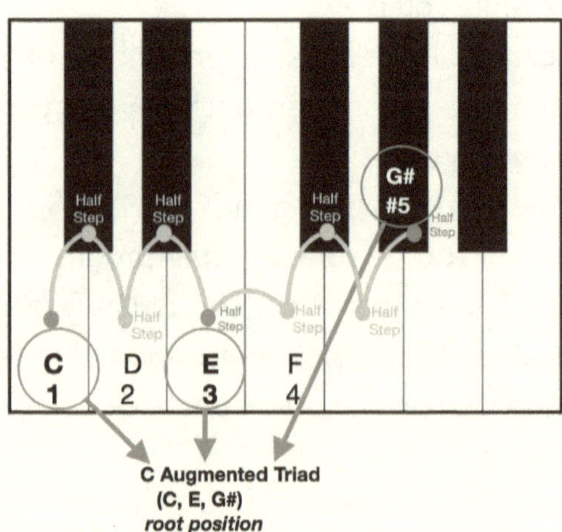

C Augmented Triad
(C, E, G#)
root position

You will notice that both these triads—the diminished and the augmented—sound *different*. You won't use them as much as major and minor triads because their sounds are so distinctive. However, they are awesome when used sparingly. (Unless you're stirring up some sweet jazz—then you'll probably use them more liberally.) Here are a few examples of well-known songs that use diminished and augmented chords:

- "Bennie and The Jets" by Elton John has a verse that features a progression including G Major to G# diminished to A minor.
- "We Are the Champions" by Queen features a diminished chord in the chorus.
- "No Particular Place to Go" by Chuck Berry opens with a D augmented chord.
- "For Once in My Life" by Stevie Wonder has verses that open with an F Major to F augmented progression.

Playbreak 2

Finger Painting: On the keyboard, build the following chord progression:

C Major - C# diminished - D minor

Notice how the only note that is different from C Major to C# diminished is one raised pitch (c to c#). I often use diminished chords to pass between chords that occur naturally within the key. Try to build this same progression starting a little higher: F Major - F#dim - G minor. Try to sing a melody over either of these progressions. (See the end of the chapter to check your notes.)

More Advanced: The vii° chord is a sometimes-neglected diatonic substitution for the V chord. Create a harmonic progression right now, intentionally using the vii° instead of a V. Create a melody on top of your progression. If you're not sure where to start, pick any key, pick from the following progressions, and then substitute the vii° chord instead of the V:

ii - V - I - IV **or** I - IV - V - vi

Chords That Play Nice Together

Certain chords play nice together when they are all in the same key signature. These chords occur "naturally" in the key because of the scale on which the key is based. We can usually identify the key of a song by figuring out what note sounds like "home." When you figure out what that note is, you will likely find your key signature. If the g feels like home, you're probably in the key of G Major (or E minor or G minor). If you guess wrong, that's okay. We're just playing around, so take your best guess.

Each key signature has its own scale. The key signature indicates whether your scale contains sharps or flats. On the keyboard, sharps and flats are usually on the black keys. C Major is the easiest scale and key signature to learn because it uses only the white keys on the piano (no sharps or flats). If you'd like to start playing chords in some simple keys, start with the keys of C Major, F Major (one flat), and G Major (one sharp).

C Major Scale:

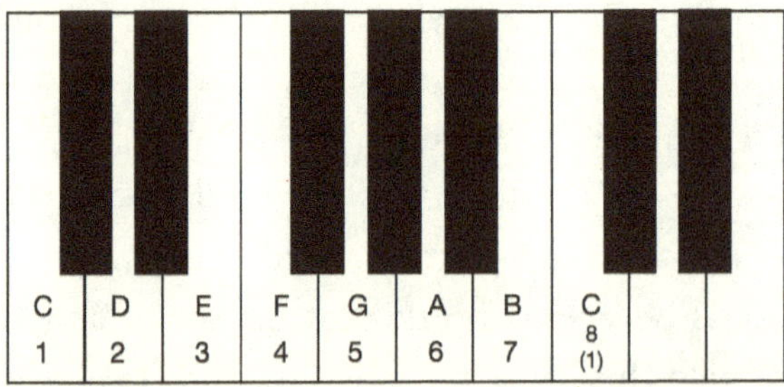

G Major Scale (one sharp):

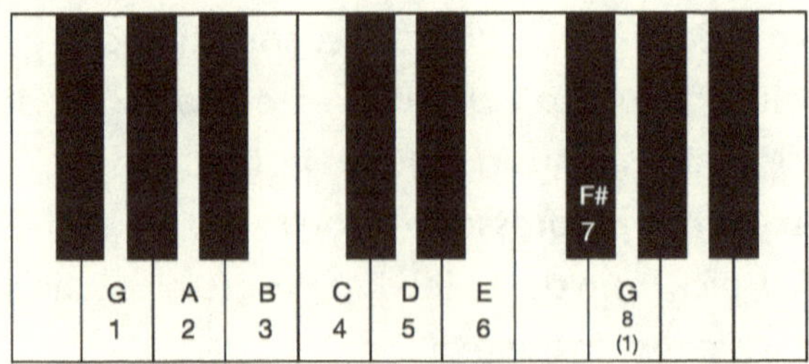

F Major Scale (one flat):

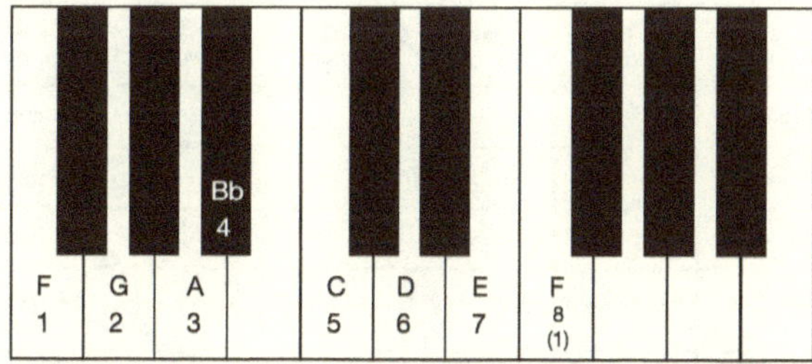

The key of D Major has two sharps (f# and c#), but it's also a pretty accessible key.

D Major Scale (two sharps):

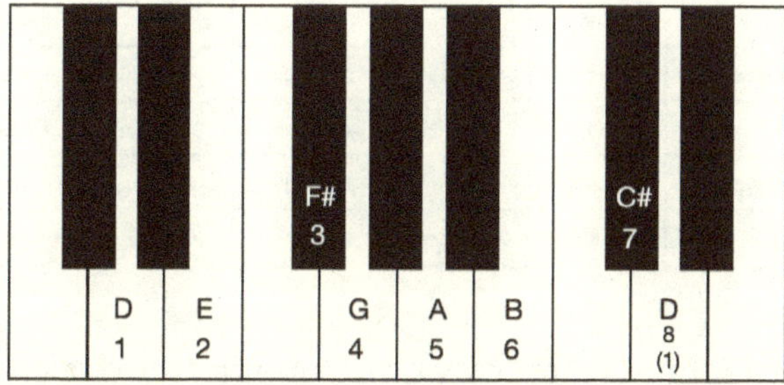

Try playing through all these scales right now. Remember, no matter the key signature or scale, the half-step principle for building triads never changes. If you can take a guess at what key you are in, you can use the half-step method to build all the triads that belong to that key. Many songs use chords that are all diatonic (occur naturally) within one key. Look up the chords and listen to the following examples for hit songs that only utilize diatonic chords:

- "Let It Be" by The Beatles in the key of C Major
- "Our Song" by Taylor Swift in the key of D Major
- "The Scientist" by Coldplay in the key of F Major
- "Ring of Fire" by Johnny Cash in the key of G Major

If you can guess your key signature, you can use this handy little chart below and figure out what chords fit in that key signature:

CHEAT SHEET FOR ALL 12 MAJOR KEYS							
KEY	**I (MAJOR)**	**ii (minor)**	**iii (minor)**	**IV (MAJOR)**	**V (MAJOR)**	**vi (minor)**	**vii° (diminished)**
C MAJOR	***C major***	D minor	E minor	F major	G major	A minor	B dim
G MAJOR	***G major***	A minor	B minor	C major	D major	E minor	F# dim
D MAJOR	***D major***	E minor	F# minor	G major	A major	B minor	C# dim
A MAJOR	***A major***	B minor	C# minor	D major	E major	F# minor	G# dim
E MAJOR	***E major***	F# minor	G#minor	A major	B major	C# minor	D# dim
B MAJOR	***B major***	C#minor	D#minor	E major	F# major	G# minor	A# dim
F# MAJOR	***F# major***	G# minor	A# minor	B major	C# major	D# minor	E# dim
Db MAJOR	***Db major***	Eb minor	F minor	Gb major	Ab major	Bb minor	C dim
Ab MAJOR	***Ab major***	Bb minor	C minor	Db major	Eb major	F min	G dim
Eb MAJOR	***Eb major***	F minor	G minor	Ab major	Bb major	C minor	D dim
Bb MAJOR	***Bb major***	C minor	D minor	Eb major	F major	G minor	A dim
F MAJOR	***F major***	G minor	A minor	Bb major	C major	D minor	E dim

Knowing the chords that "play nice" together in your key is helpful because you can pull from those chords as you are writing your song, and they will probably sound good together. However, this doesn't mean these are the only chords you can use in your song; they're just a good place to start. If you are using the chart above to write songs in a major key, don't worry so much about the diminished ones as you're starting out.

Playbreak 3

Finger Painting: Pick any ONE of the following keys: C Major, F Major, G Major, or D Major.
Build the following chord progression in your chosen key, making one triad at a time:
I - ii - IV - V (Find your key on the left column of the chart, and your chord Roman numeral at the top.)

The following is an example of how this progression would look in the key of C Major, but challenge yourself to build your progression in a different key.

I - ii - IV - V = C Major - D minor - F Major - G Major

Once you are comfortable with the progression, try rearranging the same chords in a different order. Something like this: V - ii - IV- I (Example: G Major - D minor - F Major - C Major)

Sing a melody over whichever progression inspires you more.

More Advanced: Force yourself to pick a key from the chart above that you rarely use. Explore the scale and all the chords that are diatonic to the key. Just goof around a little bit and see what happens. Try to write a chord progression and basic melody in this often-unused key.

It's a Numbers Game

Before we move beyond the basics, I want to discuss the numbers that you sometimes see added to chord symbols and briefly explain what these numbers mean. The extra numbers after the chord name caused me a lot of confusion during my finger painting years, and I hope this brief overview saves you from having to guess what those numbers signify. Basically, numbers added to the name of the chord are telling you about a *substitution* or *an addition* to the three-note triad. I'll spell out each of the chords using a C Major triad as the base for an example.

If you see a 2 added to the chord symbol (C2), you are *substituting* a 2 for the 3 of the triad. So if C = 1 3 5 = (c e g), then C2 = 1 2 5 (c d g). C2 and Csus2 are the same thing. The "sus" is an abbreviation for the word *suspended*.

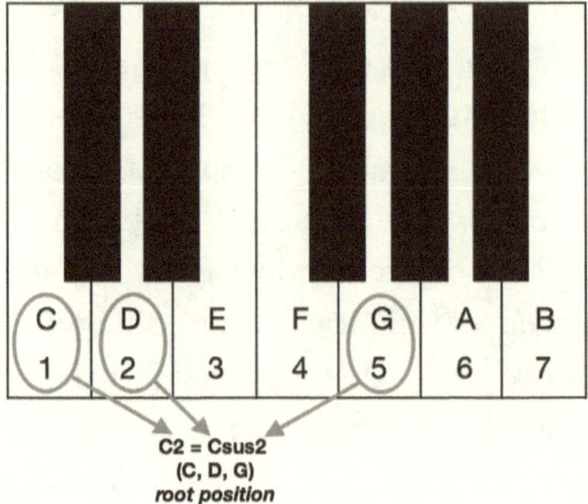

C4 is similar in that you *substitute* the 4 for the 3 in the triad. So if C = 1 3 5 (c e g), then C4 = 1 4 5 (c f g). You may see people indicate a C4 by also writing Csus or Csus4 (these are all the same thing). The *assumed suspension* is always sus4. Remember, C2 is also a suspended chord, but if you intend for a sus2, you MUST write C2 or Csus2.

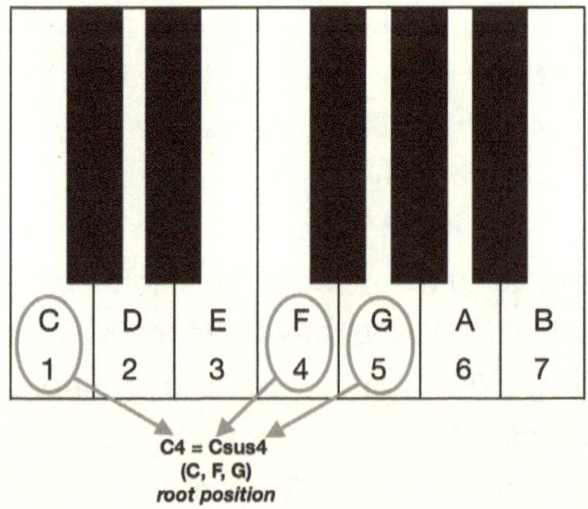

If you see a 5 next to a chord symbol, this is a power chord that *omits* the third (middle note) of the triad altogether. So if C = 1 3 5 (c e g), then C5 = 1 5 (c g). A power chord is neither major nor minor; it is intentionally ambiguous. Rock on.

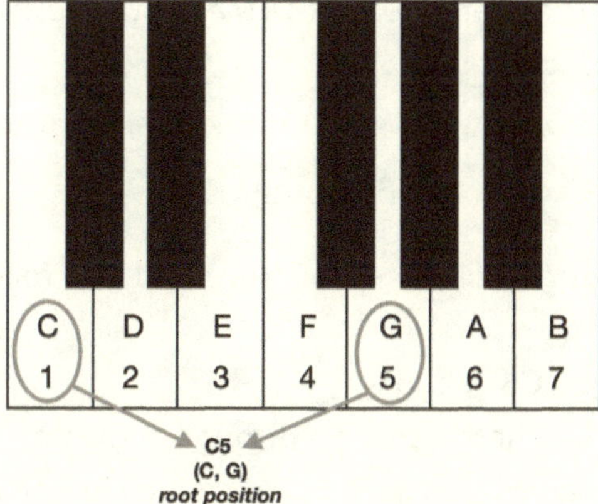

If you see a 6 added to a triad (C6), this is an *addition* on top of the 5 of the triad. So if C = 1 3 5 (c e g), then C6 = 1 3 5 6 (c e g a). This is the first *four*-note chord we have encountered so far.

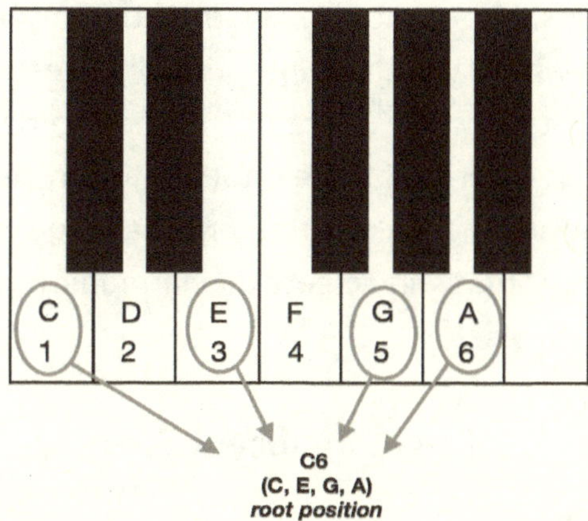

You can listen to a few examples or look up the chord charts for these songs that feature prominent "number" chords:

- "Venus" by Shocking Blue opens with a Bsus4 chord
- "Free Fallin'" by Tom Petty is an entire song with suspended chord movement
- "Smoke on the Water" by Deep Purple is one of the most famous power chord songs of all time

- "Michelle" by The Beatles features a Major 6th chord as the third chord in the verse progression

Playbreak 4

Finger Painting: On the keyboard, build the following chord progression:
C Major - Caug - C6 - Caug
Notice how the chords change through the shifting of just one pitch (g - g# - a - g#). Create a vocal melody line that follows the shape of this changing pitch as you change chords. (See the end of the chapter to check your notes.)
More Advanced: Look through the "number" chords we just covered. Are there any you don't frequently use? I avoided power chords for years, but eventually I learned that my whole writing style changes when I use them intentionally. Create a chord progression and intentionally utilize one of the chords above to see if any new ideas emerge. If there's not a category of these chords you usually ignore, then take a different challenge to write a song using ONLY basic triads and create the harmonic interest through your melody choices.

The Magnificent 7ths

We moved into the territory of additions when we added the 6 to the basic triad. If wrangling just three notes in the triad is enough for you right now, that's great. Don't push yourself so hard that you get frustrated and confused. Finger painting should be fun. If you add too many colors too soon, your painting might turn all soaky and brown. Just come back to this section of the chapter when you're ready to add more notes.

For those of you ready to handle another set of colors, we're going to move on to 7th chords. These are the four-note chords you will most often want to build. There are three types of 7th chords we will cover in an attempt to bring clarity to how to label them. We will continue to use the base of a C Major triad as we build.

We'll start with the Major 7th (written as CMaj7), which adds the major scale's 7th note to your triad chord. The technical way to think about it is not always the easiest way to think about it. Remember this: In a Major7 chord, the 7th is a half step below the root. A Major 7th will always have a "Maj" or a triangle shape appear after the chord name.

So if C = 1 3 5 (c e g), then CMaj7 = 1 3 5 7 (c e g b).

Notice that b is a half step below c:

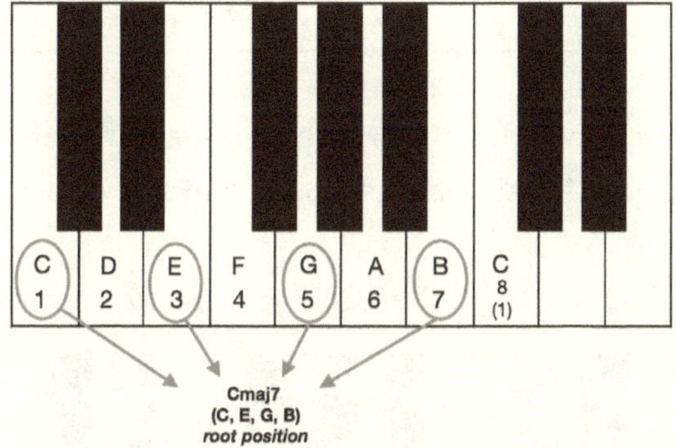

The next type of 7th, a dominant 7th, adds a note that is a whole step below the root (1) of the chord. When you simply add the number 7 to a chord symbol, like C7, you are indicating the dominant 7.

So if C = 1 3 5 (c e g), then C7 = 1 3 5 ♭7 (c e g b♭)

Notice that b♭ is a WHOLE step below c:

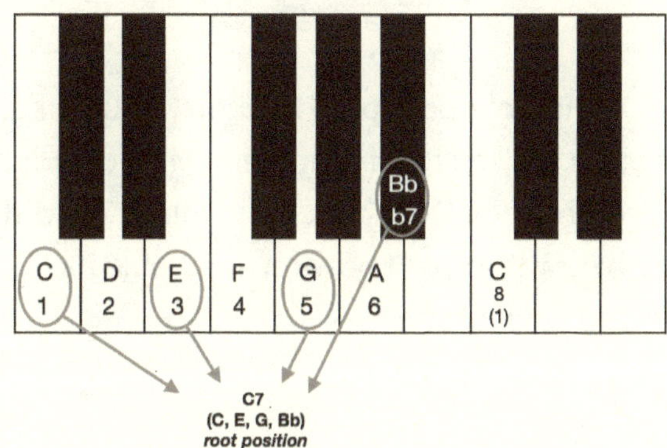

The distinction is important. Maj7 indicates the 7 that is a *half step* below the root, while a dominant 7 indicates a 7 that is a *whole step* below the root. You will most typically use Maj7 chords for I chords and IV chords, and dominant 7 chords for V chords. If I lost you there, don't worry too much about it. This is an example of what that would look like in the key of C:

CMaj7	FMaj7	G7	CMaj7
IMaj7	IVMaj7	V7	IMaj7
c e g b	f a c e	g b d f	c e g b

The last basic 7th is the 7th on the top of a minor triad. A minor 7th chord is a minor triad that adds a seventh that is a whole step below the root.

So if Cm = 1 ♭3 5 (c e♭ g), then Cm7 = 1 ♭3 5 ♭7 (c eb g b♭).

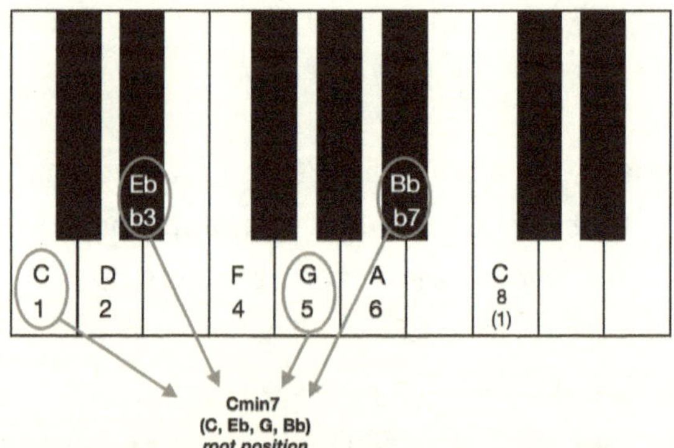

These are not the only possible 7th chords, but these are the ones you'll use most often. Broken record moment: Maj7 chords have a 7 that is a HALF STEP below the root. Dominant 7 and minor 7 chords have a 7 that is a WHOLE STEP below the root. Knowing this would have saved me years of confusion, so you're welcome.

Playbreak 5

Finger Painting: On the keyboard, build the following chord progression:
C Major7 | D minor7 | F Major7 | G7 |
Once you've got a handle on it, see if you can sing a melody while you play. (See the end of the chapter to check your notes.)
More Advanced: I like to call this one...HAND SLAM. Close your eyes and place your hands on the keyboard. Press down two random notes with your left hand and two random notes with your right hand. Do you like the chord you're playing? If so, figure out what it is. If four notes are not tricky enough for you, try "hand slam" with three notes in each hand. Some of your creations might be pretty weird, even otherworldly. Hand slam until you find a chord that inspires you. Then create a progression that utilizes your "hand slam" chord.

Reach for the Sky

For numbers added to a chord that are higher than 7 (9, 11, and 13), you will assume all notes in the triad, as well as the dominant 7th, are available in the chord. Most likely, all these notes are NOT being played; they're simply "available."

So C9 = 1 3 5 ♭7 9 =

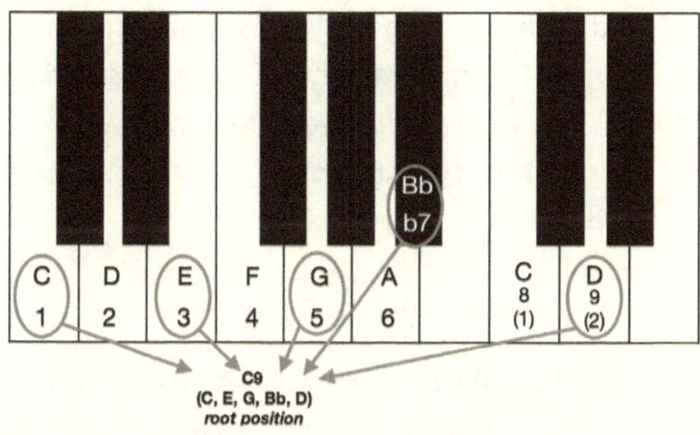

And C11 = 1 3 5 ♭7 9 11 =

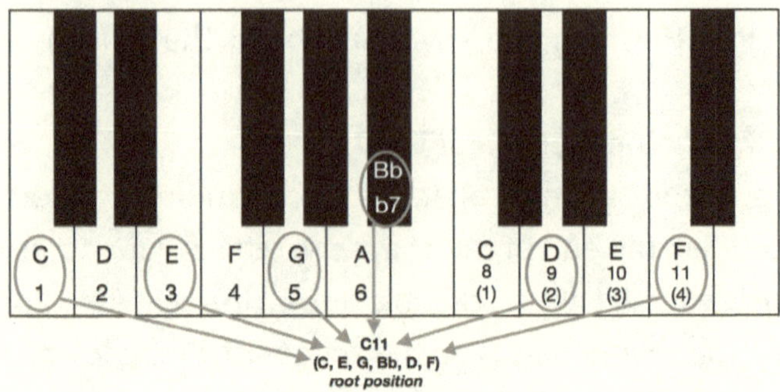

And C13 = 1 3 5 ♭7 9 11 13 =

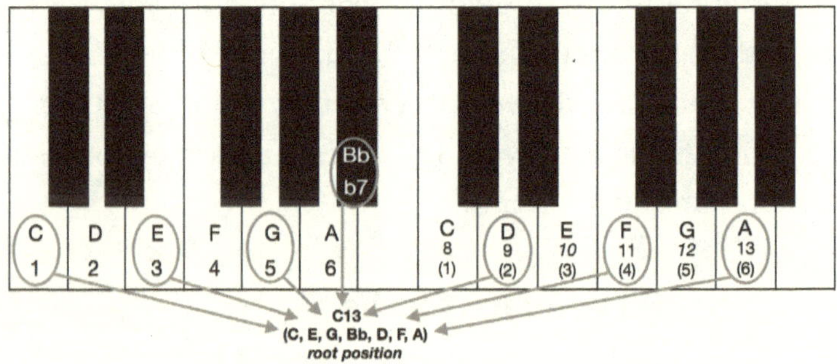

That's a lot of notes.

The dominant seventh and the notes from the triad are all "contained" within these chords, even if you don't play all of those notes at the same time!

So why does this matter? Early on, I often made the mistake of using chords like C2 and C9 interchangeably. C2 is different from C9 because C2 only has c, d, and g (no e). Remember, C2 is a *substitution* to the triad (not an addition). Long story short, if you are playing a C Major triad and ADDING the d (c d e g), this is Cadd9, not a C2, because the add9 indicates additional notes added on to the triad.

Swap Chords in the Key

Now that you're able to build all the chords within a major key, let's briefly cover how to use them. If we're in a diatonic environment (all chords within the key signature), different chords fulfill different roles. Let's look at the chords in the key of C Major to discuss these basic roles, just sticking to triads for now. We have three categories to consider when contemplating whether the harmony should be settled, unsettled, or somewhere in between. These categories are tonic, dominant, and subdominant.

I	ii	iii	IV	V	vi	vii°
Tonic	SubDom.	Tonic	SubDom.	Dom.	Tonic	Dom.
C Major	D minor	E minor	F Major	G Major	A minor	B dim

Tonic chords are the I Major, iii minor, and vi minor (C Major, E minor, and A minor in the key of C). These chords provide us with the greatest sense of arrival and resolution if our song is in a major key. Tonic chords = feel like home.

Dominant chords, which are the V and vii° diminished (G and B dim in the key of C), give us the most tension and provide the strongest pull toward resolution because they are the most harmonically unsettled. Dominant chords = REALLY want to go home.

Subdominants, the ii minor and IV Major (D minor and F Major in the key of C), don't create as much tension as dominant chords, but they also don't feel totally settled. They work well when they are *setting up* the tension (hence a *sub*dominant). Subdominant chords = thinking about going home, at some point.

Long story short, if you want your chord to give a sense of arrival, you probably want a tonic chord. If you want to maintain forward momentum and tension, you probably need a dominant or a subdominant chord (depending on the level of tension you desire).

Let's observe this in action. The following verse and chorus segment are from "Drift Away" by Dobie Gray. This song is in the key of B Major, so B is the I chord (tonic), E is the IV chord (subdominant), and F# is the V chord (dominant). Listen to how the B chord gives a sense of arrival, especially at the beginning of the chorus. Also observe how the E chord provides momentum at the beginning of the verse lines *and* at the end of the song sections to propel them forward toward "home." (If it helps you, mark the tonic chords with "T," the subdominant with "S," and the dominant chords with "Dom."

Verse 1:

E *(S)* B *(T)*
Day after day I'm more confused
E F# *(Dom)* B
Yet I look for the light in the pouring rain
E B
You know that's a game that I hate to lose
C#m E
And I'm feelin' the strain, ain't it a shame

1st half of Chorus:

B
Oh, give me the beat boys, and free my soul
F# E
I want to get lost in your rock and roll and drift away

You can also use this knowledge of harmony to add variety in your songs by swapping chords within the key that have the same harmonic role. If your eyes are starting to glaze over with all those music theory words, let me break it down in the key of C to give some practical clarity. Here's a super basic chord progression:

C Major | F Major | G Major | C Major |

In the key of C, the chords in this progression fulfill the following roles in this key:

C Major (I) *tonic* | F Major (IV) *subdominant* | G Major (V) *dominant* | C Major (I) *tonic* |

We can mix it up by simply using other chords within the key that fulfill the same roles. Remember, tonic chords are I, iii, and vi. Subdominant chords are ii and IV. Dominant chords have the strongest pull toward home with the V and vii°. Knowing these potential substitutions allows us to quickly try on other options. Play through these progressions to see how they have similar harmony roles, but sound slightly different:

Original: I IV V I
C Major | F Major | G Major | C Major |
Substitutions on first two chords: vi ii V I
A minor | D minor | G Major | C Major |
Substitutions on second and last chord: I ii V vi
C Major | D minor | G Major | A minor |

We've also got access to many chords outside of the key, and we'll cover that in the next finger painting chapter. Harmony can be complicated, so don't drive yourself crazy. It's okay if you don't have everything labeled correctly. The point is you *can* build chords, even if you're starting by counting half steps, one note at a time. Enjoy the finger painting. Use the charts and cheat sheets in this chapter to help you find new colors, but don't let them make you feel hemmed in. It's fine if your chords are messy. Messy is fun.

PLAYTIME

There are fewer activities at the end of this chapter because we really want you to do all the playbreaks. If you skipped them, please go back and do them!

Solo Activities

Reharm: Take a song you've already written and choose a new harmony. Don't just change a chord here or there; see if you can really reimagine it. You can change not only the chords but also the timing of when they change. Envisioning your song in a different genre might help you hear it in a new way.

Group Activities

Chord Association: Have the group come up with a list of random nouns, like squirrel, San Francisco, or hope. Then take turns at the piano, with each group member trying to play a chord that truly represents a noun of their choice. Broaden the exercise by asking each person to attempt writing a song section based on their favorite noun and the chord they associate with it.

Homework Challenge

The Unusual Progression: In this challenge, pick a chord progression you often use. (If you don't have a familiar progression, start with: C - G - Am - F). Then, create a new chord progression by making at least two changes to your familiar one. The goal is to break away from your usual patterns and explore new harmonic territory. After crafting your "fresher" progression, try to build a melody over it and see how the unexpected changes inspire new ideas.

Song Challenge

Minimum or Maximum Harmony: Write a song that either has very few or a boatload of chords and chord changes. Make sure your lyric's big idea aligns with your harmonic choice. Choose whichever challenge seems more challenging to you (but it's probably the minimal one).

PLAYBREAKS: Finger Painting Diagrams

Playbreak 1:

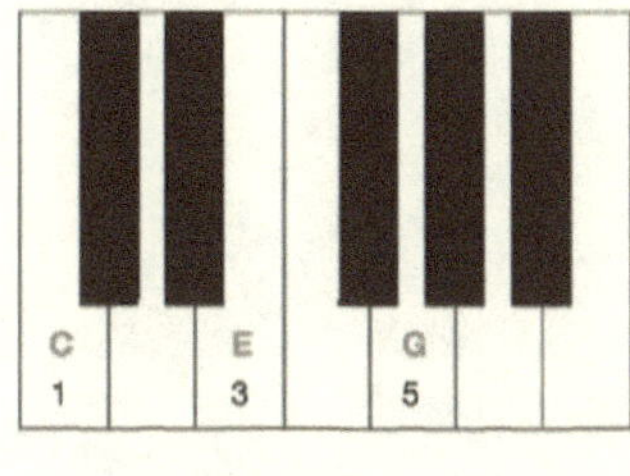

C Major

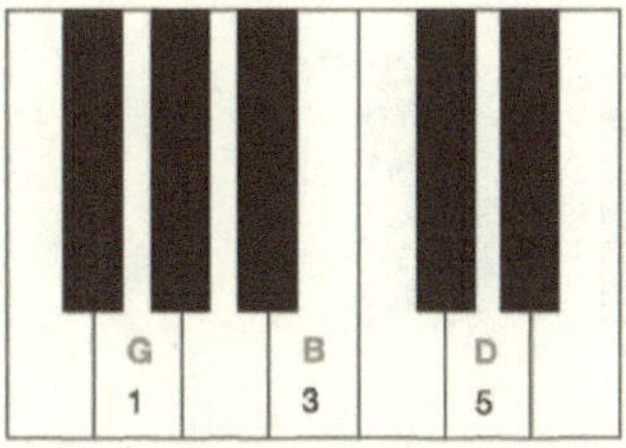

G Major

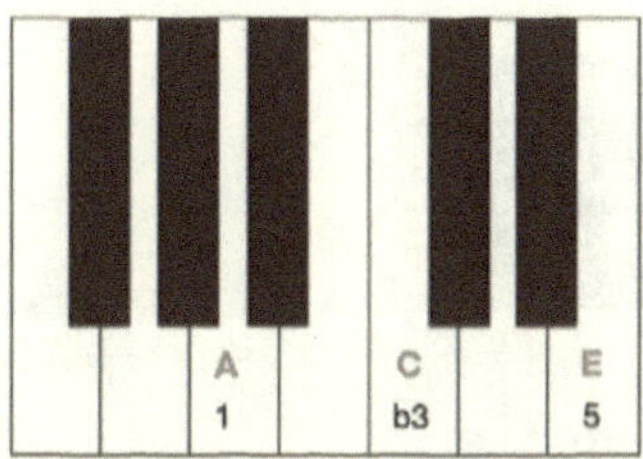

A minor

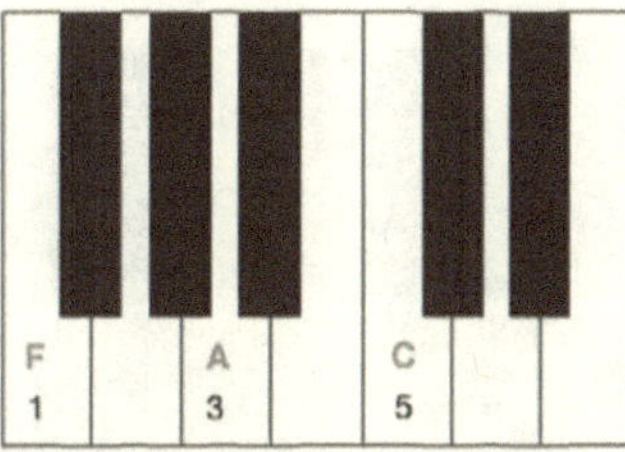

F Major

Playbreak 2:

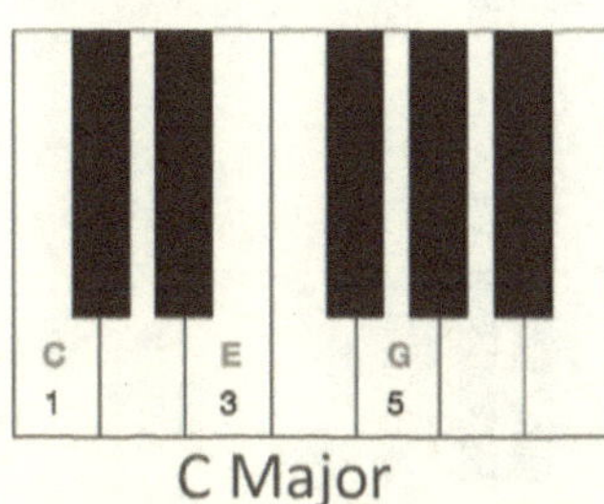

C Major

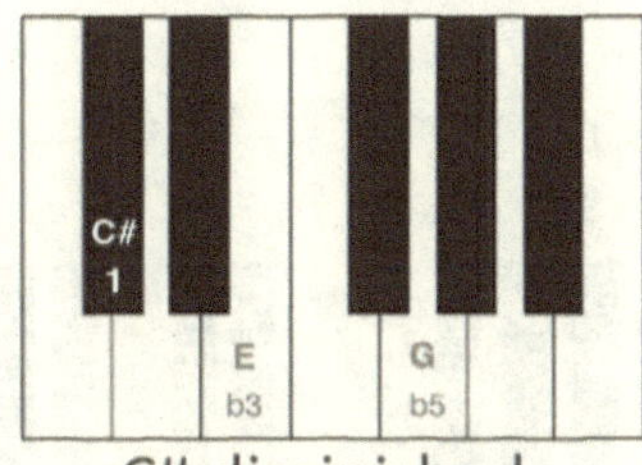

C# diminished

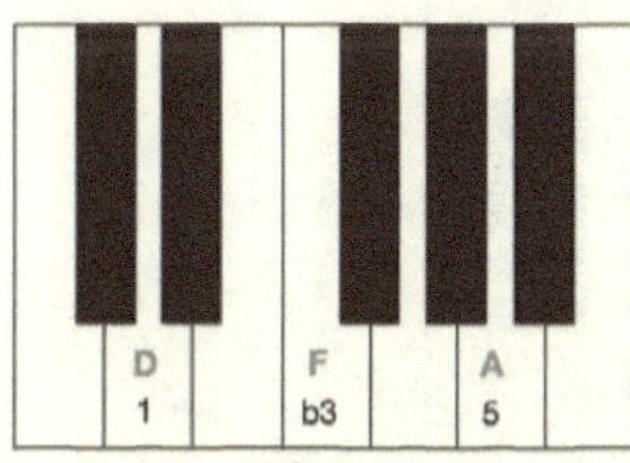

D minor

Playbreak 2 continued:

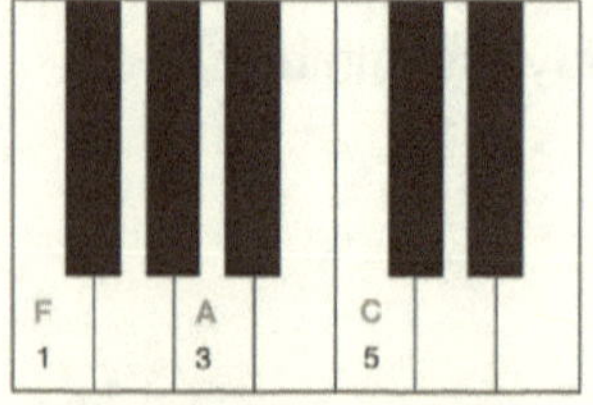

F Major

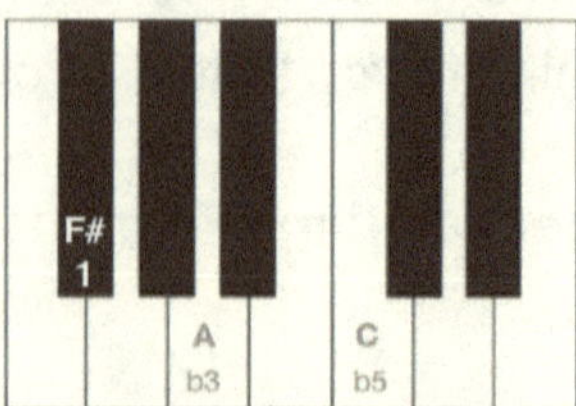

F# diminished

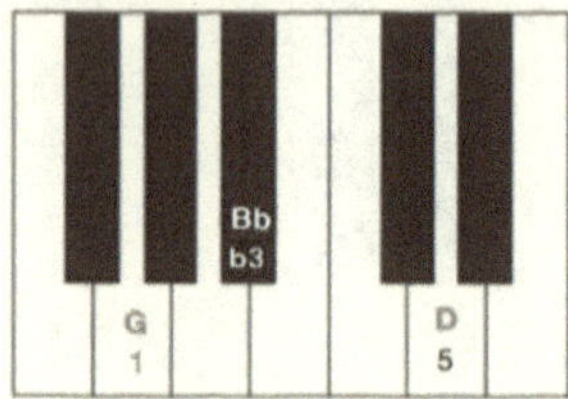

G minor

Playbreak 4:

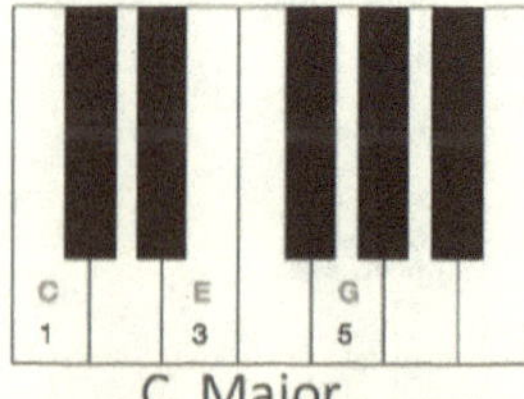

C Major

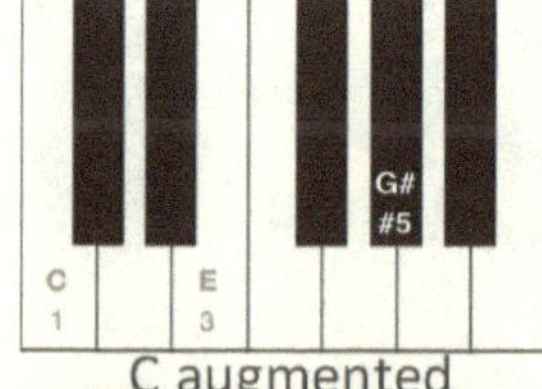

C augmented

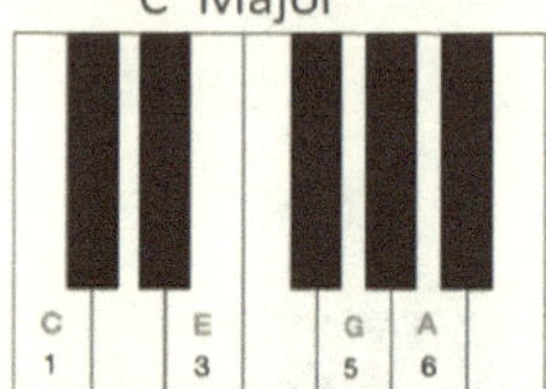

C6

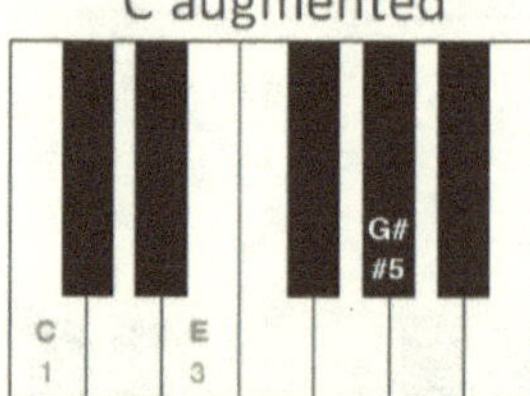

C augmented

Playbreak 5:

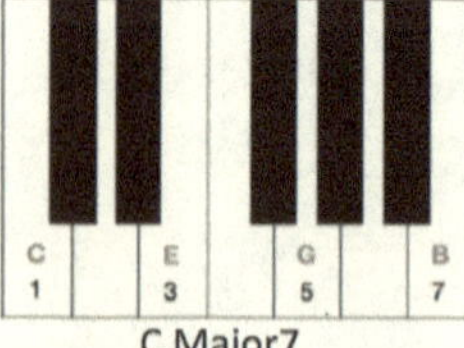

C Major7

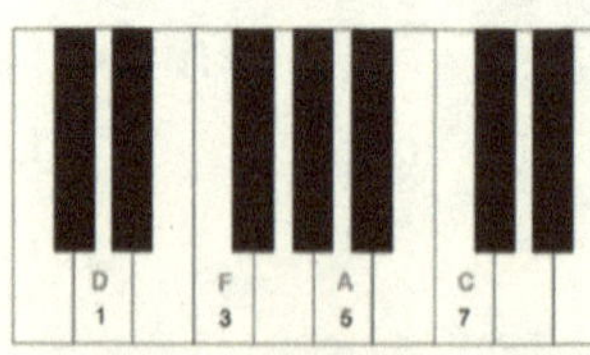

D minor7

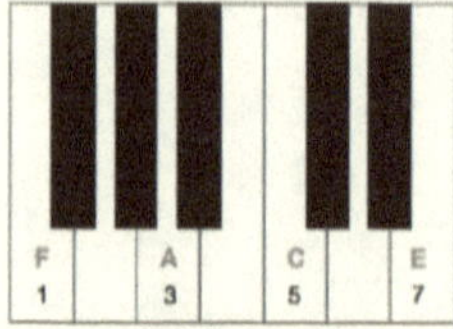

F Major7

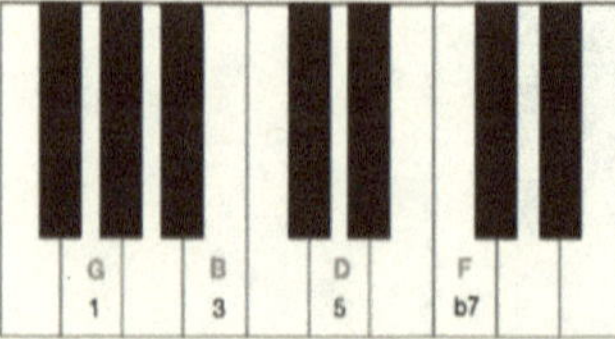

G7

CHAPTER 7

Stop Wishing on A Star

...and get out your rock tumbler

The Big Idea

"The sculpture is already complete within the marble block, before I start my work. It is already there, I just have to chisel away the superfluous material." Michelangelo

They studied and spent their whole lives watching and waiting for the promised king to arrive. Pouring over scriptures and staring at the heavens to make haste at a moment's notice. Then, all of a sudden, it was time. The star appeared. Not just any old star—*the* star they had been waiting for. The star that would guide the way to behold the Promised One. The wise men saw the star in the east and followed it. They knew the prophecies about the coming king, and they used the star in the sky to guide them on a long journey toward a new hope. They didn't really know where they were going, but they gazed intently into the distance and followed with faith.

Now, don't get me wrong, I think it's a beautiful story because it's a thrilling picture of faith and follow-through. Following the star is a great metaphor for hope…but it's an inadequate metaphor for songwriting.

In this chapter, we'll be talking about the pursuit of the "big idea." The big idea of your song is a phrase or short sentence that encapsulates what your song is all about. I've listened to countless talks and master classes by songwriting teachers discussing the "big idea." The analogy I see most often used when describing the big idea is that of the "north star."

When teachers use the analogy of the north star, they are illustrating the big idea as a guiding light, a beacon, or some sort of heavenly compass that keeps you on the right path if you follow it. They suggest songwriters should use their big idea in the same way a sailor uses the North Star to navigate. I struggle to think of the big idea as a north star because it makes the heart of our song seem distant and, frankly, unreachable. We *should* be continuously mindful of what our song is all about. But it's the *core* of the song we're after, not some flicker of light a galaxy away.

The Rock Tumbler

I want you to think about the big idea as being the core of your song. The big idea is the nucleus, the center, the "thing" whose gravity pulls all the rest of the song in toward it. The big idea isn't a separate element that drags your song along by the nose; it is the foundational center. If you neglect to understand and define what your big idea is, then your song will struggle to hold together.

While we're playing with a rock from our collection, we're gonna remember to get out our rock tumbler. The "rock tumbler" in our metaphor represents the intentionality in defining the big idea of our song. The rock tumbler helps us refine our song down to its core, and we're aiming for a fully polished core where every line is intimately exposed. Every chord choice fits perfectly with the unique shape. Why? Because your audience needs to see the emotional core of the song.

What happens if we neglect to spend enough time tumbling our rock (defining our big idea)? Our creation may end up lopsided, bulbous, and unrefined. If we've got spare rock chunks dulling our song up, it's difficult for people to see the beauty. This is what an ill-formed and messy big idea does. It's like bits of junk and dust hanging to the edges, clouding the view of the real song trapped beneath.

Big Idea Issues

Here's a boilerplate definition before we move on: The big idea is a single phrase or short sentence that defines what your song is about. This phrase or sentence should be specific and unique without being too vague or rambling. When I meet writers who haven't carefully considered their big idea, they usually face one of these three issues:

1. The writer has not considered the big idea of their song at all.

Question: What's the big idea of your song?

Answer: I have no idea.

Action steps: Define what the big idea is in a short phrase or sentence.

The caveat here is that you don't need to know the big idea of your song right when you're getting started. Initially, you explore with passion and play. However, if you keep crafting your song without regard for a big idea, you might begin to struggle. We need to at least know what we're trying to communicate.

2. The writer has a big idea, but it's too vague or broad.

Question: What's the big idea of your song?

Answers: It's a love song.

It's about loneliness.

It's about the book of Romans.

Action steps: These are all good ideas for a song, but they are not specific or unique. We should try to dig a little deeper into more nuanced ideas.

Why is it important to be more specific? At the risk of mixing metaphors, when our topic is too broad, we're offering our listeners too many flavors. If we're serving up a "love song," we're trying to put all the scoops into one bowl. Instead of giving our audience one scoop of ice cream to enjoy, we've handed them the entire ice cream shop. Our audience craves a unique flavor to taste; they can't eat all the flavors at once. I'll share more on how to make our ideas more specific later in this chapter.

3. The writer has a big idea, but it's rambling and unfocused.

Question: What's the big idea of your song?

Answer: My song is about the first time I went back home from college and fell in love for the first time. I was angry at my best friend for not understanding, and I was wrestling with whether I should stay at home or go back to school.

Action Steps: Focus on the heart of the matter and cut out everything else. (Perhaps you have more than one big idea in the song and you need to separate them.)

In the end, an idea that is rambling and unfocused suffers from similar problems as an idea that is not specific and unique. However, in this case, the unfocused big idea is trying to accomplish too much, so it's not really accomplishing any one thing. This is one scoop of ice cream with every conceivable topping piled on top. We have a lovely Butter Pecan, but the listener is getting distracted by the gummy worms and sprinkles we insisted on adding as well. This additional information does not align with the big idea and ultimately distracts from it.

Start making it a habit to clearly state the big idea in each of your songs. Defining the big idea helps us get to the core, the heart, the emotional truth of our song. If you keep tumbling, you might just discover a center of pure gold.

Melodic Hooks Are Big Ideas

People usually focus on lyrical content when wrestling with the big idea, but if you don't have a melodic core that aligns with the lyrical one, you might still have more *play* to do. Melodic big ideas are melodies that have definitive character. They are the stars of the show. We can achieve songwriting excellence when the heart of our lyrical big idea aligns with our most transcendent melodic big idea. But how do we begin to quantify what makes a melody memorable, singable, and worthy to be called a big idea type of melody?

We've already discussed that melodic rhythm (the rhythm in which the words are sung) and melodic contour (the overall shape of the melody) should be at the top of your list of things to consider when creating melody. With that in mind, we're going to play with melody again, building from the smallest unit of melody, but this time, you will create your own from scratch.

Limit yourself to two bars in 4/4 time at a medium tempo. Put a metronome on in the background at your preferred speed, then start by tapping along with the metronome to gauge what two bars feel like. Tap out your quarter notes on the table so that you can hear them out loud. Two bars in 4/4 time should sound like this as you tap:

Ex 7.01:

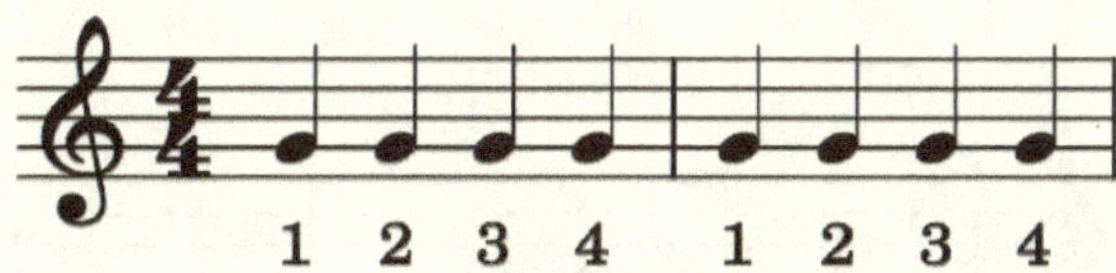

That's all the space we're going to fill with our melodic motif. Now, focus on experimenting with rhythm only. Create a two-bar melodic rhythm by tapping it out—you can choose any rhythm that feels interesting to you. You don't need to write it out; you just have to be able to remember the pattern. Keep repeating your rhythm until you find a pattern you like. I'll show you my own example below, so you can see each step as we go.

Here's the rhythm I decided on after trying several different patterns, but please create your own:

Ex 7.02:

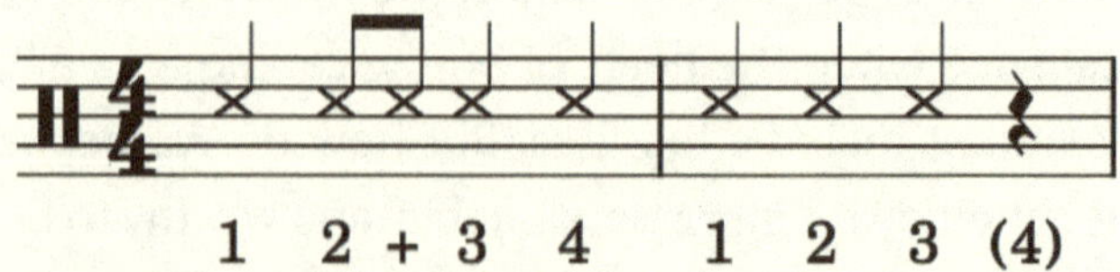

Now that we've established a rhythm, we're going to use it with some different melody shapes. Keep the rhythm the same and add pitches to it. Don't get too elaborate. Instead, try some basic shapes like "going up" or "going down."

Here's my rhythm with pitches added to make a "going up" shape:

Ex 7.03:

Or the same rhythm "going down":

Ex 7.04:

There are many shapes you can try with your rhythm, as we learned in Chapter 5. After you select a melodic rhythm and shape, you can get creative. If your melody is feeling a little basic, try inserting an interval jump to add a little sparkle.

I selected the "going down" shape to start, and then added my "sparkle" interval jump:

Ex 7.05:

Quality melodies often use satisfying combinations of stepwise motion (moving up and down one pitch step at a time) and interval jumps. If you choose to add lyrics to this melody, the sparkle interval jump probably needs to happen on an important word. Remember, don't settle on your first attempt. Keep moving notes around until you find something you enjoy singing.

Here are two other options for where I could place my interval jump:

Ex 7.06:

Ex 7.07:

Have you arrived at a "big idea" melody yet? Only you can decide. Keep playing around by shortening your melody, extending it, or playing around with the phrasing. (We'll discuss phrasing in detail in Chapter 10.)

Big idea melodies don't only have to be for the singer. Many songs are defined by stellar melodies introduced or carried by other instruments. Think about the distinctive guitar melody of "Stairway to Heaven" that is so ubiquitous it is banned in guitar shops. Can you hear the opening notes of "Smooth Criminal" or "Hotel California" after I simply mention the song titles? A definitive melodic big idea is how you immediately recognize Beyonce's "Crazy in Love" by the opening horn part.

Melodic hooks are the backbone of vibrant songs. They ground the song and give it life and staying power, so don't neglect them. A song with a brilliant lyric big idea, coupled with an ill-defined melodic big idea, is like a smooth, polished rock with no color. It is clearly defined, but there's nothing vibrant to encourage us to keep looking.

The Audience Engagement Scale

So, how do we know when our big idea is clearly defined and working? Checking in with listeners to see if they emotionally connect to the song is a good place to start. Their reaction may tell us whether our big idea warrants a little more play and polishing. I'd like to introduce you to my "audience engagement scale." This is a highly unscientific assessment tool to help gauge how much people are into your song:

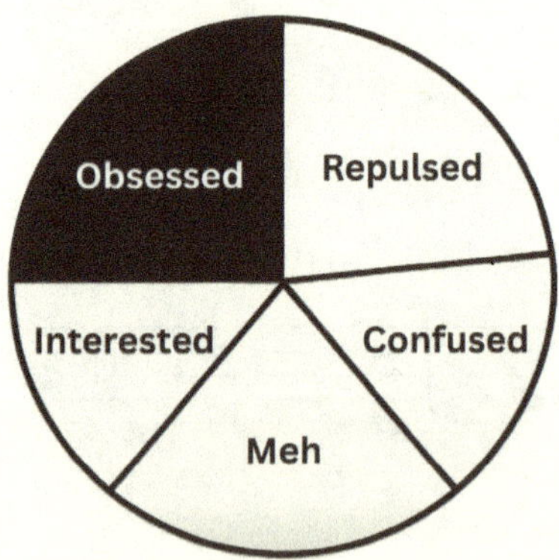

At the lowest levels of engagement, a listener is actively repulsed by the song. They dislike it and just want to turn it off. "Repulsed" might not be a bad thing; it just might mean the song is not for that listener.

In the middle, there's "meh," which is a "take it or leave it" type of neutral engagement. The listener thinks, *I've heard something very similar to this before; there's not much unique here.*

At the height of engagement, we reach "obsessed." This is a song that our listeners actively seek out over and over again. It speaks to them in an acute or evergreen kind of way. In my first iterations of this scale, it was a ladder from bottom to top. However, I realized that the obsessed category can often cycle back to repulsed if a listener becomes overexposed to a song they initially loved. I also like the visual of confused and interested being split by meh, but we'll talk more about that later.

Right now, I want to focus on the jump from meh to interested, because I believe the progression from one to the next is intimately connected to the big idea of your song. Meh songs are too generic. They don't have a unique sound or a unique story to tell. We interact with them and then move on because there's nothing terribly memorable.

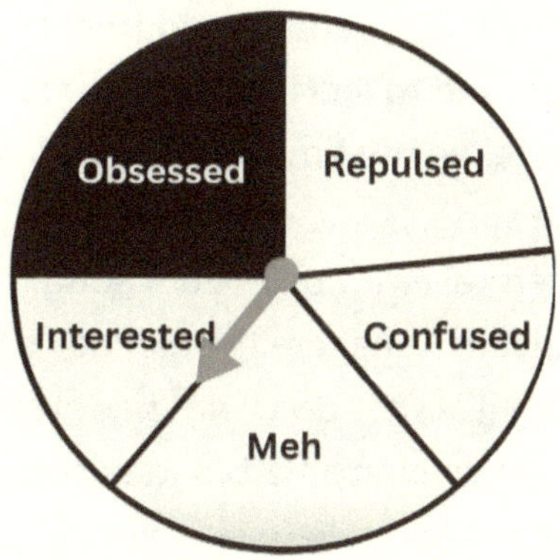

If you're getting a meh reaction from people (or if you feel meh about your song while you're writing it), consider that your big idea, lyrically and/or musically, might need some rock tumbling. Does your big idea have an interesting angle? A unique metaphor? A melodic hook that sticks with you? Here is an example of how defining a lyrical big idea can increase audience engagement:

Big Idea: *"This song is about how I love my boyfriend."* **MEH**

Big Idea: *"This song is about how I love my boyfriend in changing circumstances."* **A LITTLE BETTER**

Big Idea: *"This song is about how I show I love my boyfriend like every season of the year."* **INTERESTED**

A brief musical demonstration of elevating a meh melody to an interesting one is harder to convey in writing. But we never want to neglect the melodic component! To make the jump to interested, you're looking for a melody that you really like. The one that feels right and aligns with the identity of the song. Keep playing around until you find *that* melody. The interesting one.

Emotional Connection

For many of my early years of songwriting, I neglected the essential component of "emotional connection." I could write cool songs that were technically crafted, but when I played them for people, they didn't really walk away with anything. They didn't know what I wanted them to *feel* after listening. Were they supposed to feel inspired? Angry? Hopeful? They didn't know because I hadn't taken the time to ask myself those important questions while writing the song.

Considering the central emotion of your song is an important facet of your big idea. Ask yourself: "What are the feelings driving this song? What am I feeling when I sing it? What do I want people to feel when they hear it?" We may feel like we've crafted a big idea steeped in very real emotions, but our listeners might not be picking up on it. Have we given them enough clues to help them feel the emotions we're feeling?

There is no formula to ensure your song checks the box of "emotional connection" the way you can easily check off "consistent rhyme scheme." But you can be sure that if you *haven't* asked yourself these questions, making a genuine emotional connection with listeners will be a shot in the dark. The best way to get feedback for growth in this area is to play your song for others and ask if they feel something. Find out what their main takeaway is.

And then take honest feedback seriously. If someone says, "I don't really understand what the song is about," don't blame that feedback on your listener. Our ego's reaction might be, "Well, they just don't understand my art!" The point is, yes, they may not understand your art. Still, if you want your listeners to feel something, it usually helps if they understand what you're talking about.

Acknowledge Exceptions

There are always notable exceptions to guidelines. If you don't have a clearly defined big idea, are you doomed to never reach an emotional connection? Absolutely not. There are songs that are "universal" enough that listeners can still find themselves in the story and emotion of the song even if they don't know what the song is really about. "Losing My Religion" by REM comes to mind. I'm not asserting that you have to plainly *tell* the emotion within your song to make it crystal clear; I'm just encouraging you to keep the emotion in mind as you define your big idea.

Just Wear the Strawberry Shirt

One day, I went to Walmart for just a few basic groceries. But, in an attempt to allow myself a sense of wonder, I decided to wander the store. I drifted into the men's clothing section, and *there it was*. The most perfect strawberry shirt. It was a Hawaiian-style beige button-up shirt covered with giant neon pink and red berries. My inner voice said, "That strawberry shirt is you! You would have so much fun wearing it!" My rational voice said, "Girl...you DON'T need a strawberry shirt. Why would you waste $12 on this?" But you know what? I bought the shirt. Sometimes, things just feel right, even when it doesn't make any sense.

The bulk of this chapter has been encouraging you to tumble your rock down to the big idea, both in lyrics and melody. I also just encouraged you to consider how your song is or isn't emotionally connecting with listeners. But songwriting is not about rules, remember? Sometimes your initial big idea is pretty weird and wild, and that's okay. Sometimes, the idea may be hard for other people to swallow. Sometimes, it might be a big, bold strawberry shirt, and you just need to go for it. I had a student named Grace who wrote a song called "Green Peach Gremlin." This title (and big idea) was so weird and specific that I will never forget it.

My friend Jonathan recently talked about this same phenomenon in pop music production. He mentioned a distinctive whirly synth part that appears after the chorus in the Billie Eilish song "Bad Guy." He said, "If I'd heard that sound in the studio, I would have said, 'No way.' It's really dumb. But there's something in the intentionality of choosing something so weird and *owning* it that makes it work. It's like someone wearing bright red pants and pulling it off."

We need these kinds of risk-takers to move music creation forward. Multi-platinum record producer and neuroscientist Susan Rogers said, "The more groundbreaking a record, the harder it is to enjoy on first listen…[but] When we encounter a surprise, something special happens in our brain. The prediction 'error' can trigger an even greater release of psychic rewards."

The strawberry shirt principle isn't a hall pass to never edit your songs. It's simply an acknowledgment that sometimes, in a stroke of genius, we wander into a section of the store we never thought we'd be in and find the right thing at the right time. Sometimes, you stumble upon the perfect little thing, or a really unique idea, and when you do, you just know. Don't throw away that thing because you're afraid of what others might think. Write a "Green Peach Gremlin." And just buy the strawberry shirt.

On Rock Tumblers

So far, we've worked our way through numerous metaphors for discovering and defining the big idea. Maybe in the past, you tried to follow the north star, but it turned into a game of Marco Polo. You might have been splashing around blindly as the big idea kept shifting from corner to corner of the pool. Or perhaps you've served up songs with all the flavors and too many toppings. You may have settled for the boring old sweater instead of the strawberry shirt. But in the end, I want to bring you back to the rock tumbler. The pursuit of the big idea is about finding the core of your song—the beautiful center of that rock you pulled from your collection. I once had a student ask me how he would know when he'd found the center of the big idea. If you're not sure you've found it yet, consider asking yourself some of these questions.

Do you think *you've found it? If not, keep tumbling.*

Are you excited about your song, or does it make you feel meh*? If meh, keep tumbling.*

Do you think you're saying something true in a way no one has quite said it before? If not, keep tumbling.

It's worth it to knock away all the extra stuff that's blocking the view to the exceptional emotional center of your song. It's okay to be a little obsessed about a great big idea.

PLAYTIME

Solo Activities:

Make a Movie: Pick your two favorite actors and create a movie in your mind for them to star in together. What are they doing? What is their relationship? What is the big idea of the movie? Create a title for the movie, then journal about it for five minutes. Then, pick a "signature song" that matches the emotion of the movie. It could be a song that already exists, or hey, you could try writing one!

More than a "Love" Song: What kinds of love songs are there? Create a list to see how many types of love songs you can think of—like breakup, makeup, first love, or long-lasting love—each with a unique big idea. Pick the most compelling theme and try to write some lyrics around that big idea. Next, brainstorm what kinds of "sad songs" are out there. Make a list to see how many types of sad songs you can think of, each with a unique big idea. Some ideas to start are loss, loneliness, or defeat. Pick one and try to write some lyrics around that big idea. After you write some lyric lines for your "more than a love song" and "more than a sad song" topics, then try to create some melodies that match the emotion of each lyric (separately).

Group Activities:

3-4 Syllable Titles: Have your group make the following lists: colors, places, feelings, verbs, animals, food, sports words & random nouns. The lists can be as long as you want, but they can only contain one or two-syllable words. For example, the "feelings" list could have hope, sadness, anger, rage, despair, and joy, but it cannot have resentment or jubilation.

Pull words from all the columns to combine them into interesting three to four-syllable titles like "Texas Twist," "Sandwich Sadness," or "Green Peach Gremlin." Let the group pick a few titles that inspire them and write what the big idea of that song might be about. Have each person pick one title they love to set to a melody.

100,000 Pyramid: Have the group leader write the following list of themes on the board: heartbreak, victory, leaving home, faith, and grief. Taking each theme one at a time, have group members call out as many physical objects as they can think of that are associated with each theme. For example, if the theme is "victory," objects could include trophy, battlefield, eagle, or Olympics. Have each group member select a theme/object combination that speaks to them and have them journal about that connection. Redo this exercise by using the same theme categories and have your group members individually create melodies that capture the essence of each theme.

Homework Challenge:

Watch an Episode: Watch an episode of one of your favorite TV shows. Then, create 10 titles based on dialogue or scenes. Keep in mind that you're not trying to write a song about the whole show. You're just using dialogue for inspiration. Then select one of the 10 titles and make a song map. A simple song map summarizes what each song section might try to accomplish lyrically. If you're unsure what that means, refer to the chart below.

SONG MAP

Title:
Verse 1 is about:
Chorus is about:
Verse 2 is about:
CHORUS
Verse 3 is about:
Optional Bridge is about:
CHORUS

Conversation Observation: Be out in the real world for this homework. Go to a coffee shop, park, or grocery store to watch and listen. Make a list of interesting sights and snippets of conversation. Submit a list of at least 20 things you saw and/or heard. Pick one or two things from your list and write one sentence for each about how that thing could connect to a song idea.

Song Challenge:

Strong Feelings Response Song: Think of a song, not written by you, that you have strong feelings about. It could be a song you really love or one you always come back to for some reason. Write a song "in response" to this song. How you "respond" to this song is totally up to you. You could give the counterargument or the total opposite perspective. You could answer a question the original song asks. *(This prompt idea is from Sara Groves and her work with Art House North.)*

A Strawberry Shirt Song: Write a song with the weirdest and wildest big idea you can conceive of. An "I've *never* heard a song about this" kind of song. Try to include a hooky melody that's so distinctive, it couldn't be confused with anything else. It's okay if you don't *achieve* this prompt; the point is to try.

CHAPTER 8

I Spy

Point of View & Point in Time

"What we do with our attention, in short, is at the heart of what makes us human." Rob Walker

My favorite, albeit somewhat antagonistic, way to play I Spy with my kids is to pick something that is quite obvious from my perspective, but difficult to see from theirs. My favorite choice is usually whatever color happens to be blazing bright on whatever character is adorning the center of their t-shirt.

Let me set the scene here: We're in the car, and it's hour five of a desperately long road trip.

"I spy with my little eye something red," I say with a smirk.

"Red?!" My poor kid says, exasperated as he looks around everywhere. "I don't see any red in the car!"

"Guess you'll have to keep looking..." I say, as I wink at the red Power Ranger on his chest.

I have the advantage in the game because I anticipate viewpoints beyond my own. Playing I Spy is a gamified way of living a life of noticing, which is a songwriter's life. The game is also a helpful reminder that what is obvious from one point of view may be seen quite differently, or not seen at all, from another perspective.

Many people start songwriting mainly for catharsis—to wrestle with emotions and pour them all out in song. While songwriting helps us process our feelings, problems arise when every song starts to read like a diary entry or a breakup note. Eventually, we need to broaden our horizons. We do this by considering viewpoints beyond ourselves, outside our personal space and time. We relate to each other when we connect the stories we've lived with the stories of others. We begin to see how individual events relate to universal truths when we learn to view things from multiple perspectives.

In this chapter, we will discuss point of view, point in time, and a little bit about aesthetic beauty. Understanding how to manipulate these narrative points of reference will open up new worlds of possibility and perspective. Neglecting to consider them can cause confusion in our lyrics and hinder our potential to create emotional connections with listeners.

The Audience Engagement Scale

Let's quickly glance at the audience engagement scale again:

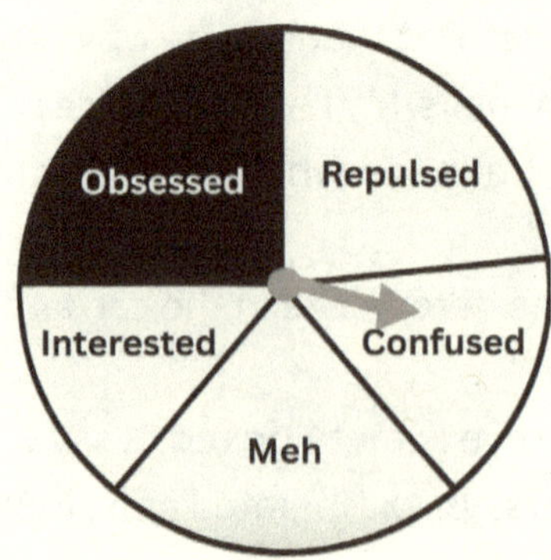

Many quality songs are lost to the "confused" category because there is a lack of clarity in the song's point of view or point in time. When I encounter a song that confuses me, I usually ask my students one or all of the following questions:

Who is the singer?

Who are they singing to?

What is the context of the present moment? (When is the now?)

And sometimes...

Can you define the relationship between the characters?

We don't want to leave our listeners in the land of confused. Answering the questions above can help us be more intentional about defining our point of view and point in time. The answers to these questions can significantly alter the meaning and impact of the song. We want to take our listeners from feeling confused to much higher levels of engagement, and we can start by being clear about our singer's point of view.

Point of View

Understanding the four primary points of view at your disposal as a songwriter is being aware of multiple vantage points in the ultimate game of I Spy. Your song will communicate and emote differently depending on the point of view you choose. A basic understanding of how the point of view works will enable you to "try on" all your options.

From now on, I'm going to abbreviate the phrase "point of view" to POV.

Many songwriters stick to the first POV they choose when they start writing their song, whether it was the best option or not. For example, if the first lyric line you write down is "Do you remember when we met?" then a POV has already been selected. The POV of direct address has been chosen because there is an "I" singing to a "you." This is an acceptable POV to use, but the songwriter should keep considering whether it remains the *best* choice as the song develops.

Typically, consistency is key for effective use of POV. Neglecting to remain within one POV can result in situations like this one. The opening verse lyric says, *"This is my song about how he did me wrong,"* but the chorus follows with *"You're to blame, blame, blame."*

Our listeners may be left with a confusing narrative about whether the bad guy is the "he" from the verse or the "you" from the chorus. Sticking to a consistent POV throughout a song is usually best because it minimizes confusion. And minimizing confusion usually enhances emotional impact. Your listener is going to have a hard time connecting to your song if they have no idea what's going on or which bad guy to hate. (Is *he* the bad guy? Am *I* the bad guy? Who am I supposed to be mad at?)

There are plenty of examples of songwriters breaking this guideline—and doing so effectively—when they *intend* to shift the POV because it serves their song. Corporate worship songs often shift from talking about God to singing directly to Him. Sometimes love songs start off talking about the girl, but then shift to singing directly to her. These variations to the guideline of maintaining a consistent POV usually do so to enhance the intimacy of the lyrics as the song progresses. When done right, they can add to the overall emotional impact instead of detracting from it. However, these are the exceptions.

Instead of leaning into the exceptions, we're going to focus on giving you a confident grasp of the available POVs so that you can gain mastery to stay within one. The hope is that you will experiment and try them all on to see which one works best, song by song. My students often have a hard time recalling all the available POVs, so I made a catch phrase for each one:

Direct Address: "The Conversation"
You and I
First Person: "The Confession"
I (no you)
Second Person: "The Character"
You (no I)
Third Person: "The Chronicle"
No I or you (only he/she/they)

Let's dig deeper into each POV and talk about when and how they can be used effectively. We'll start "up close" first with direct address.

Direct Address: The Conversation

Direct address involves both an "I," representing the singer, and a "you," referring to the intended audience or listener. It establishes a direct line of *conversation* between the singer and the audience or listener. Here are some examples of direct address found in popular song titles:

"I Will Always Love You"

"My Life Would Suck Without You"

"You Were Meant for Me"

Direct address works well for songs with intense relationship drama, from "I love you" to "I hate you" and all the complicated spaces in between. It's the first point of view to consider if you have something important to say to a significant someone, and you need to tell them to their face.

There can be "he/she/they" characters contained in a song using direct address, but "he/she/they" are not the *main* characters. Look up Paula Cole's song "I Am So Ordinary" for an example of this. If you discover that "he" or "she" is the main character in your song, you might want to reconsider your choice of direct address.

If direct address is the most intimate of the POVs, why would we ever choose anything else? Because sometimes we want to navigate the experience for our listener in a different way. Sometimes, a less "in-your-face" approach works better for the big idea of our song. Other times, we want the listener to come along with us as we tell them a story. If the story is deeply personal, we might decide to give the listener a glimpse into our lives by leaving the "you" out of it altogether. The first option we will look at when leaving "you" out of it is first person.

First Person: The Confession

Think of first person as a kind of confessional for the singer. The main character is "I." If there are other characters in the song, those characters are "he/she/they" and *not* "you." The singer is telling their story to the audience, but that story doesn't directly involve a "you."

Often, we default to direct address when writing our first draft of a song, but first person is more appropriate if the song isn't really about a "you." A common "POV pitfall" I see is a writer mentioning an erroneous "you" once in a lyric that will pull it to direct address. Removing an unessential "you" and committing to first person is usually the stronger choice. Popular songs that effectively use first person include Sia's "Chandelier," The Beatles' "Norwegian Wood," and The Allman Brothers Band's "Ramblin' Man."

Let's take a moment to consider "Ramblin' Man" because there is a caveat here. In the chorus of "Ramblin' Man," we find the lyric "I hope you'll understand." Here is the line in the context of the entire chorus:

Lord, I was born a ramblin' man
Tryin' to make a livin' and doin' the best I can
And when it's time for leavin'
I hope you'll understand
That I was born a ramblin' man

We might be tempted to label this song as having a direct address POV because of the one lyric that contains a "you." However, the intention of this line is a "universal" you, rather than a specific one. Nowhere else in the song does the lyric mention a specific "you." So even though we see a "you" in "Ramblin' Man," the overall spirit of the song remains in first person POV. It's a confession. It's the "ramblin' man" telling his story.

If you have chosen direct address but then realize the singer is having a conversation with a "you" where they're telling "you" a lot of information "you" should have already known, consider a rewrite to first person. One of my favorite songs, "Blue Velvet," is in first person. Here's the second A section of the song:

She wore blue velvet
Bluer than velvet were her eyes
Warmer than May, her tender sighs
Love was ours

This first person POV is an effective choice because the song is recounting all the details about the singer's lost love. He's singing it *about* her, not *to* her. If the songwriter had chosen direct address, the lyric would have read:

You wore blue velvet
Bluer than velvet were your eyes
Warmer than May, your tender sighs…

Direct address feels awkward here. It doesn't make sense for the singer to be singing these things *directly* to their long-lost love. Typically, if you want the singer to tell a story about their life or process something they're going through, the first person POV is probably best. Just leave the "you" out of it.

But maybe the story you're trying to tell isn't about "I." What if you want to build a character and create an intimate connection with the audience? Then we can explore the most rarely used POV in songwriting, second person.

Second Person: The Character

Second person is a POV that songwriters often forget about. A song in second person addresses the listener directly (a whole lotta "you"), but the singer isn't really part of the story (no "I"). Beginning songwriters might not be used to trying on second person because their first instinct is often to look inward and process their own experiences. In a way, second person is more challenging to wrestle with because it removes the singer from the story. However, experimenting with second person is an excellent way to expand your scope and build empathy as a songwriter because it's centered on character development. I call this point of view "the character" because the all-knowing singer is building the character of "you" by describing who "you" are, where "you" have been, and possibly who "you" could become. The singer is defining who the "you" is line by line.

If "the character" is too hard to remember, you could also call second person the "dancing queen" POV. My students have an easy time remembering second person when they sing the chorus of Dancing Queen. Notice how "you" defines the chorus of this song, and there is no mention of "I."

You are the dancing queen
Young and sweet
Only seventeen…
You can dance
You can jive
Having the time of your life…

There is not an abundance of popular songs that are exclusively in second person. It's a POV that doesn't often work, but when it does, it can be really interesting. Sometimes songs that aren't entirely in this POV can have the "spirit" of second person. "She Loves You" by the Beatles is a good example because the most important characters in the song are "you" and "she." In the literal sense, "She Loves You" is direct address because it is a conversation between the singer "I" and the listener "you." But we get the spirit of second person because the singer is not the main character. Check out the verse and observe how all those "yous" and "shes/hers" outweigh the singular mentions of "I" and "me."

You think you've lost your love
Well, I saw her yesterday
It's you she's thinkin' of
And she told me what to say
She says she loves you
And you know that can't be bad
Yes, she loves you
And you know you should be glad

Try on the spirit of second person sometime if you'd like to try writing a song where the singer is the "middle man" negotiating the communication in a relationship song.

Second person is also a great POV to try if you're crafting a hero or villain. You can use this POV if you don't want the bad guy to be the singer, but still want to achieve an intimate point of view. My student, Maggie, brought a song entitled "The Mouse King," based on the villain from The Nutcracker. She initially chose first person as her point of view:

I've got a devilish smile
And a cold stoned heart
I'm a king who's prideful
Ruthless, savage, and smart
I'm the Mouse King
I'm the antagonist in this story…

Maggie and I discussed that unless she intended this song to be a soliloquy-style villain ballad for a musical, then this song might be hard for listeners to connect with. Who wants to call themselves the Mouse King as they sing along? I suggested to Maggie that this song might be the perfect candidate for a second person POV transformation. By shifting the lyric to second person, she would allow the song to create "the character." Listeners could relate to the lyrics if they recognized someone in their life who was quite similar to the "Mouse King." Here are the same lyrics in second person:

You've got a devilish smile
And a cold stoned heart
A king who's prideful
Ruthless, savage and smart
You're the Mouse King
The antagonist in this story…

I liked this version much better. It still packed a punch without the singer being the bad guy. The inverse can also be true if you'd like to craft a hero song. Sometimes it can sound awkward for the singer to sing about their own heroic self. But when the second person POV is chosen, the heroic character is "you." Check out the Steely Dan song "Kid Charlemagne" for an example.

Lastly, we'll cover the POV that is useful if you want to have some emotional distance from the characters, for both the singer and the audience. Perhaps you want to tell a story from above, all knowing and privy to every detail. For this kind of view, we turn to third person.

Third Person: The Chronicle

The word *chronicle* is defined as a "factual written account of events," but don't let the word *factual* trip you up. Third person POV is telling us a little story about "Jack & Diane"—who they are, where they went, and what they think about life. It leaves the "I" and the "you" out of it as the singer becomes the storyteller delivering a tale in which they are not directly involved. The singer invites us to see what we can learn about life through tales like that of Eleanor Rigby, Father McKenzie, and "all the lonely people." You can still utilize third person even if your story *is* personal because songs grounded in reality can have an easier time feeling honest.

Seeing this in action will bring some clarity. My student Leah had a song called "When She's Not Laughing, She's Crying" about her mom processing Leah and her brother getting older and moving on. Leah knew she wanted to sing the song about her mom, not *to* her mom, so the character of her mom was referred to as "she" in the lyric.

In her first draft, Leah was "I," her mom was "she," and her brother was "you." Because the song had an "I" singing to a "you," Leah had chosen direct address where the singer ("I") was singing directly to her brother ("you") about their mom ("she"). This was the first verse:

We were backing down the driveway
When she realized
We won't live under the same roof
For the rest of our lives
Because you found a love
That you'll need more than hers

From Leah's perspective, the story made a lot of sense, but as a fresh listener, I was confused by the choice of direct address. Because the song was ultimately about Leah's mom, not necessarily about the relationship between Leah and her brother, the intimacy of direct address between the siblings was pulling away from mom being the central character of the story. It's also difficult for listeners to untangle the nature of the relationships when there are this many different pronouns flying around as a song begins. As writers, we've got to make the story and the nature of the relationships between the characters clear enough for our listeners to follow.

Leah ultimately chose third person to solve the problem and shift the focus back to her mom. Here was her rewritten first verse:

They were backing down the driveway
When she realized
They won't live under the same roof
For the rest of their lives
Cause her son found a love
That he needed more than hers

When the new POV was selected, the focus shifted back to where it was supposed to be: on mom. This POV also allows the listener to develop greater empathy for Mom, which increases the potential for emotional connection.

I've provided some clear and simple categories here for POV, but in reality, it's a bit more complicated when you start to analyze other songs. Often, songs in third person (The Chronicle) will still mention a "you" or an "I," but they are NOT the main characters in the story. Figuring out POV is all about understanding who the song is really focused on. **Check out the lyrics to "She Works Hard for the Money" by Donna Summer or "Betty Davis Eyes" by Kim Carnes to see how songs can stay in third person while mentioning an "I" or "you."**

Ultimately, there is no one POV that is always the best to use. Simply take a minute to question the POV you've chosen at the end of a first draft. The key takeaway is that you should be aware of which POV you're choosing and know how to try the other ones on. You might be surprised how dramatically your song could improve by using a different point of view.

Point in Time

When I was in college, I earned extra money by working as a substitute teacher at the high school where I graduated. One day, while I was on duty as a sub, a teacher yelled at me for going into the teacher's lounge. "Stop right there! You absolutely can't go in there!" they shouted. The teacher recognized me, but they still thought I was a current student. They didn't take the time to slow down and notice my substitute teacher badge. They got my "now" confused. Sometimes people misunderstand because they don't know when your now is.

Just like a consistent and suitable point of view helps bring clarity and emotional connection to your listener, so does keeping a consistent now. In Chapter 3, we learned that scene setting and physical spaces are significant because we are embodied creatures. We are also temporal creatures, and the "when" we are in time also affects our perspective. Basically, we need to know when now is in our song.

Paying attention to tense (past, present, future) can help us establish a now, but it's not as simple as keeping everything in your song in the same tense. We need to clearly define what moment is *now* for the singer, especially in relationship songs. Defining a specific now helps your listener understand whether the conflict is something you've gone through, are experiencing presently, or is something you're expecting. All of these cannot be happening at the same time.

Defining the now acknowledges that we live life one moment at a time. We can still recount memories and past experiences in the lyrics, but we have to choose the correct tense to differentiate between what happened in the past and the current situation. Just as jumping between POVs can confuse your listener, being unclear about "when is the now" can also cause your listeners to disconnect. They'll have a hard time relating to your story if they can't figure out the timeline. Read this lyric and see if you can understand the nature of the relationship between the characters.

We'll spend the night under the stars
You're breaking my heart
I want to hold you again
Say you're my best friend

Now, perhaps you could wrestle meaning out of this straining to find some kind of story. But we should probably help our listener make some sense of what's going on. This lyric needs some serious DTR (defining the relationship), and we can do that by establishing when the now is. Consider the following rewrite options to see if they make more sense. Pay attention to what's past tense, present tense, and future tense.

Option 1:
We spent the night under the stars
Then you broke my heart
I want to hold you again
Hear you say, "you're my best friend"

Option 2:
If we spend the night under the stars
Will you break my heart?
Will you hold me again
But then say that we're just friends?

Option 3:

We're sitting under the stars
And you could break my heart
You're holding me again
Saying I'm your best friend

If we make small changes to a few words and tense, then the now is more firmly established. In Option 1, we are remembering a special night in the past and longing to go back there. In Option 2, we are anticipating a relationship that might be going somewhere. In Option 3, we are present in the moment with our significant other. It becomes easier for the listener to go on the emotional journey if they clearly know *when* the singer's present moment is.

My kids love the song "Seven Years" by Lukas Graham. This song covers multiple stages of life within the story of the lyrics. However, it's important to note that this song does a good job of establishing one now. Read through some of the lyrics below and see if you can figure out when the now is. Look for the *present* tense:

Once, I was seven years old, my mama told me…
Once, I was 11 years old, my daddy told me…
Once, I was 20 years old, my story got told…
<u>I only see my goals, I don't believe in failure</u>…
Soon, we'll be 30 years old, our songs have been sold…
<u>I'm still learning about life</u>…
Soon, I'll be 60 years old, my daddy got 61…

Did you catch it? The now is between 20 and 30 years old, at an age when the singer is presently seeing goals and still learning about life. As the song progresses, the singer shifts between telling us things that happened in the past, things that are happening in the present, and the anticipation of things that may happen in the future. But there is only one now.

Asking yourself the question "when is the now" gets at the emotional center of your song. While it's true that we can experience multiple emotions at the same time, it can be difficult for a listener to relate to multiple emotions experienced over a large stretch of time within a three-minute song. I'm not saying it's impossible, it's just difficult! It might cause your song to feel emotionally inauthentic if you try to tap into too many emotions and too many "how I feel right now" statements as the narrative of your song progresses.

The characters in your song, whether they are I, you, or he/she, can have a rich past and lots of hopes for the future, but they should only exist at one point in time. And if the *movement* of those characters is also happening when you're using present tense, they also occupy one space at a time, in time.

Point in Space

Most songs contain narrative flow and pacing, even if they aren't specifically "story songs." When I ask my students to start infusing tactile details into their songwriting, they sometimes worry that I'm trying to force them into being country or folk songwriters. I reassure them that I'm not trying to turn all their songs into "story songs," but rather, I want them to understand that narrative flow helps a lyric to emotionally progress. Jewel's narrative flow in "You Were Meant for Me" walks us through the monotony of a post-breakup day, from sunrise to sunset.

Selected lyrics from "You Were Meant for Me":
From Verse 1
I hear the clock, it's six a.m.
I feel so far from where I've been
I got my eggs, I got my pancakes too...

From Verse 2
Put on my coat in the pouring rain
I saw a movie it just wasn't the same...

From Verse 3
I brush my teeth, I put the cap back on
I know you hate it when I leave the light on
I pick a book up and then I turn the sheets down…

We're not filled in on *every* step and *every* moment the singer experiences, but the progression from one point in space to the next feels natural.

Leah showed me a song about a budding relationship. It was by no means a "story song," but it still had a narrative flow, whether she liked it or not. At the beginning of the verse, the characters were so close in physical proximity that one of them was getting a kiss from the other. However, by the end of the same verse, she asks her new love if she can sit next to him on a bench.

From Leah's first draft of "November 6th":
November the 6th
1st kiss on the neck
We'll take a picture
We won't soon forget
Polaroids are expensive
But what the heck
Can I sit next to you?
Where we'll be close enough
To confess…

There was a lyrical disconnect here because the narrative flow, which seemed to be linear in the present, was interrupted. How did her love teleport from neck-kissing distance to being seated far away from her? We've got to try to hear our songs the way our listeners will hear them: from top to bottom, one line at a time. They don't have all the memories and context we have in our own heads as we write the song. If you're going to move the characters around in your song, make the movement natural. Consider where they were, where they are now, and where they might go next. Please save unexpected teleporting for sci-fi space operas.

Intentional, Not Incoherent

This chapter was all about the beauty we risk losing if we are incoherent. Confusion arises about our song's message when we lack a clearly defined point of view or haven't given our listeners a clear understanding of "when is the now" (point in time) or grounded them in a coherent narrative space.

I once tried to give a songwriter feedback about a lack of clarity in his song's point of view. I couldn't tell who the singer was or to whom he was singing because the point of view changed multiple times within the song. I told him that I thought his song could have incredible emotional power if he would just pick one POV and stick to it. The writer pushed back and said choosing the confusing point of view shift felt more poetic because it allowed him to cover multiple perspectives. Ultimately, he's the writer, and he has to do what he feels is right. But in my opinion, he wasn't making his song more poetic or beautiful. His choice to be incoherent in his point of view detracted from the beauty and message of the song.

Lastly, and perhaps most importantly, beauty can be lost when we are unintentional. Since you're here to study songwriting, I think you already believe that beauty can be found when we choose to craft our songs with care. Passion provokes us toward intentional pursuit. My programmer husband often talks about beautiful code in the same way I talk about my favorite songs. He marvels at the beauty found in efficiency. He was pontificating once on a particular piece of code he had just studied. He said, "How could 400 lines of code accomplish so much in such a small space?" Not a single dash or dot was wasted. So in the same way, songwriter, take care with every word and every note that you choose. Be intentional about your point of view, point in space, and point in time. You have so many beautiful stories to tell.

PLAYTIME

Solo Activities:

POV Jukebox Journey: Find four songs that each use a different point of view discussed in this chapter (direct address, first, second, and third person) and reflect on how the point of view creates emotional connection and narrative clarity. With each of the songs, try writing an additional verse that can be added anywhere in the song, staying consistent with the point of view and continuing the narrative forward. If you need help getting started, analyze the following songs: "Set Fire to the Rain" by Adele, "Let It Be" by The Beatles, "Captain Jack" by Billy Joel, and "The Trapper and the Furrier" by Regina Spektor.

The "Now" Navigator: What is the moment you find yourself in right now? Journal or try to write lyrics in the present tense to anchor yourself in this moment, writing about your senses, your surroundings, and your emotional state. If you find a few lyrics that really speak to you, compose a melody that enhances the emotional tone. Perhaps you'll come away with a new rock to add to your collection.

Time Traveler's Tune: Brainstorm one place that you could find yourself occupying in the past, present, and future for each verse of one song. *For example, "I can see myself on the back porch of my parents' house when I was a child, at my current age, and at some point in the future."* Write lyrics that reflect a narrative that goes from past, to present, to future, but stays in the same physical location. Write verse 1 in the past tense, verse 2 in the present tense, and verse 3 in the future tense. The narrative of your song can cover past, present, and future, but remember, there is only *one* now.

Group Activities:

Time Capsule Songwriting: Assign each group a historic time period. Look up some visuals to help ground the group in the culture of the time period. Each group will pick a theme or emotion that corresponds with their time period (e.g., loss, hope, transformation). Start with a 5-minute journaling, then have each group co-write a verse or chorus that reflects their assigned time period and theme. Remember: Just because something happened in the past, doesn't mean the song has to be in past tense!

DTR in Pairs: Break into groups of two. Going one at a time, have each partner tell the story of a complicated relationship they've been in. The other partner will be the scribe, capturing interesting phrases and details. Have the partners swap notes so that the storyteller has what their scribe recorded. Then, each person will create a song map with a title and the narrative flow for a song about the history of the complicated relationship. They can choose to write the song from any point of view, and they must be specific about their chosen POV and "when is the now?" (Is it the middle, end, or long after the end of the relationship?)

Homework Challenge:

Shifting Perspectives: Choose a topic you are currently obsessed with (sci-fi novels, gardening, baking pies, politics, etc.) and write a long verse that ends in a refrain line about this topic. If you're not sure what a verse ending in a refrain line looks like, reference Bob Dylan's "Ballad of a Thin Man." After you finish, go back and discover which point of view you chose. Now, try to rewrite your lyric, trying on all the other POVs you didn't use in your first draft. Did a more interesting POV emerge?

Timeline Exploration: Choose a significant event you personally experienced as the theme for your song, like a graduation, a funeral, winning the spelling bee, or your first time driving. Do three journalings: one describing the past event in vivid detail, another reflecting on its emotional impact on you in the present, and a third envisioning its future implications on your life. Attempt to write song sections from your journaling using the first as material for your verses, the second as content for your chorus, and the third as inspiration for a bridge. If that song map doesn't work for you, use your journalings however you like to inform the lyrics.

Song Challenge:

Middle Man: Write a "middle man" relationship song in the style of "She Loves You" where the point of view is direct address, but there's a spirit of second person because the main characters are "you" and "he or she."

The Character Song: Write a song truly in second person. Build a character and then call that character "you." If you need help, work backward from third person. Create an interesting character—a hero or a villain, perhaps—and describe them in detail. Then, instead of referring to them as "he/she," adjust the pronouns to "you."

CHAPTER 9

Climbing Trees

Songwriting Priority Tiers

"He is like a tree planted by streams of water that yields fruit in its season, and its leaf does not wither. In all that he does, he prospers." Psalm 1:3 ESV

Previously, I argued that melody is king, lyrics are queen, and harmony is the kingdom that they live in. In this chapter, we will pursue a more symbiotic metaphor to help you think about how the pieces of songwriting interact and grow together. Songwriting is of the organic, natural realm. In a way, it's less like a king building his kingdom and more like a tree that is flourishing where it's planted. It's alive, awe-inspiring, and connected to deeper things beneath the surface.

My younger brother and I were tree climbers as kids. It was fun to find the perfect little nook or cranny where my foot could take hold. I'd climb to the next spot, finding a gentle curve in the tree and leaning against its wooden skin, listening to the leaves rustle. I'd look down and enjoy a new perspective on the world. Not just a higher perspective, but a freer, slightly otherworldly one—seeing the ground through a magical shimmer of green. I remember the last time I ever really climbed. I was in college and had gotten high up on a tree at the edge of campus. Suddenly, I realized I cared much more about falling than I did about the joy of climbing. I had to briefly mourn the fact that the fearless tree climbing part of my childhood was behind me.

Engaging with a great song is like climbing a beautiful, unique tree. It's somehow thrilling, peaceful, and satisfying all at the same time. This chapter uses the visual of a tree to help you differentiate the three basic parts of a song—melody, lyrics, and harmony—and discuss ways to keep these pieces interacting in a cohesive and cooperative way. In my new analogy, melody is the tree's body, lyrics are the foliage (leaves, flowers, fruits), and harmony is the environment (ground, grass, sun, clouds).

A Bold Statement

I'm gonna go where most songwriters won't go and make a bold statement: Melody is more important than lyrics. It's probably obvious that I believe this because of that whole "king" chapter, but to many songwriters, this statement feels provocative. Lyricists the world over clutch their pearls and shake their fists. I hear them cry out, "A powerful lyric can move mountains!" and "You need thoughtful lyrics to have an emotional connection!" And I wholeheartedly agree. Lyrics *are* important. At one point, I even considered myself a much stronger lyric writer than a melody writer.

But here's the rub. Craft a brilliant lyric over a forgettable melody, and your song is dead on arrival. Can you think of many songs with transcendent lyrics but mediocre melodies? I can't. I struggle to remember beautiful words if the melody doesn't stick with me. However, if a subpar lyric is pasted on top of a brilliant melody, well, I can give you more hit songs than I can count. And what about the harmony (the chord changes)? Ultimately, harmony usually takes a back seat to both in most cases.

I'm going to argue that melody and lyrics live on the top priority tier of songwriting, with melody being slightly more important in a foundational way. Harmony (chords and arrangements) is a second-tier priority in what defines a song. These three components, while all significant, should not be given equal footing when you are creating, playing with, and refining a song. Genre considerations may change this balance a little bit, but again, we are working with guidelines, not rules. If we can grow our song tree while keeping these priorities in mind, we can foster a tree that is alive, awe-inspiring, and connected to deeper things below the surface.

Which Comes First?

Almost every time I play a show, a curious member of the audience will approach me afterward and ask, "Which comes first, the music or the lyrics?" Creating songs feels magical to people who don't yet do it, and so I am always happy to engage the question. And analyzing this question will help us untangle some things. First and foremost, we've got to establish what a "song" is before we deal with the importance of each component. So when we are asked, "Which comes first, music or lyrics?" We must start with: "Well, what do you mean by *music*?"

For this chapter, we're going to separate "music" into two categories: melody and harmony. If music is the combination of melody and harmony, then the original question of "What comes first, music or lyrics?" helps us identify the three components of what makes a song: melody, lyrics, and harmony. I'm sure you can think of examples of instrumental songs that don't have lyrics, or a cappella songs that don't have harmony, but *most* songs have all three of these elements. However, should all of these elements carry equal weight?

Songwriting commentaries and texts usually lean heavily into addressing one of the three aspects of song craft, neglecting the others. I once read an online article titled "How To Get Started Songwriting," and most of the steps involved learning basic chords and copying chord changes from popular songs. However, learning basic harmony is not of primary importance when writing a song. Many of the songwriting resources you will engage with will focus about 90% on lyric writing because lyrics are easier to discuss on paper. But lyrics are not of 90% importance to songwriting. People talk more about chords and lyrics when discussing songwriting because these elements are easier to articulate than melody. There aren't enough books and resources about crafting hooky melodies for modern songwriters. I have most of them; they could fit in one hand.

If you ask people for feedback on your song, most of the time, they will comment on the lyrics. They may even suggest alternative chord changes if they play an instrument. However, it is rare for someone to give you critical feedback on the quality of your melody. Why? Because they can't see the melody written down, and also, even if they could, it's hard to know what feedback to give. Most people won't question the composition of an existing melody and wouldn't know how to begin critiquing it or suggesting alternatives.

Since people don't often question the beauty, intention, and crafting of your melody, this is exactly where we should start. The tree analogy helps us establish "priorities" while still giving respect to the beauty of all parts of a song thriving together. These three components of songwriting can fail to thrive if we treat them functionally as equals. To have a healthy, thriving song, we need these elements to support each other in an organic, yet ordered, way.

Melody: The Body of the Tree

Interacting with a well-crafted melody is like discovering the body of a captivating tree, which includes the trunk *and* branches. This is the most important element of our thought picture because it provides the shape, structure, and identity of our song. Without the tree, we have an empty field of harmony and a pile of dead leaves. It could be a beautiful field, but it's a field nonetheless. We need a melody worthy to be the centerpiece. We should aim to craft melodies sturdy and interesting enough to support all our lyrical leaves. The leaves find their cohesive shape within the structure of the tree branches. They cannot thrive without a branch that will keep them connected to the soil and rising toward the sun.

Sturdy trees can withstand the weight of years and the berating of weather. In the same way, sturdy melodies have staying power—not just on our own lips but passing from one generation to the next. Are you crafting a melody that can withstand the test of time? Strong tree trunks support and enable extensive branches. Interesting melodies—with twisting, reaching, and arching phrases—draw us into their unique beauty. The melody, like the body of a tree, might not be what we focus on most, but its interest and integrity shape the experience. Are you crafting a melody that surprises and delights? Are you crafting a melody that allows your lyrical leaves to be featured and flourish?

In the real world, no single type of tree can grow in every climate, but several trees are adaptable to many different climates. Likewise, well-crafted melody trees should be resilient and capable of thriving in various conditions. My student Clay had an epiphany one day during our songwriting lesson. He realized that just because he conceived of one of his songs as folk, that didn't mean it couldn't also make the jump to rock. And that's the kind of melody we are trying to craft: one that is resilient in many different harmonic contexts. Ever notice how the best songs can be reinterpreted in many genres? I think of the group Postmodern Jukebox, whose bread and butter is reimagining modern songs in musical styles from decades past. How could an alt-rock song from the 1990s be so perfectly reimagined as a 1930s-era big band number? A resilient melody is how.

People don't usually declare their love for a song is motivated by the melody. But again, praise and criticism for melody isn't really something most people know how to do. What they do know how to do is hum. Or sing at the top of their lungs in the shower, in the car, or at karaoke. People betray the importance of melody through the ways they interact with a song over and over again. If we craft beautifully intricate lyric leaves and place them on a shriveled melody trunk, we've got dead or dying leaves. However, a tree with very simple leaves, or without any leaves at all, can still be stunning and interesting. Don't believe me? Go look up the song "Land of 1000 Dances" right now. Sing along to the chorus and come back to me. (Spoiler alert: the lyrics are na-na-na-na-na-na-na-na.)

Songwriter and author Billy Seidman argues that the most timeless melodies utilize three different things:

1. Stepwise motion
2. Interval jumps
3. "Cool" rhythm (my dorky terminology, not his)

One could argue that without any of these things, you wouldn't have much of a melody at all. Acknowledging these components of timeless melodies (stepwise motion, interval jumps, and cool rhythm) is important because it makes us aware if we are habitually ignoring one of them. It also helps us determine which category is leading the way, or defining the heart, of a melodic big idea.

Your melody tree should have a unique character through definitive melodic motifs. This is what makes it memorable, special, and sets it apart from other trees. As much as I hate this about me, I'm going to talk about "Wrecking Ball" again. **Go and listen to the first verse, pre-chorus, and chorus right now, paying special attention to the movement of the melody.** Talking about melody can be hard, especially if you can't read sheet music or if analyzing lead sheets feels overwhelming. Often, I draw out basic shapes to help me visually understand what's going on in the melody across song sections. I'll do this as we discuss "Wrecking Ball," so you can observe the motion of what I would consider to be a pretty "timeless" melody.

In the verse, the melody is defined by interval jumps. The rhythm is pretty simple, but the interval jumps capture our attention with their hypnotic push and pull. The verse lines end with a bit of stepwise motion.

"We clawed, we chained our hearts in vain, we jumped—never asking why..."

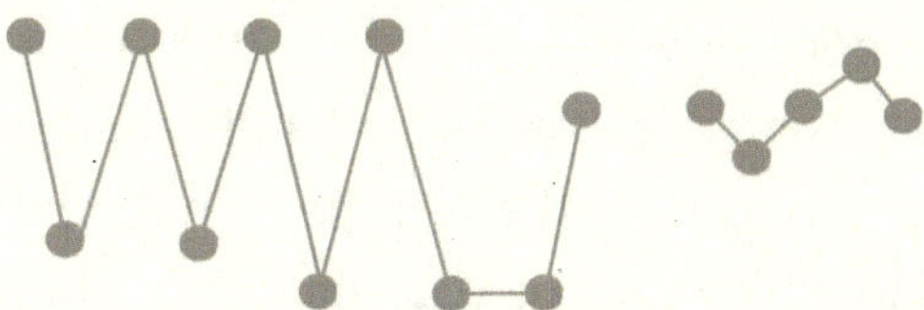

In the pre-chorus, we get a contrast of shapely descending lines that feel more like cascading stepwise motion.

"Don't you ever say, I just walked away, I will always want you..."

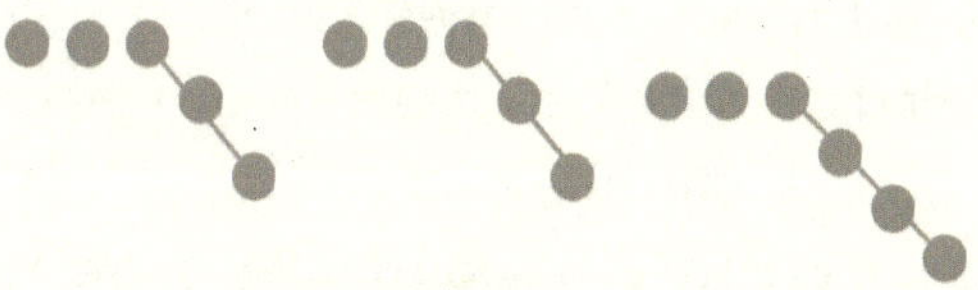

Did you notice there are three lines in the pre-chorus? The first two are melodically identical, and the third is a slight variation starting on a lower pitch. That's productive repetition. In the chorus, we are punched in the gut with a (front-heavy fa) rhythm that drives the nature of the lyric home. It's a combination of a flat rhythmic shape and short, wavy stepwise motion.

"I came in like a wrecking ball, I never hit so hard in love..."

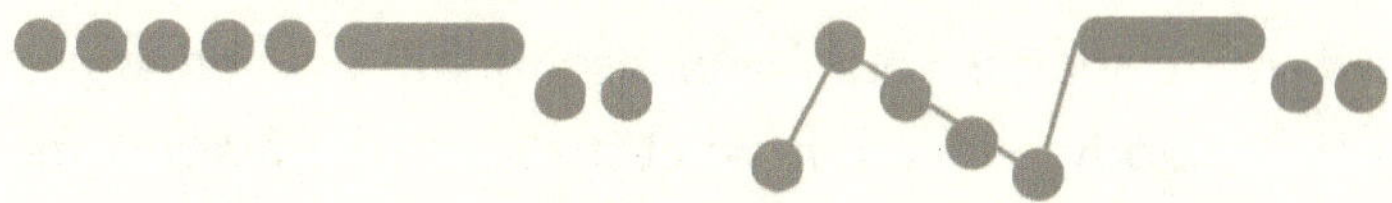

It's an incredible melody because it utilizes all the components. There is stepwise motion at the end of the verse, pre-chorus, and mid-chorus. There are significant interval jumps in the verse and between the pre-chorus motifs. There is "cool" rhythm in the chorus. Not only that, but this melody applies the components with repetition *and* variation. We're going to spend a lot of time talking about repetition and variation in Chapter 14, but for now, I want you to keep these three components in your pocket when considering which part of your melody is shining. Ultimately, it should be a group effort. No one component should be completely neglected.

Is this all starting to feel like a lot of puzzle pieces to manage? If you are feeling overwhelmed when thinking about growing a melody tree, remember to roll things back to a melodic motif (roughly two bars of melody). Find a motif you love and then start to play with it through repetition and manipulation, making small changes. Repetition helps reinforce and reimagine your melodic motifs. I will never argue that only complicated melodies can be truly beautiful trees.

There's so much more we can add to this picture. How much more enchanting will our melody tree become when we adorn it with green? Let's move forward, considering the foliage—the lyrical leaves hanging from our melody branches.

Lyrics: Foliage

Now that we've established the importance of crafting a resilient melody tree, we can turn our attention to the foliage. In the end, the foliage may be what really emotionally sticks with your listener. Remember, I didn't say lyrics aren't important; I'm just saying that your carefully crafted lyrics need a melody to hold them up. The lyrics may ultimately be the reason that your favorite song is your *favorite* song. but I would argue that the shape of the melody beneath is what makes those lyrics come alive to you. The branch of that melody rose and fell at just the right moments, allowing you to be captivated by the leaves rustling in the wind. The shapes of our branches matter. They guide our leaves into a structure that shows the world what our tree is all about.

Let's get practical. What if all of our tree branches (melody pieces) were the exact same length, shape, and all pointed in the same direction? Try to picture a tree like this. Then try to imagine a song that would sound like this. Seems a little too symmetrical and not organic, right? Or perhaps we find ourselves crafting a mismatch, like trying to pull pinecones out of a palm tree. We might have weeping willow lyrics flowing from a fern of a melody. To have a beautiful tree, our melody and lyrics must find alignment. Our lyrics and melody should work together, but we should care *just a little* more about tending to the melody when things go awry. Reworking your leaves to fit your foundational melody is usually a better choice than taking a machete to your melody to save a few lyrical leaves.

It's important to note that just because melody provides the foundation for your lyrics, it doesn't mean that melody is where you have to start. I've written many songs inspired by a journal entry (words first) or by a title. It's fantastic to find a combination of words that makes us want to sing. The point of the tree metaphor isn't that the trunk and branches must be created first. Instead, the point is that prioritizing them is foundational to the success of a lyric.

My student Clay once brought a poem to his songwriting lesson. He said, "I know it's a poem and not song lyrics, but I was doing what you said and rotating the crops. I watched an interesting movie, and then this poem just came spilling out." My teacher's heart is always encouraged when I see songwriters experimenting with other artistic mediums, whether they feel skilled at them or not.

"What do you want to do with the poem?" I asked.

"Well," he said, "maybe it could become some song lyrics, but I don't know where to start."

I asked him to read the poem and observe which words jumped off the page, which ones he felt especially drawn to. After reading, he picked out a few phrases. Then, still a little stuck, he asked me about my own process. "How would you choose your favorite words?" he asked. "What's the next step you would take toward using words from a poem to write a song?"

It was a practical and interesting question. I told him that I look for the words that *sing*. To me, this moment is the birth of a tree. As I ruminate on the words on the page, I ask myself:

- Which words do I hear out loud?
- Which words have a natural rhythm?
- Which ones can I feel the shape of?
- Which ones feel good in my mouth?
- Which ones make me feel like grabbing an instrument?
- What words sing?

As we read and speak, there are technical things that draw our attention to certain words that make them feel "singable." In Clay's poem, I was drawn to the phrase "love is a lion." It's possible I gravitated toward these words because I enjoyed the alliteration of the double "l" in *love* and *lion*. There was also inherent rhythmic potential contained in the words, and I was drawn to the strong metaphor that declared love *is* a lion.

But to be honest, I didn't actively think about any of those things. When I saw the phrase "love is a lion," I immediately knew how I would sing it. That's why I was drawn to those words. This may not be your process when engaging with words you've written, but it's always a question worth asking when you're engaging with a journal entry or any sort of text that could be a lyric: What words make you want to sing?

Taking a Break from Trees for the Backstreet Boys

Let's "rotate the crops," so to speak, and stop talking about trees for just a minute. I want to talk about boy bands instead. The Backstreet Boys had a huge hit in 1999 called "I Want It That Way." The version most people know, the huge hit, almost didn't see the light of day. Max Martin, a prolific songwriter who went on to have hits for decades, wrote the original version of the song you know now. The Backstreet Boys recorded Martin's version, but the executives at Jive Records had a problem: They thought the lyrics were too confusing. The issue was that Max Martin, who also famously wrote Britney Spears's smash hit "Baby One More Time," was not a native English speaker. Jive felt Martin's lyrics to "I Want It That Way" were awkward and confusing, and would fail to connect with audiences. The record company ordered a new version of the song to be written with significantly revised lyrics. These lyrics, on paper, made way more sense. After the song had been rewritten, the Backstreet Boys re-recorded it. Then, they compared the new version with the original for feedback.

Portion of the original lyric:
Tell me why
Ain't nothing but a heartache
Tell me why
Ain't nothing but a mistake
Tell me why
I never wanna hear you say
I want it that way

Same portion of the rewrite:
No goodbyes
Ain't nothing but a heartache
No more lies
Ain't nothing but a mistake
That is why
I love it when I hear you say
I want it that way

Ultimately, they chose Max Martin's original version. Why? Because even though his version made less sense, it sounded more "right." Why did this unclear string of words sound better together than a cohesive lyric with what *should've been* a stronger emotional impact? It's hard to say. Maybe the original had just the right amount of lyric repetition for a pop song. Or perhaps the ambiguity in the original lyric allowed listeners a more universal entry point—making it easier for them to see themselves in the story because they could interpret the song's meaning however they wanted. Or it could be some less quantifiable reason, like the "mouthfeel" of certain words and how they interacted with the melody and rhythm. Ultimately, some words just click, and some don't.

My point is that sometimes "better" lyrics are not better lyrics. Sometimes, the mouthfeel of a word, the inherent rhythm of it, the vowel sound, and how it sings can be more important than the meaning of the word. You might not be willing to explore or embrace this idea if lyrics are the top priority in your songwriting. When lyric writing becomes the primary driving force behind our song craft, we might overwork them. We may be creating beautiful leaves without considering the tree that they're hanging on. It's okay to keep a word in a lyric just because it feels right and sounds right—even if you can think of a "better" or more clever word. If you get pushback for your weird lyric that feels right and sings well, just tell people, "I want it that way."

Harmony: The Environment

The environment is the song's atmosphere. In our thought picture, chord changes, arrangement, and production are the grass, the air, the clouds, and the sun. The environment is important to the tree, but it's not the tree itself. Intentional crafting of these elements is crucial for a song's success, but they don't define what makes a song a song. If you're a songwriter who is gifted at feeling out harmony and arrangement, we love you and we need you. But the truth is, as of right now, you can't copyright chord changes and grooves, though people have tried. And re-harmonizing a song usually doesn't change the bones and essence of what a song is.

Producers and instrumentalists may push back that riffs and production can often be a foundational starting point for songwriting. Don't come at me! I believe distinctive riffs are *melodies*. Important synth and bass lines or guitar hooks can also serve as melody instead of harmony and environment within this thought experiment. The key is separating what musical motifs are essential to the song's essence from those that are background elements surrounding it.

Our chosen environment *does* have perceived genre implications. I would argue that what makes a song sound country or R&B has a lot more to do with the harmony, groove, and production than it has to do with the melody or lyrics. But we shouldn't let harmony or perceived genre be the driving force behind our creation. We are not cranking out commodities; we are creating art.

So if the environment is secondary, should we care about it? Absolutely! Our song tree needs healthy soil, sunshine, and an environment that allows it to thrive. Knowing our tree well helps us understand what environments might be most suitable and what atmosphere might highlight the unique beauty and character of our tree.

Trees don't all come in the same shape and size, and they don't have to be huge or intricate to be healthy. Some find their beauty in their accessibility and simple form. The environment can become essential in elevating these melody trees—just think of how a basic fir tree becomes the centerpiece of an elaborate Christmas display, complete with garland, a roaring fire, and a pile of presents.

A Basic Melody Elevated

For an example of a simple melody elevated by its environment, let's consider "Heat Waves" by Glass Animals. This was the number-one Billboard song of 2022. **If you're unfamiliar with the song, check it out right now and pay special attention to the *chorus* melody.**

The melody is simple and repetitive, yet effective. Why? There are no big interval jumps or sweeping contours. There is some catchy melodic rhythm, but the only bit of "sparkle" found is in the suspended note at the end of the lines. The lyrics are not terribly compelling, but they do have great mouthfeel as they shift from bright to dark vowels in each line ("I" to "oo" sounds, then "A" to "ow" sounds). They also have a trance-like couplet rhyme scheme.

Sometimes all I think about is you
Late nights in the middle of June
Heat waves been fakin' me out
Can't make you happier now

Remember, sometimes it's more important to find words that are fun to sing, even if they aren't the most interesting to read or contemplate.

Repetitive melodies like this rely on their harmonic environment to be effective. Just as Andy Warhol painted a Campbell's soup can in many colors, harmonic recoloring enhances basic and repetitive melodic ideas. The magic of "Heat Waves" and many modern pop songs is that the vocal melody is re-colored as the harmony shifts underneath it. The harmonic environment becomes vitally important for the song's overall interest. **Sing the first two lines of "Heat Waves" playing the original chords. Then sing it again with these chord rewrites to feel how much duller the melody could have sounded.** (The sung pitch of c# on the word *you* is a critical moment.)

Original:

C#m B
Sometimes all I think about is you (c#)
G#m F#
Late nights in the middle of June

Rewrites with a "less effective" environment:

B F#
Sometimes all I think about is you
B F#
Late nights in the middle of June

Just Fooling Around?

I also think a lot about the song "Fooled Around and Fell in Love" by Elvin Bishop. This song has a repetitive chorus melody where the shifting harmonic environment beneath it *creates* the sparkle note. **Take a listen to the chorus of this song now. Note how the lyrical "leaves" of the chorus remain the same four times in a row:**

I fooled around and fell in love
I fooled around and fell in love
I fooled around and fell in love
I fooled around and fell in love

The melody is highly repetitive, with a slight variation at the end of the phrases. There is an interesting interruption to the melodic rhythm in line 3, but otherwise it is consistent. So where is the melodic magic amidst all this repetition?

The magic happens at the intersection of the melody and the harmony. We'll pay special attention to the third chord in the progression, the E♭ Major. Here are the chorus chord changes:

F *Am*
I fooled around and fell in love
E♭ *B♭*
I fooled around and fell in love
F *Am*
I fooled around and fell in love
E♭ *B♭*
I fooled around and fell in love

The melodic note sung on the word *fooled* is in an a♮ every time. This note is very spicy in an Eb Major chord.

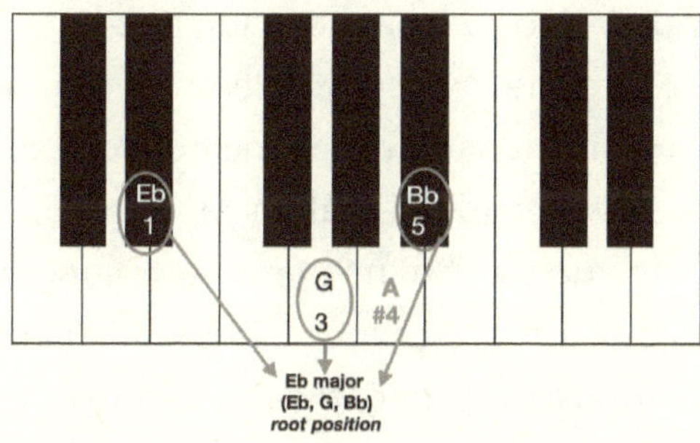

The spell is cast when the melodic note a♮ crashes into the unexpected Eb Major chord, which is *not* diatonic in the key of F. In fact, this a♮ in the melody is a tritone away from the root of the Eb chord, one of the crunchiest intervals in all of music. Again, I'm not writing a music theory textbook for you, but I do want to be clear that while I think the harmonic environment is secondary to the melody and lyrics, there are many examples, like this song, that prove the environment can be crucial to the thriving of melody trees.

Add More Grass

My friend Rachel sent me a song she loved, but she felt the chords were drab and basic. When I listened to her song, I agreed with her assessment. She had a beautiful melody tree body and appropriately placed lyric leaves, but the harmonic environment wasn't allowing her tree to flourish. The problem was that her harmonic rhythm—how *often* the chords changed—was a bit too sparse. We needed to metaphorically "add more grass" to the environment, and this was as easy as introducing a new chord at each bar.

We took the verse harmony from this:
Cm | Cm | Cm | Cm |
And adjusted it to this:
Cm | Fm | Cm | Gm |

Adding more chords isn't always the solution for harmony hangups—this just happened to be what her song needed.

Sometimes we face the inverse problem: far too many chords clogging up our song, making it hard for the melody to breathe. I would liken this to grass that's so wild and tall that it's blocking our view of the tree. This was a personal struggle of mine in my early songwriting days. I was addicted to complicated chord changes, but I didn't consider how starting with complex chords could negatively affect my melodies. My melodies were getting lost and buried in the weeds of all those crazy chords.

When I started to craft melodies I loved *before* I thought too much about the environment around them, my songs began to thrive in a way they never had before.

Struggle with Harmony

Ultimately, I see harmony/arrangement environmental issues as micro problems. You can still write incredible songs without having mastery over harmony. If you struggle with incorporating a harmonic environment, I encourage you to collaborate with others who find harmony, production, and arranging to be their strengths. You can still bring them a fully formed song idea with a melody and lyrics, and then they can help you find the environment that allows the song to thrive.

Harmony and arrangement are on the secondary priority tier of what you *need* to make a song because all the fancy production or intricate chord changes in the world can't save an uninspired melody and lyric. However, this doesn't mean we can't start the songwriting process with the environment. I often encourage my students to experiment with drum or synth loops if they are feeling stuck in their songwriting practice. A great loop, the right beat, or fresh chord changes can be what sparks new creativity. The environment can also be the thing that enables us to begin to hear melody and lyrics emerge. We just can't get so caught up in our environment that we miss the heart of the song.

The Curious Case of Viva La Vida

"Viva La Vida" was Coldplay's first number-one song in both the US and the UK. Even more, it became their highest-charting single and was named Song of the Year at the 2009 Grammy Awards. This was one of the biggest songs by one of the world's most renowned bands at the time. But why? How could a song that has a chorus lyric featuring lines like "Roman calvary choirs are singing" and "my missionaries in a foreign field" find the most universal and widespread acceptance from fans and critics alike?

I believe this song has magical transcendence because its priority tiers are in alignment:

1. The melody is memorable. There is a delightful combination of stepwise motion and interval jumps. It has cool melodic rhythm and utilizes productive repetition and reinvention.
2. There is uniqueness beyond the vocal melody, particularly in the melodic rhythm of the opening string riff. This countermelody to the vocal melody provides important melodic and environmental elements to the recording.
3. There is one definitive lyric line that establishes the big idea and makes it stick.

This song is a shining example of prioritizing the melody above the lyrics. As songwriters, we tend to fuss and agonize over words, but oftentimes, people don't remember all those words. Maybe they remember one very important set of words like "when I ruled the world," but the words surrounding that big idea lyric might not matter as much as we think they do. That's not to say that a unique and compelling big idea isn't worthwhile. The big idea of this song, exploring the concept of a "falling from grace" through the lens of the French Revolution, does give tactile and vivid imagery to give context to what it feels like to "rule the world." But my point is that the lyrics aren't the king of this mountain. Our takeaway is to use spellbinding big ideas in support of and in alignment with spectacular melody.

A Tree of Divinity

When talking about the daunting task of crafting a "perfect" song, Jeff Tweedy once said, "I've accepted the fact that it's also impossible to make the perfect tree—there's no perfecting it. There's no reaching some conclusion that you've made *the* tree." There is no such thing as a perfect tree or a perfect song. We should not aim for perfection but rather for beauty, truth, and goodness. Joyfully creating with unique twists and turns, leaving no two creations exactly alike. Some trees are massive, and some are delicate. Some have pinecones, and others have palm leaves. You find some in the mountains and some in the deserts. But wherever you find a thriving song tree, you find the elements of melody, lyrics, and harmony working together.

A song tree may reach divinity if we can build a beautiful melody and pair it with words that stick inside the soul. Can you hear it? To me, it's the way Fleetwood Mac sings "you can go your own way." Or how John Mayer sings "your body is a wonderland," making us blush. And how Bruce Springsteen taught us what it feels like to be "born in the USA." The melody means more *because* of the lyric, and the lyric comes alive *because* of the melody. You need both parts to be divine.

But what about harmony? Again, I would argue it is crucial, but not essential, for most songs. Why? When the melding of melody to lyric reaches divinity, songs like these can survive the jump to new harmonic interpretations, fresh arrangements, and even entire genre shifts.

Don't neglect the body of your melody tree just because you're spending all your time fussing over the lyric leaves. Don't lose your tree in the tall grasses of too much harmony. Strive to raise up trees that are alive, awe-inspiring, and connected to deeper things beneath the surface. Trees where the birds of heaven can make their nests in the boughs. Trees of divinity that become something greater than the sum of all their parts. Those are the trees we're after.

PLAYTIME

Solo Activities

R-E-S-P-E-C-T: Find an interesting noun or verb that you think would make a good song title, like "Respect" or "Gloria" or "Staring." Now, spell this word out and put it into a melodic rhythm the way we hear Aretha Franklin spell R-E-S-P-E-C-T in the chorus of "Respect." Once you can spell your word on a melodic rhythm, add pitch. Then loop your word several times and turn it into a chorus. If you don't want to fill out the chorus only using the spelled word, try adding a "call and response" second line that would come after the spelled word. For examples of how this works, check out the chorus from "Respect," or "Gloria" by Van Morrison, or "Staring Problem" by No Doubt.

Exploring Emotional Contours: Take the following lists and choose one melodic contour and one emotion; any combination is fine. Create a melodic motif (roughly 2-bar melody) using your chosen contour and emotion. For example, if you select "going up" and "calm," try to create a melody that goes up in pitch and feels calm. You aren't writing lyrics to convey the emotion; you are embodying the emotion through the melody you create. If you like the melody, keep going and try to compose the melody for the whole song section.

Melody Contour (shape)	**Emotion**
Going Up (Ascending)	Joy
Going Down (Descending)	Grief
Flat (Stationary)	Rage
Hill (Arch)	Anxiety
Ditch (Inverted Arch)	Craving
Going Up to Flat	Nostalgia
Going Down to Flat	Calm
Yo-Yo (Big Interval Jumps)	Indifference

Group Activities

Power of Three: Break into groups of three. Each group will be composing a song section. Have one member of the group take the melody, one take the lyrics, and one take the harmony. Have the lyric person create a line of lyric, then let the melody person add melody to the lyric, and lastly, let the harmony person add chord changes. Complete this activity as many times as you like, switching which group member has which role, and then switching the order in which you compose the song sections. (Start with harmony first, or melody first, etc.)

A New Pairing: The group leader will pre-compose three different melodic motifs and three different short lyric phrases. Present them one at a time. Sing the melodic motifs one at a time, without lyrics, and ask participants to craft lyrics that align with each motif. Then present the lyric phrases one at a time. Have each person individually craft a melody that aligns with the lyric. For fun, see if any of these new pairings emerge as a strong song start idea.

Homework Challenge:

Song Deconstruction: Choose a well-known song, preferably one with a strong melody, and deconstruct it into its three elements: melody, lyrics, and harmony. Analyze how each tier contributes to the overall impact of the song. For melody, focus on a motif and how it appears and reappears. For lyrics, consider the title placement, "show," and big idea. For harmony, analyze the chords and arrangement. Submit a reflection on how each element is working together to support the overall song. If you're not sure where to start, analyze "Fire and Rain" by James Taylor or "Pink Pony Club" by Chappell Roan.

Solo Tiers: Take one of your original songs in process and experiment with adjusting the emphasis of each song priority element. Start by focusing solely on the melody, setting aside lyrics and harmony. Adjust the melody through more intentional repetition of your melodic motifs, adding sparkle notes, or being picky about the hookiness of your melodic rhythm. Then start adding lyrics back in, choosing only those that fit with your newly adjusted melody. Once you've settled on updated lyrics for your new melody, add harmony. Focus on making sure the harmony reinforces what your melody and lyrics communicate. Finally, reflect on the impact of the adjustments. Did soloing the priority tiers help you make decisions and move the song forward?

Song Challenge:

A Song about a Tree: Consider an actual tree that triggers a memory. Write a song inspired by your experience(s) with or within proximity of this tree. The tree can be a starting point; it doesn't have to be the central subject matter of the song. If a specific tree doesn't immediately come to mind, pick a memory of a specific outdoor space like a backyard, garden, or field instead. Let the image of this tree or outdoor space inform the emotion of your melody and harmony.

A Tale of Two Trees: Pick two very different trees (anything from birch to banyan, sequoia to sycamore). Look up lots of pictures of your two trees. Which tree is really speaking to you? Select this tree and study its shape, its leaves, and its environment. Try to write a song that evokes the emotional quality of this tree. I know it's weird. Just try it and see what happens. If you're a little stuck, try to imagine someone or something that would live in that tree. Do a journal entry about it and create a story. It's okay if it goes a little off the rails; be as creative as you want. Use your journaling as inspiration for lyrics or a big idea.

CHAPTER 10

Finger Painting Part 2

Progressions & More Play

Scan Me

"Art is a circulation of energetic ideas. What makes them appear new is that they're combining differently each time they come back." Rick Rubin

My oldest daughter is a painter. She paints on canvases, but often she goes rogue and decides to resort to unusual mediums. She will paint on her arms and legs, index cards, and ceiling fan blades. She especially loves to create tiny paintings inside plastic bottle caps, creating an entire landscape in a Coke screwtop. She's a whiz at one-inch majestic mountaintops and loves giving these mini masterpieces away to her friends at school.

In our first "finger painting" chapter, we learned how to build basic triads and also make substitutions and extensions to those triads. We learned how to build chords and label them with letters and numbers. Writing harmony using chords diatonic to a key—chords that occur naturally in a key signature—is kind of like painting on a canvas. It's a great place to start. But we want to give you some "bottle cap" options if you're ready to venture outside the key signature. We're going to briefly cover easy ways to access extensions and minor keys and then move on to talk about borrowing chords from other keys and modes. Then we'll do an inventory of our harmonic habits while learning from some inspired progressions.

Let Your Left Hand Wander

I discovered that finding chords beyond triads in root position came easier to me if I found them in a roundabout way. Instead of building them from the bottom up, all clustered together, I started to let my left hand wander. I would begin by building a triad in my right hand and start with the root of the chord in my left hand. After that, I would keep my right hand in the same place and let my left hand roam. Allowing your left hand to wander will help you become more aware of bass movement, which will really help your understanding of how your harmony functions.

Try it right now. Make a C Major chord in your right hand (c e g) and play a lower octave c with your left hand. Now keep the C Major chord in your right hand and lower your left hand down to an a. This creates an A minor 7 chord (a … c e g) just by lowering the left-hand note.

Thinking of your hands separately (as in left hand bass, right hand chords) isn't always the best way to learn piano long-term, but it can help you get past initial hurdles into new harmonic territory.

I began to make interesting combos through left-hand wandering. If I played a G chord in my right hand and a c note in my left hand, I would notate that as G/C (a G Major chord over a c note in the bass). I began to write this way because it helped me remember how I was voicing the chords.

You will often see these "slash" chords in charts to indicate which note should be on the bottom (and which note the bass player in the band should be playing). Don't get too hung up on labeling correctly; just give yourself a good way to remember the combinations you create.

Playbreak 6

Finger Painting: Try out this progression so you get comfortable with the idea of slash chords:
F | F/G | C |
Reminder: if there's no "m" after the chord symbol, always assume it's a major triad.

For F/G, you will have F Major in the right hand (f a c) and a g note in the left hand. Remember the second letter of the slash chord (F/**G**) is a *single bass note* in the left hand, not the entire chord. After you get the hang of this progression, let your left hand wander. Make major and minor triads in your right hand and try different notes underneath with your left hand. Try to create a four-chord progression using slash chords. Find combinations that you like; it doesn't matter if you label them correctly. Something like this: F | F/G | F/Bb | F/D |
More Advanced: Compose a melody over this descending bass line progression:
C | G/B | Am |Am/G | F | C/E | Dm7 | G |

Minor Keys

Choosing to write your song in a minor key can also expand your palette of available chords. When you're starting from a natural minor scale, the types of chords that occur naturally in the key get a little "reversed." Let's stick with the white keys and show you the chords that occur in the key of A (natural) minor. **Play each one of these triads in a row.**

i	ii°	♭III	iv	v	♭VI	♭VII
Am	Bdim	C	Dm	Em	F	G

But this is just A *natural* minor. The fabulous thing about minor keys is that they're built from minor scales. Minor scales are a little weird and wonderful because there's not just one basic pattern for a minor scale; there are three basic patterns to choose from: natural, harmonic, and melodic minor.

Again, we're starting to get into the theory weeds, and that's not what this book is about. To help you get started, I'll give you an example of some of the chords you can access if you're writing a song in A minor when pulling from all the minor scales. All of these chords should sound pretty good if you're writing a song in the key of A minor. Try playing all of them now:

Am	Bm	C	Dm	D	Em	E	F	G
i	ii	♭III	iv	IV	v	V	♭VI	♭VII

The key takeaway is that minor keys can contain minor *and* major triads of some of the chords. In this key, notice how we have access to D minor, D Major, E minor, and E Major all in the middle. That's a lot of sturdy chords to choose from.

Look at this verse from "Hotel California" transposed into the key of A minor. Notice how this verse uses both D Major in the second line and D minor in the fourth line:

Am E7
On a dark desert highway, cool wind in my hair
G D
Warm smell of colitas rising up through the air

F   C
Up ahead in the distance, I saw a shimmering light
Dm
My head grew heavy and my sight grew dim
E7
I had to stop for the night

Playing with minor keys can help build your confidence to branch out harmonically. If you haven't written in a minor key before, try to keep the i chord (Am in the key of A Minor) as an important chord featured at the beginning and/or end of song sections to keep you grounded in the minor key. Let's continue to venture a little farther to find even more harmony to play with.

I'm Only One Key Away

What if you want to go beyond the chords that are diatonic to a major or minor key? Borrowing from close keys can give you access to a few more chords. In her book *How to Write a Song that Matters*, Dar Williams refers to this concept as "visiting a neighbor key's house." In this analogy, each key signature is built around a small set of basic chords. When you get tired of looking at the same walls in your house, there's a house next door you can borrow from. To borrow chords from a "neighbor" key, you simply add or subtract a sharp or flat to the key signature, depending on the key you're starting in. If you're looking at a circle of fifths chart, you're going to be borrowing chords from the key one step to the right or the left of your starting key. If your starting key is C Major, your neighbor keys are F Major and G Major. If your starting key is G♭ Major, your neighbor keys are D♭ Major and B Major.

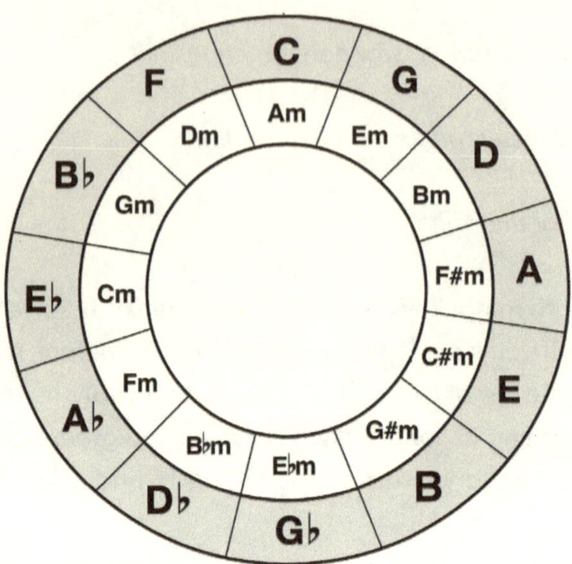

**Note that the outer ring is made of major chords, while the inner ring is each major key's relative minor.*

Simply look up the chords to your "neighbor keys" to find new chords to play with. For example, if these are the chords in the key of C: C Dm Em F G Am Bdim, then our neighboring keys of F Major and G Major will give us access to additional chords like Gm, B♭, Bm, and D.

Key of C: C Dm Em F G Am Bdim

Key of F: F **Gm** Am **B♭** C Dm Edim

Key of G: G Am **Bm** C **D** Em F#dim

But you don't have to limit yourself to "neighbor" keys only. I learned from Sara Groves that The Beatles habitually used a distinctive chord palette that let them access chords outside of the key. I figured if it was good enough for The Beatles, it was good enough for me. I'm going to skip the complicated theory explanation and ask you to trust me that they were borrowing from the keys three half steps above and three half steps below the key they were in. (In the Key of C Major, they'd be borrowing chords from A Major and E♭ Major.) It gives choices that look like this:

Key of A	A	Bm	Cm	**D**	E	F#m	G#dim
Key of C	C	Dm	Em	F	G	Am	Bdim
Key of Eb	E♭	Fm	Gm	Ab	**B♭**	Cm	Ddim

Notice how in the chorus of "In My Life" (transposed here to the Key of C) that the B♭ chord in line two is borrowed from the Key of E♭ and the D chord in line three is borrowed from the key of A:

Am   F
Though I know I'll never lose affection
B♭   *C*
For people and things that went before
Am   ***D***
I know I'll often stop and think about them
F5   C
In my life I love you more

Astute observers will realize that the chords B♭ and D became available to use through the neighbor key method *as well as* the Beatles palette. So which keys were they actually borrowing from? Doesn't really matter. The point is, don't be afraid to borrow chords from closely related keys.

Playbreak 7

Finger Painting: Play around with this chord progression in the key of C, which borrows a chord from a neighbor key:
C | F | Dm | B♭ | C |
In this example, we're borrowing the B♭ chord from the neighboring key of F. (B♭ is the IV chord in the key of F.) Check the end of the chapter to check your notes.
More Advanced: Use the Beatles palette to create a song section. Push yourself to make an unconventional chord choice work melodically.

Modes

Until now, we've been building our chords by making triads from the scale of our chosen key or borrowing from keys next door. As we move away from major and minor keys, we're getting into murkier harmonic waters. As we go a bit further, we wade dangerously close to something called modes. A mode is a system of structuring tonality outside the basic major and minor scales. Modes are difficult to understand, even for music majors. Many a level 3 music theory student has wanted to quit school over modes. So what I'm *not* going to do is try to fully explain modes. Instead, I'll give you some CliffsNotes and examples from popular songs so you can dip your toes into modes if you'd like.

There are seven modes to choose from in "western" music, and they all have funky Greek names. Two of them you already know. The major scale is the Ionian mode, and the minor scale is the Aeolian mode; we've essentially covered those. I want to introduce you to two other modes you may see in popular music: Mixolydian and Dorian. In Mixolydian, we have a scale that features a ♭7 (just trust me).

So if the C Major scale is: c d e f g a b
Then the C Mixolydian scale is: c d e f g a b♭

Because of the change to the scale, all the chords you would have made using b♮ now use a b♭. Why do we care? Because in C Major, our vii° chord is Bdim (which isn't super useful). But when we transform that b♮ to a b♭, it can lead us to very useful progressions like this:

I	♭VII	IV	I
C	B♭	F	C
c e g	b♭ d f	f a c	c e g

If you're truly writing in Mixolydian, your melody notes will also feature b♭s (not b♮s). You may notice that C Mixolydian and the key of F share the same key signature—one flat, which is b♭. So, what's the difference between C Mixo and the key of F? It's which root note and chord feel like *home*. In C Mixo, the harmony will be pulling towards the C Major chord as home (instead of F Major). Mixolydian is useful if you're writing music with a bent towards the blues, but it applies across genres. Pop singer-songwriter Lorde is in *love* with Mixolydian, and many of her songs use this mode. Check out this chorus from her song "Royals":

D
And we'll never be royals it don't run in our blood
C
That kind of lux just ain't for us
G
We crave a different kind of buzz
D
Let me be your ruler you can call me Queen Bee
C
And baby I'll rule, I'll rule, I'll rule, I'll rule
G (D)
Let me live that fantasy

This song is in D Mixolydian. This mode gives us access to that important ♭VII chord (which is C in this key). If you'd like to start playing with Mixolydian, pick an easy key and focus on the I, IV, and ♭VII chords. Just make sure the I chord feels like home. Here's a cheat sheet.

Basic Mixolydian chords in easy keys:

	I	ii	IV	v	vi	♭VII
C Mixo	C	Dm	F	Gm	Am	B♭
D Mixo	D	Em	G	Am	Bm	C
G Mixo	G	Am	C	Dm	Em	F

The other mode you might stumble upon more regularly in popular music is Dorian. Dorian is a little more complicated because it sounds like a natural minor scale with a raised 6th (shudder).

This is A minor: a b c d e f g

And this is A Dorian: a b c d e f# g

Again, why do we care? Modes can be fun because they give us access to unique harmonies. The distinctive sound we're looking for with Dorian is the IV Major chord occurring in a minor-sounding key. It's like a "happy-sad" sound. Look at this progression from the song "Mad World" by Tears for Fears, transposed to A Dorian. Listen to how the fourth chord sounds "brighter" than it ought to in a minor key:

from Verse 1

Am C
All around me are familiar faces
G ***D***
Worn out places, worn out faces

Try playing the chord progression above again and substitute D minor instead of the D Major, and you will hear the significant difference.

I can feel your eyes starting to glaze over with all this talk of modes. Knowing this stuff isn't mandatory, but it just makes for more opportunities for exploration. Don't work too hard to force yourself to use modes. The main thing is to establish what note feels like "home" using chords that aren't in a regular major or minor setup. Make sure your melody is grounded in the note corresponding to the name of the mode: for example, the pitch a in A Dorian. If you'd like to play around, here are some Dorian modes in easy keys:

	i	ii	♭III	IV	v	♭VII
A Dorian	Am	Bm	C	D	Em	G
D Dorian	Dm	Em	F	G	Am	C
G Dorian	Gm	Am	B♭	C	Dm	F

Playbreak 8

Finger Painting: Write a song section using a Mixolydian or a Dorian chord progression:
D Mixolydian: D | C | G | D | or
D Dorian: Dm | F | C | G |
More Advanced: Try to write a song section in Phrygian or Locrian (just melody and harmony). Good luck and godspeed.

Avoiding Same Old Same Old

Let's talk about harmonic infatuation. It's normal and natural. Recently, I went through a "mixolydian phase," and somehow those were the only chord changes and melodies I could write. Early on in my songwriting career, I was completely smitten by the iv6 chord. (In the key of C, this chord is Fm6.) I used it as the next-to-last chord in almost every chorus I wrote, but it sounded so epic. But when all my songs ended with that "epic" cadence, it didn't sound so epic anymore. I use that chord very sparingly now because I know that this chord, for me, is a temptress.

There's beauty in falling in love, but it's potentially hazardous if you're so obsessed with a new harmonic sound that you can't get away from it. We've got to learn how to give new sounds some respectable space so they're not overused. How do we do this? We "rotate the crops" harmonically. We can play in new keys, new modes, or introduce limitations, such as avoiding certain progressions or writing on an instrument with which we're less comfortable. The point is not to allow yourself to fall into the same patterns of music making.

Let's take a moment to do an inventory of your go-to harmonic patterns. The next Playbreak will ask you to review three of your most recent songs. Write out the Roman numeral analysis of your progressions if you can, and take notice of what chords and chord progressions you are using. Are you finding there's enough variety in your chord changes? Or do you tend to use the same progressions (and keys) over and over, always changing the chord at the same time?

What I'm arguing for is variety, not complexity. Some of the greatest songs of all time have very simple harmony. "Dreams" by Fleetwood Mac is essentially built around two chords that rotate back and forth throughout the entire song. I'm not suggesting complexity over simplicity, but rather variation in your creations *across* your catalog.

Playbreak 9

Finger Painting: Look at three songs you've written and analyze the harmony. Set them side by side. What patterns in the chord changes do you notice? Take one of the songs and try to make some harmonic adjustments to differentiate it from the other songs based on your observations. It could be as simple as transposing it to a key you don't normally write, taking away a few chords, or doing some diatonic substitutions (swapping chords within the key).

More Advanced: Take a broader look at your catalog. Have you been venturing outside of diatonic harmony? Have you experimented with modes? Select one song for your catalog that would improve with "elevated" harmony and try some rewrites.

Trusty Progressions

Again, there's nothing wrong with using basic chords and progressions. Some of the greatest songs of all time feature very "predictable" and oft-used harmonic progressions. My teaching assistant, Hallie, showed me a video compilation of over 100 hit songs that all used the same chord progression (I V vi IV), so if you're ready to write a hit in the key of C, get started! Gary Ewer and many others refer to this progression as the "Axis of Awesome" because it features strong root movement and a slightly deceptive ending that listeners tend to love.

There's nothing wrong with noticing progressions that work in other songs and then playing with them to make them your own. And they don't have to be overly complicated. Some of the most "famous" progressions are only four chords long. Here are a few trusty progressions if you'd like to start with time-tested harmonic environments (I'll give them in C Major or A minor):

The Axis of Awesome	|C |G |Am |F |	I – V – vi – IV
Vintage Doo Wop	|C |Am |F |G |	I – vi – IV – V
The Minor Loop	|Am |G |F |G |	i – ♭VII – ♭VI – ♭VII
The Royal Roads	|F |G |Em |Am |	IV – V – iii – vi
Rock On	|C |E |F |Fm |	I – III – IV – iv
The Pachelbel	|C |G |Am |Em | |F |C |F |G |	I – V – vi – iii – IV – I – IV – V

Playbreak 10

Finger Painting: Figure out the chords for the "Axis of Awesome" in the keys of D and A Major. Select one of those keys and compose a song section (with melody) on top of the "Axis of Awesome" progression.

More Advanced: Compose the melody and lyrics of a song section using the "Pachelbel" or "Rock On" progression.

I want to make sure you're leaving this chapter with plenty of new harmonic toys to play with. I usually don't suggest letting chord changes be the primary driver of your melody making, but sometimes a fresh chord progression can be inspiring. Since chord progressions are not copyrightable things, here are some chord progressions from some of my favorite songs. I've removed the titles of the songs and changed the key signatures so you won't be tempted to recreate a melody you might be familiar with. Try to make some melodies on top of these chord changes:

Chord Progression 1:

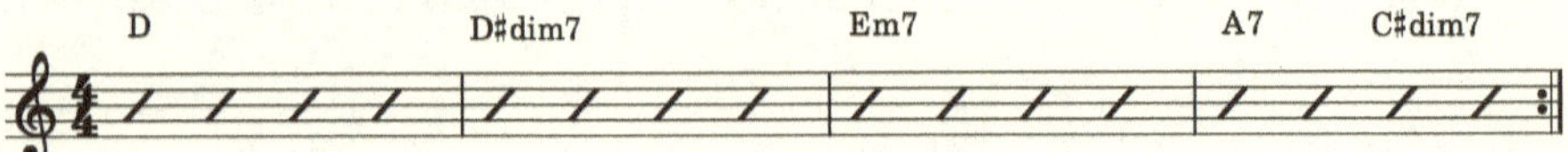

Chord Progression 2:

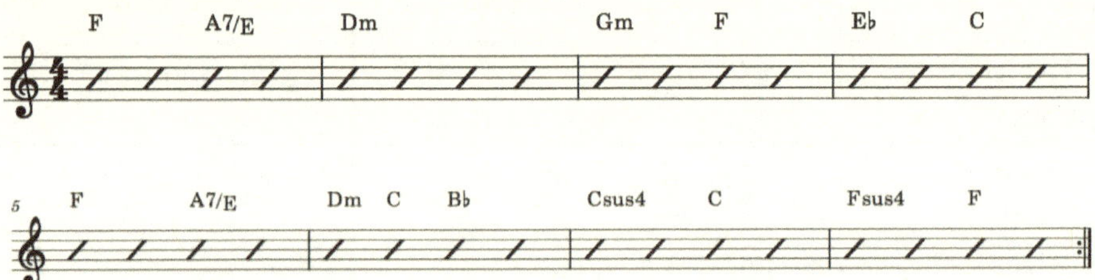

Chord Progression 3:

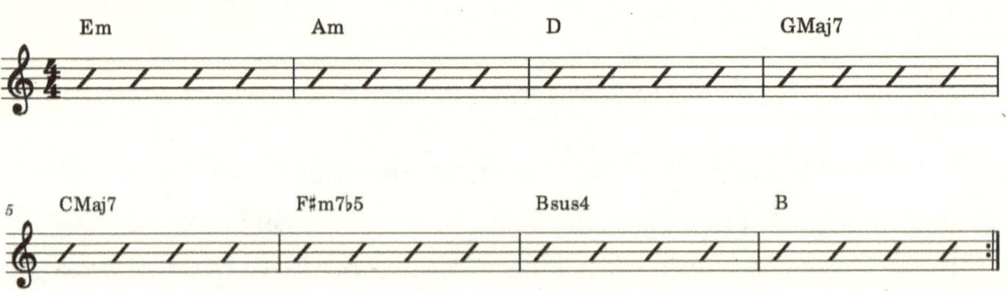

Did any of these progressions speak to you? If drawing inspiration from new progressions works for you, you can literally do this anytime you'd like. Find a song you love and borrow its chord progression. I suggest changing the key and tempo to help you avoid mimicking the melody of the song you're "borrowing" the chords from.

Why Harmony Matters

As I see it, harmony has three principal functionalities for the songwriter: momentum, emotion, and recoloring. There is definitely overlap in these categories, but the key point is that harmony serves a purpose in its interaction with melody and lyrics.

Harmony can affect the overall momentum of your song, especially at cadences (ends of lines and ends of song sections). Ask yourself: Should your melody and lyrics be arriving and settling or propelling forward? Put another way, should the harmony be used as a stop sign, a temporary pumping of the brakes, or the green light forward, depending on the moment you're at within the song? Momentum choices often need to take into account the emotion of the lyric.

Considering the emotional content of the lyric is important in selecting the harmony that aligns with it. Unsettled thoughts and feelings might not work as well with settled harmony. This is why it's worth considering if a tonic, subdominant, or dominant chord would best translate the emotion of your lyric. You can also consider using non-diatonic harmony to give a special-sounding chord to highlight a significant word or phrase.

If you have a lyric that deserves repetition, try recoloring it with harmony changes to add depth. Harmony recoloring can be used for both lyric and melodic repetition. Simple and repetitive melodies can be dramatically elevated by changing the harmony underneath. (Remember Heat Waves?) In the end, don't just settle on the first chords that come to mind. Think about how your chord choices influence the song's momentum, amplify the emotion, or add interest through recoloring.

Harmony is a secondary aspect of songwriting that sits just below melody and lyrics in terms of songwriting importance, but that doesn't mean it's insignificant. Harmony can alter the mood of your song. Harmony can interact with your melody to bring it to life. Harmony shouldn't be a total afterthought; it's still a critical piece of the puzzle. Just remember that the more you *play* and have fun, the more you'll enjoy engaging with harmony. You don't have to be a pro at the piano or guitar to be a proficient songwriter, but the more you're willing to play, the more colors you'll add to your palette.

PLAYTIME

There are fewer activities at the end of this chapter because we really want you to do all the playbreaks. If you skipped them, please go back and do them!

Solo Activities

Harmonic Exploration: Create a simple melody for a song section (like a verse or a chorus) and create three different harmonic accompaniments. For the first version of your song section, only use the I Major, IV Major, and V Major chords. For example, in the key of C, you could only use C Major, F Major, and G Major. For the second version, try adding in some diatonic substitutions (use Em or Am instead of C, and Dm instead of F). In the third version, try using some chords *outside* of the key.

Group Activities

Reharm a Friend: Have group members bring a copy of one of their songs with all the chord changes removed so it looks more like a lyric sheet. Pair up group members so that in each pair, one person is adding chord changes to the other's song. Make sure the partner has not heard the song before. The person who brought the song can only sing the melody; they cannot suggest harmony.

Homework Challenge

Harmony Resurrection: Revisit a song you wrote a long time ago, and sing through it to just a metronome. Try to forget all the previous chord changes. Then, do a harmony resurrection, reimagining what the harmony of your song could be, starting from the a cappella version. Use the accompanying instrument you are least skilled at.

Song Challenge

(Finger Painting) Minor Key: Write a song in a minor key and try to play with chords outside of the natural minor. For a lyrical challenge, try to incorporate the word "awesome" somewhere in the chorus. If this doesn't seem challenging enough, write in Mixolydian or Dorian.

(More Advanced) The Split Personality: Write a song where the chorus is in a different key than the rest of the song. You don't need to go too crazy—you can choose a neighboring key—but make sure the transitions between sections still work musically. Have a lyrical reason to justify this key shift in the chorus.

PLAYBREAKS: Finger Painting Diagrams

Playbreak 6: F | F/G | C |

F: (F Major triad in right hand, f note in bass)

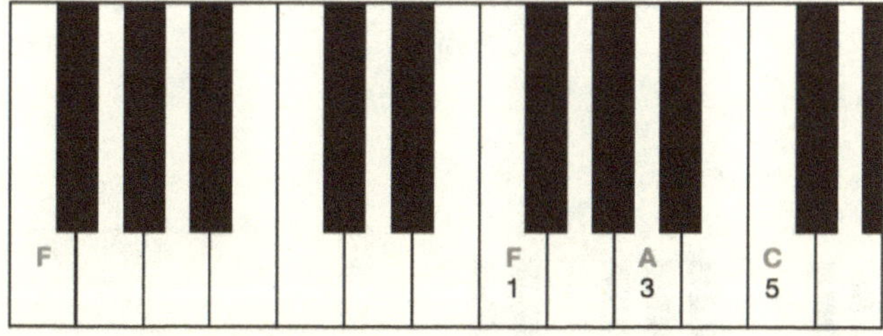

F/G: (F Major triad in right hand, g note in bass)

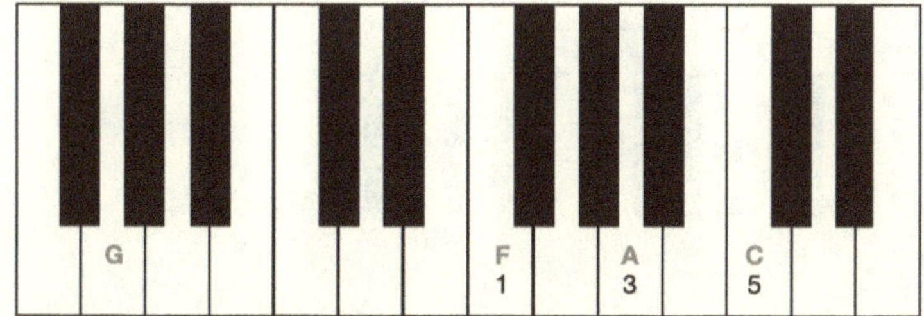

C: (C Major triad in right hand, c note in bass)

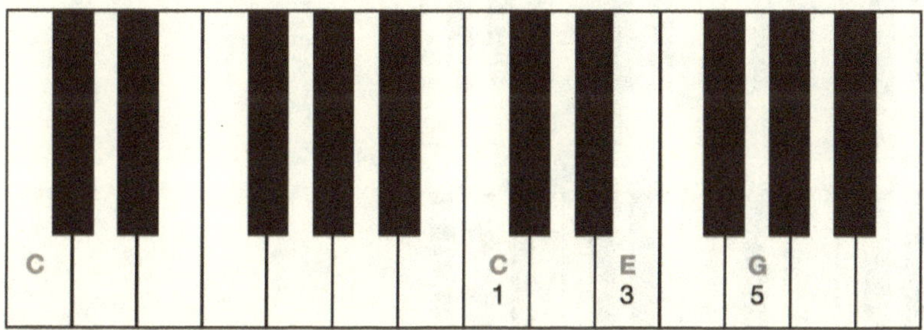

Playbreak 7:

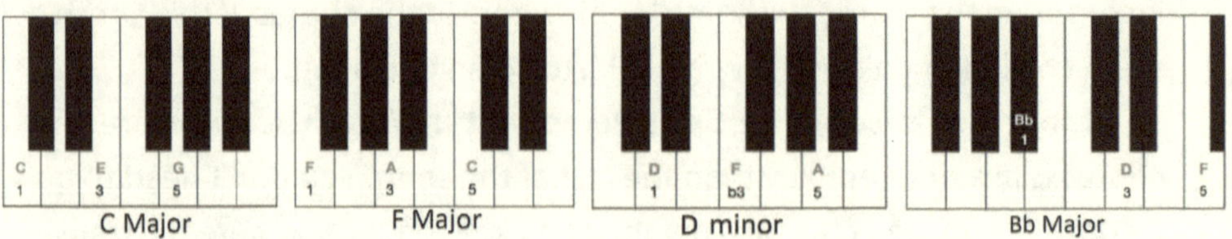

Playbreak 8:

D Mixolydian Progression

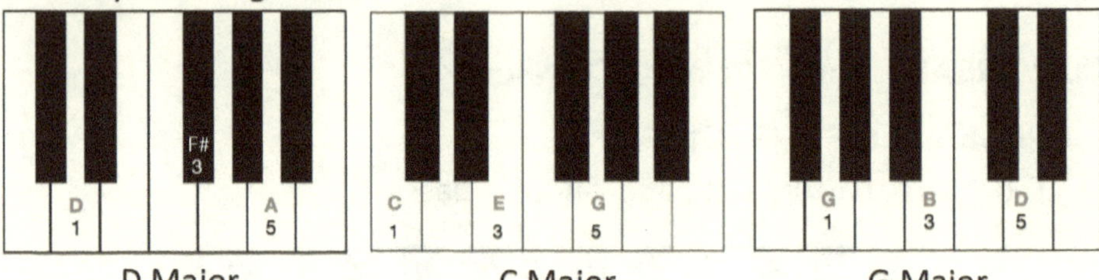

D Major C Major G Major

Playbreak 10:

I – V – vi – IV in the keys of D and A Major

Key of D

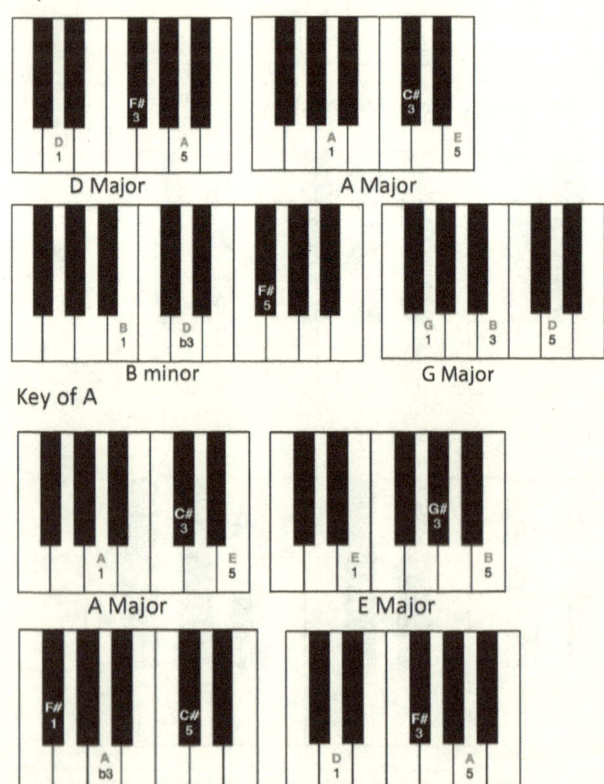

CHAPTER 11

Jumping Rope & Telephone

Phrasing & Setting Lyrics

"You don't have to swing hard to hit a home run. If you got the timing, it'll go." Yogi Berra

My mom was an elementary school PE teacher. She had an '80s perm, neon wind suits, unmatched creativity and work ethic, and was, objectively, the greatest PE teacher of all time. My childhood was filled with tetherball, Four Square, and Knockout. I learned that playground games are all about timing, pacing, momentum, and a lot of yelling. I learned to master jump rope, hopscotch, and monkey bars as I began to understand when to move, when to stop, and how to adjust based on progress—usually while yelling. Understanding this concept has a lot to do with songwriting as well.

Jumping Rope: Understanding Phrasing

Did you ever have to jump rope in PE class? I remember the kind of ropes we had when I was a kid: red plastic handles connected by a limp noodle of white string. The string was encased in little white and red plastic cylinders that jostled and clicked together. These ropes looked like beaded uncooked penne pasta whizzing through the air, just waiting to make contact with the back of your legs. The inevitable sting felt like a punishment for mis-timing your jump. It's tricky in the beginning, but once you get the hang of the timing, jumping rope can be fun. Having a feel for the best time to jump makes the motion and the experience invigorating and fluid.

Learning how to manipulate lyrical phrasing is a little like learning how to jump rope. If I get to be the first person to introduce you to the concept of "phrasing" in songwriting, I feel honored to be the one to show you this shiny new toy. It's gonna change the way you write lyrics and how you think about songwriting.

I was introduced to this concept by Pat Pattison. I was lucky enough to study under him for a couple of years at the Berklee College of Music, and I will never forget his class on phrasing. He made us listen to an entire song by The Cars. And I mean the entire song. At the time, I was an impatient student, and spending five entire minutes of a lecture just "listening" seemed startlingly indulgent. (I've since learned the error of my ways and embraced the paramount importance of active listening in learning.) In this exercise, we were instructed to pay attention to *where* the lyric lines interacted with the downbeat of the music. This was something I had *never* considered before. It mattered *where* the lyric line began in relation to the musical downbeat? I didn't even realize this was something I was supposed to be thinking about.

So we listened to the entire Cars song, start to finish, line by line. At the end, the big revelation was that only one lyrical phrase in the entire song was phrased differently from the rest. The lyrics in that one line began at a different place in relation to the downbeat than all the other lines, and the choice to phrase it differently affected the emotional impact. This just happened to be the one line in the whole song with the big emotional tell: "I miss you." Where a lyric started in relation to the rhythmic bar lines was a brand-new concept for me. I realized I had been jumping rope and placing lyrics clumsily for years because I had never considered when I should touch the ground.

Not understanding how phrasing works can feel like jumping rope as a beginner. You like the lyric you've written, but for some reason, it feels like it's not working. Instead of making an emotional impact and hitting you in the heart, the lyric feels clunky and misplaced, much like what happens when the rope stings the back of your legs. Or maybe you know how to jump rope in the realm of phrasing, but you're stuck in a rut and keep using the same pattern over and over again. Your phrasing has become predictable and boring. Skip skip skip. Perhaps it's time for some fancier footwork.

In this chapter, we're going to break down the phrasing choices and experiment with them by focusing on the emotions, meaning, and important words contained in our lyrics. We will also consider phrasing as a tool for much-needed compositional variation. To get started, we need to cover the three types of phrasing defined by how they interact with the downbeat of a measure (in order of their rhythmic appearance):

Early Phrases: The melody/lyric line starts *before* the downbeat.
On-Time Phrases: The melody/lyric line starts *with/on* the downbeat.
Late Phrases: The melody/lyric line starts *after* the downbeat.

Phrasing choice is a way to communicate emotion, so let's break down how each phrasing type can help to get your meaning across.

Jumping Rope: Emotions

Early phrases are ones in which the singer begins singing the lyric line *before* the downbeat. Like they're a little "early" to the musical party. This is usually before the chord hits, if that's helpful for you to think about it.

Remember the famous king "front-heavy fa"? He's an example of an early phrase. In fact, many songwriting texts will call early phrases "front-heavy" and late phrases "back-heavy." I have discovered my students have a difficult time understanding these terms, so we've gone with the simpler terminology of "early" and "late" to bring clarity. On a lead sheet, early phrases are melody lines for the singer that look like pickup notes leading into a song section.

Notice below how the lyric starts before the downbeat and the chord change that goes along with it. Now, you may be asking, "Why isn't the first quarter rest in the first measure considered the downbeat?" Envision this lyric as the first line of a verse or chorus. The singer begins singing before the music of the song section begins. In that way, it is *ahead* of the musical bars, so it is "early."

Ex 11.01 Early Phrasing:

Early phrases often feel like they are launching, anticipatory, or as if they are running toward an explosion. They are eager to get to the good stuff. Emotionally, early phrases will suit lyrical content that's about going somewhere, making a change, or taking action. They don't always have to be "positive" emotions, but these phrases feel like they're leading up to something.

In on-time phrases, the singer begins singing right on the downbeat, usually where the chord hits. Because on-time phrases line up so strongly with everything that's happening musically, this phrasing will suit statements of stability, security, resolve, or confidence. These are phrases that feel more firmly planted.

Ex 11.02 On-Time Phrasing:

Late phrases are ones in which the singer begins singing the lyric line *after* the downbeat. (Again, imagine that this chord hit on beat 1 is the beginning of a new song section, and that will make the timing feel clearer.) On a lead sheet, you will notice rests preceding these lyric lines that align with the chord change. If it's helpful, think about it this way: The chord hits first, and *then* you sing.

Ex 11.03 Late Phrasing:

Late phrases are the type most underutilized by beginning songwriters. To use them, you must be comfortable with the rest space and the sensation of being slightly adrift. Emotionally, late phrases can feel held back, reticent, confused, aimless, stifled, uncertain, or conflicted. If you're looking to tap into other emotional spaces, late phrases could also feel relaxed, meandering, sluggish, or seductive in a "slow burn" sort of way.

Did you notice in the examples above that I used a different lyric for each phrasing option? The emotional content of the lyric guided my choice of the phrasing. The meaning of the lyric "taking my time" feels like it would be a late phrase. But there's no cut-and-dry formula here. There is not just one right phrasing for every lyric. The important thing is to ask yourself, "What is the emotion of this lyric?" and then, "Have I chosen a phrasing placement that is helping me to clearly communicate that emotion?" These questions will change the way you write. Sometimes it's not just *what* you say, it's *when* you say it.

Jumping Rope: Important Words

The second thing that should inform your phrasing choices is considering the importance of words in your lyric line. Start by identifying which words in the line are the most vital in communicating the meaning. Nouns and verbs tend to be the most consequential words in a lyric, but context and implied tone are significant. Anyone who has taken a basic acting class has learned that there's more than one way to say a line. The same is true for considering phrasing placement. The words that land on strong musical beats matter. Did you mean to say:

<u>MY</u> heart is breaking like waves
My <u>HEART</u> is breaking like waves
My heart is <u>BREAKING</u> like waves
My heart is breaking like <u>WAVES</u>

Awareness of the important words and how they interact with the melodic rhythm and placement within the bar should affect phrasing choices. We'll talk more about this later on when we discuss setting lyrics, but for now, be mindful of emotion and important words as you play with phrasing. Look at the lyric below, phrased three different ways. Play the chords in the indicated spots as you sing the lyric. Which one emotionally feels the most right to you?

Ex 11.04 Early Phrasing:

Ex 11.05 On-Time Phrasing:

Ex 11.06 Late Phrasing:

There's not necessarily a "right" answer for how to phrase "I don't know how to move on," but the late phrasing feels the best to me because of the emotional content of the lyric.

Jumping Rope: Variation Potential

The third thing you need to consider with phrasing is its potential to unlock variation and differentiate your song sections. Now that you're aware of the concept of phrasing, you may realize that your default phrasing for individual lyric lines and song sections as a whole is dominated by on-time and early phrases. But all is not lost. Adjusting the phrasing in *some* song sections can help bring much-needed contrast to the song as a whole.

When I'm working with students in songwriting lessons, I'll usually do a quick inventory of their phrasing choices throughout their song. Adjusting phrasing can be a quick fix when the emotion feels slightly off or if song sections are sounding too similar. Willingness to play with phrasing also helps us be more flexible about our line lengths. Rigid thinking leads to rigid writing, and we are looking for a balance of straightforward and surprise.

Perhaps the thing your verse needs to set itself apart is not a weirder melody or flashy lyric, but a different phrasing choice. Does your chorus feel *almost* right but not confident enough? Maybe cut out those pickup notes and start right on the downbeat for an on-time phrase. What if your song feels "plodding" and predictable? Perhaps some early phrases in a bridge or pre-chorus will give the song a little boost of anticipation if all the other sections start squarely on the downbeat. The point is to utilize phrasing choices to provide contrast in your song sections, setting them apart from one another.

We are constantly looking for ways to hook and then surprise our listeners' ears. But we also have to respect the way they process language. Phrasing deals with where we place a lyric line in relation to the downbeat. Zooming in further, we will consider how to satisfy our listeners' ears by setting individual words in a way that feels natural to how we speak. We achieve this through awareness of the words we emphasize in our melodic and rhythmic choices, taking special care with lyrics that contain multi-syllabic words. Strategic phrasing is important, but if we want our listeners to lock in and understand our words, we've got to be sure we're setting them up for success.

Telephone (Setting & Mis-setting Lyrics)

Time-travel back with me to elementary school: You're sitting in a circle on the ground, glancing around from giggling face to giggling face. Your teacher has decided to "entertain" your class with a game sure to inspire laughter (and a little bit of seated peace). She whispers a word to the girl three kids away to your left.

[Teacher whispers in the little girl's ear]
"What??" The little girl squints and wrinkles her nose in confusion.

[The teacher whispers again, a little louder]

Now she's got it. The girl leans over to the boy seated next to her. She cups her hands around his ears and tries her hardest not to whisper too loudly.

"Whaaaat?!" He exclaims.

And on it goes.

By the time the game of telephone reaches your young ears, you're pretty sure the word is *jellyfish*. Or was it *smelly pits*? If only you could have some context. If only the conditions were more suitable for understanding. Oh well, the game is better when it gets silly and weird.

The game of telephone is hilariously fun because the words are so easily misunderstood and mangled. However, in the game of songwriting, we want to *avoid* mangling words in ways that might cause them to be lost or misunderstood. To communicate effectively, we aim to set our words with precision. We want to give proper timing and context so our words hit naturally. Effective lyrical communication isn't just about the words you choose; it's also about aligning your lyrics rhythmically in a way that "respects the natural shape of the language." (This is another phrase I learned from Pat Pattison.)

The setting and mis-setting of lyrics starts with knowing the following:

1. What are the emphasized *beats* in your measure?
2. What are the emphasized and un-emphasized *syllables* in the words you are using?

Let's keep it simple and start in 4/4 time, where beats 1 and 3 are the strongest in each measure. If we have lyrics aligned with beat 1 or beat 3, we want to make sure they are interesting words. If they are multi-syllabic words, the stres*sed* syllable should land on beat 1 or beat 3. Mis-set lyrics occur when an unimportant word or unstressed syllable is placed on an important or stressed beat.

I know this sounds a little complicated. Rest assured, you don't need to write down your melodies on sheet music in order to figure out what's going on. All you need is a metronome or your fingers for snapping to keep time. Say your lyric is "peanut butter." In this lyric, we have four total syllables, and the first half of each word has the emphasized syllable. If we write it out with this in mind, it looks like PEA-nut BU-tter. How do you know which syllables are emphasized? It's easy—just say it with the opposite emphasis (pea-NUT but-TER) and you'll discover which one sounds right. We want to make sure the "pea" and "but" are landing somewhere around beat 1 and/or beat 3 in the measure because these are the emphasized syllables.

Here are some ways we could accomplish this:

Ex 11.07:

Ex 11.08:

Ex 11.09:

In each of these examples, the emphasized syllables of one or both words land on the most important beats in the measure. This is how we set lyrics for maximum clarity and impact. When lyrics are mis-set, pronunciations get mangled, and words become misunderstood or missed altogether. And what's the harm? At best, a cool lyric can be lost on the listener when it's mis-set. At worst, the emotional impact of the song is limited, and a chance at real connection has been lost. Ouch.

Let's see some examples of "peanut butter" that are mis-set so you can compare. Try to say them out loud while you snap in time. Again, you will notice the words jump out like "pea-NUT bu-TTER" when they are rhythmically mis-set.

Ex 11.10:

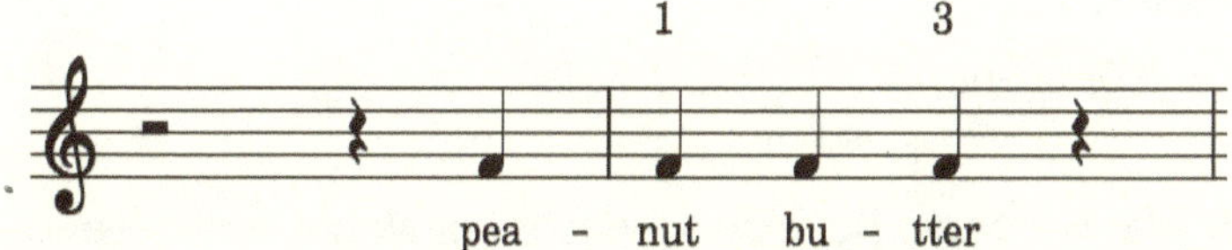

Ex 11.11:

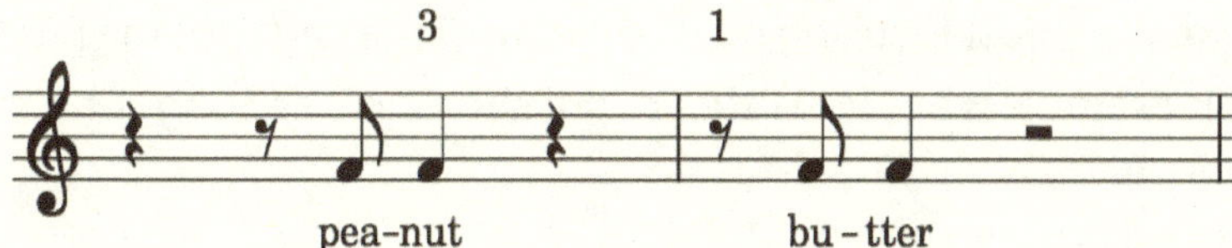

Those examples may seem a little ridiculous. But even professional songwriters sometimes let these things fall through the cracks. I'm gonna pick on a song right now explicitly for the purposes of showing you what a mis-set lyric in action sounds like. I'm not the kind of person who wants to hate on other people's creative work. I'm strictly picking on this song for the enhancement of your education!

Let's look at the lyrics of the first half of the chorus with no emphasis added. Read these lyrics out loud, and don't sing them! Even if you know the tune.

Unconditional
Unconditionally
I will love you
Unconditionally

The following is how you would read and speak the words if you were speaking naturally, putting the emphasis on the correct syllable. Read them again.

UN-con-DI-tio-nal
UN-con-DI-tio-nal-ly
I will love you
UN-con-DI-tio-nal-ly

Now that we know how these words speak naturally, we will witness an epic mis-set of this big multisyllabic word. In the recorded version of the song I'm referencing, what follows are how the words of the chorus sound when they are sung. Keep in mind the "TIO" makes the "shuh" sound. We're just focusing on the *rhythm* of the lyric, not the pitches. Look at this example while you listen to the chorus of the song "Unconditional" by Katy Perry:

Ex 11.12:

The setting of this lyric lands all the unstressed syllables of the word *unconditional* on the important musical beats, and the result is a totally mangled word. It feels weird, it sings weird, and ultimately, I believe this is part of why the song hasn't been as successful as her others. How can a listener believe this love is unconditional when the singer can't even pronounce the word properly?

Listen: I don't want you to start overthinking every lyric you write. If rhythmic lyric setting feels overwhelming, begin by focusing on which word or syllable of your lyric would be best served by landing on beats 1 and/or 3 if you're in 4/4 time. If you're in 6/8 time, beats 1 and 4 are the emphasized beats as you subdivide: 1 2 3 4 5 6. Try to make the important words and emphasized syllables land on those beats. If you make it a habit to always snap a beat when you record voice memos of song ideas, it will help a lot on your quest to set your lyrics for maximum singability.

Recalling the tree and the songwriting priority tiers, we're going to try not to change a great melody in deference to lyrics. Sometimes the best solution to a mis-set lyric is to keep the melody intact and change the lyrics. You do this by noticing which notes are important in your melody. What notes are the highest, the longest, or the most interesting? Which notes land on beats 1 and 3? Important notes crave important words.

Now, let's look at a lyric that succeeds in setting the important words on the important beats.

Ex 11.13:

In this example, important words and their emphasized syllables fall on beats 1 and 3. The "O" in *O-ver* lands on beat 3 because that's how we naturally say the word. **To compare, listen to the song "Over My Head (Cable Car)" by The Fray. Notice how it sounds like o-VER in the chorus.** This song was still a hit, but that word is straight-up mis-set, and it drives me a little crazy.

I'm not suggesting that you sit down and write out the rhythm to your melody every time you have a song idea. For most of us, that probably doesn't feel like a natural way to write songs. Matching your words and syllables to strong rhythmic beats takes some intuition and plenty of practice, but the first step is simply to start *listening* for it. If you sing a lyric and it feels off, there might be something about how your lyric interacts with the rhythm of your measure. If you realize you're singing an unimportant word at the same time you're landing on an important beat, it's time to take a closer look at how your lyrics are lining up within the bar.

Another great starting point is to consider whether it's easy to remember how you sang your lyric line. Generally, if it's hard for you to remember how your lyrics are sung, you might have an alignment problem that's making the timing less memorable. When I'm writing a new song, I often underline the word of the lyric that I'm landing on, aligning it with the downbeat, to help me remember the phrasing. This also helps me notice if I'm emphasizing an important word. If I've selected a late phrase, I'll leave a blank to indicate that I'm singing after the downbeat. It looks like this:

Am
I'm never giving up
G
I'm never letting go
F
Forever hanging on
Dm
____ *I'm hanging on* (late phrase)

Finding a solution to a mis-set lyric problem is usually not difficult. For the most part, we can nudge words a beat one way or the other by adding rests, adding or subtracting syllables, or reordering the lyric. We'll come back to that in a little bit. For now, take comfort in the fact that just because you have a mis-set lyric, it doesn't mean you have to completely rewrite the whole thing from scratch.

What's Important?

I've been talking a lot about important and unimportant words, but I haven't yet taken the time to differentiate between the two. Let's define "unimportant" words as those that don't often deserve our rhythmic emphasis. Typically, these are connector words that don't add vivid information—they aren't nouns or verbs. Words like *in, at, the, to, an, are, have,* and *be* are usually not important enough to emphasize. Sometimes, these words might be interesting depending on the context, but most of the time, they're not.

For example, if the lyric is "have a little sugar in your tea," then *have* is probably not the word you want to choose to emphasize (along with *a, in,* & *your*). Words like *sugar* and *tea* will be better served to land on beat 1 or 3 if you're in 4/4 time.

However, if the lyric is "I gotta have you," then *have* might actually be the word you want to emphasize. *Gotta* might also be a good choice.

Pronouns are also usually on the list of unimportant words. Words like *he, she, they, I, you, them, his,* and *her* are usually dull because the verb or noun coming after them is going to be more interesting. I most often observe this problem in lyric lines that start on the downbeat of the measure when the lyric begins with a pronoun.

For example, if the lyric is *"He walks the road,"* perhaps the first draft of the lyric placed *he* on the downbeat. This example gives the words *he* and *the* the most emphasis (say it and snap it):

Ex 11.14:

However, rhythmically emphasizing the words *walks* and *road* are the better choices as they are the verb and the noun in the lyric. By simply shifting the phrase one beat forward or one beat backward, the more important words are now aligned and shine rhythmically!

Ex 11.15:

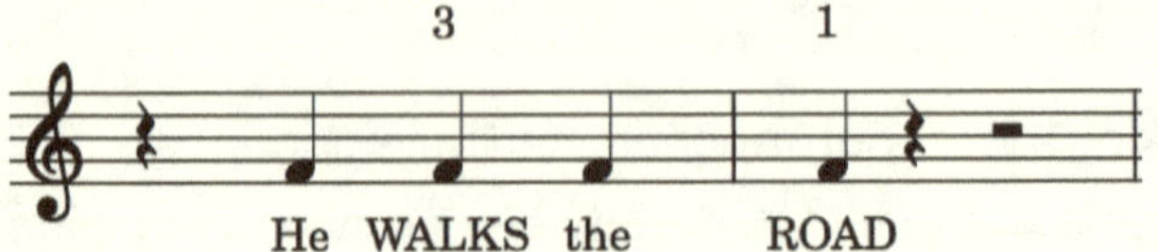

Ex 11.16:

Too Much Talking, More Playtime

Let's play around to further understand lyric setting. I want you to manipulate a lyric line to avoid placing unimportant words and pronouns in the emphasized rhythmic spots. You can do this through rewriting words (picking synonyms and substitutes) or by reordering the words in your lyric. I will give you examples of several potential manipulations. I have intentionally mis-set most of this lyric:

Ex 11.17:

We've started with all quarter notes and a phrase that begins on time, which is right on the downbeat. Right now, we have fairly uninteresting words on all the strong rhythmic beats (*you*, *my*, *my*), and there is also a mis-set word in *embrace*. It is mis-set because the word is em-BRACE when we speak it. If one of those two syllables should land on a strong rhythmic beat, it should be -BRACE.

Let's do a quick lyrical "shove" to see if it helps. All I'm going to do is add a rest upfront and turn this into an early or late phrase instead of an on-time phrase. Whether it's early or late would depend on where the chord change is occurring.

Ex 11.18:

This isn't the world's best lyric, but at least now it is dramatically improved by the phrasing. Simply by adding a rest and shoving the lyric one beat over, the words *are*, *hearts*, *-brace*, and *dear* are on the important beats. The word *are* isn't the best choice for an emphasized word, but we're getting away with it because of the internal rhyme with the word *hearts*. We fixed the mis-set word problem by prioritizing more interesting words and demoting unimportant words from the important beats.

Let's try another solution in action. Remember, here is our first draft of the line:

Ex 11.17:

The following example is another "shoving" that combines two words.

Ex 11.19:

In this solution, we have *you're* on the downbeat, which isn't ideal. However, this allowed us to maintain the on-time phrasing and shift all of the other important words to important beats. Of course, there is never just one solution. Your options and alternatives are as many as you're willing to dream up. Maybe instead of shoving, we could find substitute words that have the same meaning but fit the rhythm better (if we've decided we don't want to change the melodic rhythm).

Measure two of our original example is:

Ex 11.20:

This setting sings like "EM-brace MY dear" because of the rhythm. So instead of changing the rhythm, we could substitute with other words that have a similar meaning and also the appropriate emphasis:

Ex 11.21:

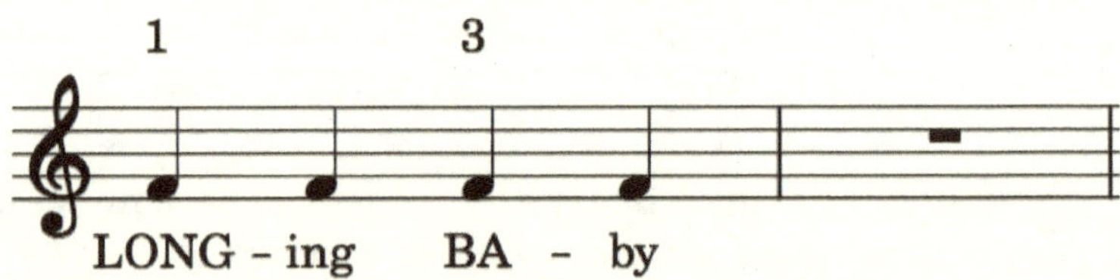

"Longing baby" works much better with this rhythm because both of these words have a first syllable that is emphasized, which aligns with the rhythm we selected. Again, don't drive yourself crazy. Just be mindful that words have inherent rhythm. If you want to start with words before melody, try to speak before you sing the words with a metronome to discover the natural rhythm of the words.

So Much More Momentum

Throughout this chapter, we've primarily focused on the "micro" level of momentum and timing in individual words and lyric lines. However, there are also "macro" considerations regarding momentum within your songs. For example, you can think about the overall pacing of your lyric narrative and how it develops across song sections. We've already discussed how our choices in harmony and melody also allow us to create tension and resolution, as well as instability and stability. We absolutely need both in a song to generate momentum. Ultimately, we are chasing the arc of climax and resolution—a wandering and a return home.

As the preacher once said, "There is an appointed time for everything." A time to speed up, and a time to slow down. The point is, you should know how to change the momentum of your song if it's not doing what you want it to do. I know it's a lot to think about, and I don't want you to get overwhelmed. I just wanted to introduce you to new playground games. The more you play them, the more you get comfortable with the timing, the balance, and the strategy.

It's also like playing with playdough: It's easier to make defined shapes when you have specialized tools. As you grow as a songwriter, you're going to have a more specific vision. You'll want to manipulate things like phrasing, rhyme scheme, and lyric setting to execute precisely what you feel. Small shifts in momentum and timing can lead to big payoffs in the overall emotional impact of your song. Don't start your writing session trying to hold all these concepts in your head. Write fearlessly, unfiltered, and unhindered, *then* come back and play our playground games. Once you play them for a while, they will begin to become second nature to you. Just like a hop, skip, and a jump.

PLAYTIME

Solo Activities:

Phrasing One Line at a Time: Write one line of lyric. Speak it over and over again, emphasizing different words each time. Once you find a rhythm for the words that feels good, add pitches. Lastly, begin to play around with phrasing. Playing only one chord, try singing your line *before* you play the chord, then at the *same time* you play the chord, and then *after* you play the chord. Which phrasing choice matches the lyric the best? Starting with this line, complete the song section, being mindful of phrasing as you go.

Setting the Multi-Syllabic: Write a one-line lyric that contains at least two multisyllabic words.

Examples: "The universe is a mood machine" (universe = 3 syllables, machine = 2 syllables)
"My thinking is combustible" (thinking = 2 syllables, combustible = 4 syllables)
"Impossible wonder" (impossible = 4 syllables, wonder = 2 syllables)

Say the lyric out loud several times in order to understand the natural way these words flow when spoken. Analyze the words within your lyric and underline all stressed syllables. Intentionally line up the stressed syllables with strong beats when selecting a rhythm for your lyric. Add pitches last.

Group Activities:

Phrasing Roulette: Let each member of the group select a lyric from the following list and a phrasing option (either early, on-time, or late). Then, have the group members take turns creating a simple melody and singing their lyric in their chosen phrasing as the group leader plays one chord. Keep it simple and use C Major or A minor. Choose from the following:

"I don't even know you"
"Never gonna say never"
"Disco 'til you die"
"Flowers ain't enough anymore"
"Spinning my wheels again"

Words for the Rhythm: Write out a collection of very short rhythms for the group ahead of time. These rhythms should have 2 to 4 notes. Present the rhythms one at a time, asking group members to first clap/speak the rhythm and then create a list of words (or short phrases) that correspond to each rhythm. For example, on this rhythm:

The following words or phrases will align with the rhythm to respect the natural shape of the language: *mood machine, eloquence, Prince of Peace, Mary Beth, bowl of soup.*

Homework Challenge:

Lyrical Phrasing Emotion: Write a four-line verse lyric describing a scene that feels "hopeful." Next, write a four-line verse lyric that describes a situation requiring "endurance." Then write a four-line verse lyric that describes a scene about "loss." Keeping these verses separate, add melody and phrasing to each verse. Be intentional about choosing phrasing that helps communicate the lyrical emotion. Keep the chord changes minimal.

A Better Setting: Rewrite the following verse where every line has the exact same pattern of stressed and unstressed syllables as the first line.

Feel free to change, add, and omit words in order to mimic the exact pattern. Match this pattern: PA-per PLANES are FALL-ing DOWN (7 syllables).

Paper planes are falling down
The wind and water are pummeling them
My hopes and dreams feel the same
I always lose and I never win

After you rewrite all four lines following the same pattern, next rewrite lines 2 and 4 selecting a new stressed/unstressed pattern that match each other.

Song Challenge:

Multisyllabic Title Setting: Pick a long and interesting word that would make a good song title. The word must have at *least* four syllables. For example: *unconditional*, *apologize*, *Carolina*, *hallucinogenic*, or *revolutionary*. Use this multisyllabic word as the foundational lyric for your chorus. You can have other words in the chorus, but this is the primary word and big idea. Make sure you set the multisyllabic words for maximum clarity and emotional impact. Once you've written your chorus, be intentional to have different phrasing in the verse from the phrasing you've selected for the chorus.

Cars and the Important Words: Write a song where all the lines have late phrasing, with the exception of the chorus, which has to be an on-time phrase and can only have 10 words or fewer. Make sure the first word of the chorus is important because it's going to be the first time a lyric line lands on a downbeat.

CHAPTER 12

Tetris

Song Form

"Form is important, we should learn form, but we should also remember to fill form with life. This takes practice." Natalie Goldberg

I was born in 1983. My brother and I shared a first-generation Game Boy that only played 2D games in black and white. He preferred the challenge of games that required learning maps, perfecting the timing of jumps, and a bit of daring to succeed. He was a Mario Bros. fan all the way, but games like that were a little too stressful for me. I couldn't get lost in them, and I'd get frustrated facing the same failure repeatedly with each misstep. I preferred logic and strategy games—ones where the payoff felt more intellectually rewarding (probably because I never had the hand-eye coordination my brother did). Tetris was *my* Game Boy addiction. There was something satisfying about knowing the shapes, pacing the build, and discerning the odds when managing the larger pieces that were sure to give you trouble. The best part was the satisfying thrill of multiple lines blinking out of existence all at once when a big piece lined up perfectly.

Tetris is a game that challenges players to understand how different pieces can fit together. Sometimes they all seem to come at you in the right order, and everything lines up as easy as pie. Other times, you get brick after brick that just won't build easily from one to the next. You're forced to get creative and pivot, so you start making a plan for how all these pieces could work together eventually. In Tetris, you always have to hold your plans loosely because you're never really sure what's coming next.

Much like the game of Tetris, song pieces can come in different shapes and sizes, each functioning in its own way. Some are more versatile, while others require more planning and intention from the writer. It can sometimes be hard to know which piece you need at what time. Keeping all this in mind, this chapter will cover common song form sections and how writers tend to use them. Understanding how song form works should give you more possibilities as a writer, not less. We're not going to be straightjacketed by rules, but I will share plenty of guidelines for strategies that work best—most of the time. After all, you're more likely to succeed if you're utilizing a difficult Tetris piece intentionally.

Form matters because it has dramatic impacts on balance, momentum, and ultimately, communication and emotional connection. We need to understand the patterns that continue to connect with music listeners across generations. In his book *The Song Machine,* John Seabrook notes that "it's striking how little the basic form of the popular song has changed. The delivery mechanism is in constant flux...but the emotional mechanics of songs have largely remained the same, whether they're embodied by Al Jolson's ivories or Slash's lead guitar." We're looking for a song form that tells a story and keeps the listeners engaged the entire time. So let's discuss standard song form sections and what they typically attempt to accomplish within a song.

Verse

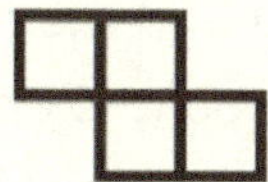

A verse is your listener's entry point into the *context* of a song. It attempts to answer some of the questions about who, what, when, where, and why. Verses tend to lean on sensory language to set the scene of the story. They not only paint the picture but also help you hear, smell, taste, and touch it. We talked at length about this in Chapter 3, when we discussed the importance of "showing" rather than just "telling." Verses are a perfect place to help listeners connect the tactile world with a greater meaning and story. That's the joy of songwriting: inviting people to see the world in a new and different way.

Verses are also where you earn the right for your listener to care about the emotions in the chorus or refrain. If there's no grounding in specific details or imagery within the verse, then the listener probably won't have the emotional buy-in to feel what you're trying to make them feel in the chorus. Our craft as songwriters shines when we help people see the physical context of emotions.

Here's an example of a verse that tells and a verse that shows. Which one do you like better?

Tell:
Do you ever feel aimless and wandering
Like you're drifting and wanting to start again?
Do you ever feel, feel so vulnerable
Like you're unstable and could easily tumble?

Show:
Do you ever feel like a plastic bag
Drifting through the wind, wanting to start again?
Do you ever feel, feel so paper thin

Like a house of cards, one blow from cavin' in?
(from "Firework" made popular by Katy Perry)

Verse lyrics tend to set up the lyrical big idea in the same way that verse melodies set up the primary chorus or refrain melodic hook. Verse melodies should be interesting and memorable, but they usually don't capture a sense of "arrival." Most of the time, they also tend to linger in a lower register than other song sections, leaving us wanting something more.

Structurally, with the exception of intros, verses are often the first section in a song. If you open a song with a verse, it's important to remember that it will be the first lyric and melody your listener encounters. How you open a song is crucial because listeners experience your song one section at a time—not all at once. If they don't get hooked on the song from the beginning, they might not make it to the actual hook!

There are many genres and circumstances where opening the song with the chorus—or, more rarely, another section of the song—might be called for. But for now, let's remember that a verse needs to make a strong impression. Musically and lyrically, it should entice the listener to stay and set the stage for what's next. Next, we'll consider the role of choruses, since verses and choruses tend to be the foundational sections of most modern songs.

Just remember, there is absolutely no right order in which to compose your song sections.

Chorus

The chorus of the song should feel like that big piece we've been waiting for; the moment of arrival. Everything has been building up to it musically and lyrically. A chorus should be able to stand on its own, like it somehow still feels complete even without the rest of the song. It's the part people should probably remember most. If it's not the part they remember, then it's probably not the chorus. The chorus is the essence of the big idea—the big Tetris piece around which all other song elements need to fit.

Lyrically, a chorus comes to a sense of "arrival" and completeness by giving a more straightforward presentation of the song's big idea. The intent of the song and its core emotions are more exposed. Usually, but not always, the song's title can be found here. It's important to note that a chorus should remain narratively true and relevant every time it's repeated. If verse 2 changes the emotion or the plot, you may struggle to return to the chorus.

Musically, this sense of arrival in the chorus is often achieved by aligning a "grounded" harmony with a melody that is distinct, hooky, and memorable. What makes a chorus melody stand out could be its melodic rhythm, its range, or its use of interval jumps. However, what's really important is that it has something special that our ears long to come back to.

Usually, repetition is a more crucial element in this song section. This could be repetition of melody, repetition of lyric, or how easily you can repeat the entire chorus. Productive melodic and lyrical repetition helps create that unquantifiable "stick with you" feeling. If your chorus doesn't feel memorable, powerful, or worthy to be repeated, then it's probably time to make some edits.

After reading the last few paragraphs, you might already be thinking about a song that needs some edits. That's great! First things first: you should enjoy singing your chorus. Now, I don't mean that singing it makes you happy. I mean that singing it feels right, even if you're singing about something sad. The chorus should feel right when you start singing, and it should land when you finish. If you don't enjoy singing it, keep working on the melody. If you don't like how the words sound when you sing them over and over again, keep tweaking the lyrics. Is the big idea or core emotion of your song conveyed by your chorus? If not, try rewriting it. For many of my students, the main issue with their choruses is that they're too long. If yours feels heavy or rambling, try cutting everything except your favorite lines, then find ways to repurpose the magic in them.

The connection between the verse and chorus is a key moment in the song to consider. The next song form sections we'll look at serve as connecting pieces between our foundational sections. Perhaps the jump from verse to chorus feels too sudden. Or maybe you've captured the main idea within a chorus, but the song demands to see things from another angle. Sometimes there's more depth to the story. If you have more to say musically and/or lyrically, your song would probably benefit from a pre-chorus, a bridge, or a post-chorus.

Pre-Chorus

A pre-chorus is a highly flexible song form section. Most are short—or at least shorter than other parts of the song—but some are as long as the verse that came before them. Some pre-choruses create momentum, but others provide needed variety or space. Many connect the content of the verse to the chorus, yet some ask us to step back and rethink things. Well, dagummit then... What does a pre-chorus actually do?!

In a literal sense, a pre-chorus is any song section that directly precedes the chorus but is *not* the verse. They work best only if you *really* need them. If you *don't* need it to help the chorus land musically or lyrically, a pre-chorus might hamper your momentum. Sometimes, we don't set out to craft a pre-chorus; it simply becomes a section that is needed when a verse doesn't connect well with the chorus. (Caveat: This might not apply if you're building songs from tracks. Genres with stricter "form building," like pop or EDM, sometimes mandate an 8-bar pre-chorus as the standard operating procedure.)

Why might we need a pre-chorus? Since it can serve more than one purpose, we'll briefly discuss how they can function as a connector, spacer, or intensifier.

A pre-chorus can act as a "connector" when it's launching the verse toward the chorus. This can be achieved lyrically by bridging the context of the verse to the emotional big idea of the chorus. Melodically, a pre-chorus can add movement that maintains continuity between the verse and the chorus. Harmonically, it can provide a ramp to keep things moving forward. At the risk of you thinking I'm a superfan, **check out "Firework" by Katy Perry again for a great example of a "connector" pre-chorus.**

As you listen, notice how the lyrics connect the ideas of the verse to the chorus. I want you to observe how the melody quite literally ramps up from the verse toward the chorus hook.

Last Line of the Verse
'Cause there's a spark in you

Pre-Chorus
You just gotta ignite the light
And let it shine
Just own the night
Like the Fourth of July

Chorus
'Cause baby, you're a firework...

But "connecting" is just one potential function of a pre-chorus. Pre-choruses can also serve as a "spacer" when the listener needs a break. This happens in songs where the verse and chorus have a similar feel in line length, melodic rhythm, or range. When the verse and chorus are too similar, the pre-chorus gives the song some room to breathe. It adds a bit of variety that keeps the verse and chorus distinct yet connected. **To hear**

a "spacer" pre-chorus in action, listen to the transition from verse to pre-chorus to chorus in "Bad Blood" by Taylor Swift.

Last Line of the Verse
Salt in the wound like you're laughing right at me

Pre-Chorus
Oh, it's so sad to think about the good times
You and I

Chorus
'Cause baby, now we got bad blood…

Lastly, beyond creating connection or providing space, a pre-chorus can function as an "intensifier" to build energy and add an additional hook. You might see this sort of longer pre-chorus development in dance or pop-leaning genres. Let's take a look at a portion of Lady Gaga's song "Bloody Mary":

I'll dance, dance, dance
With my hands, hands, hands
Above my head, head, head
Like Jesus said…

Did you know this section of the song is the pre-chorus, not the chorus? Some would argue it's the hookiest part of the whole song. It definitely builds intensity and adds an additional hook, almost to a fault. In most cases, though, we're not hoping for our pre-chorus to be the star of the show. A pre-chorus usually makes a way toward the song's centerpiece—our long block, if you will—the chorus.

Once our song has gone through a chorus a few times, we might need a break. We might need to look at things from a fresh perspective during a bridge.

Bridge

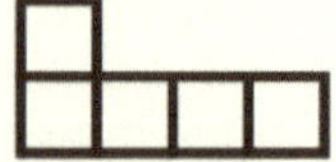

A bridge song section is another highly malleable song form piece. Its purpose depends on the context. In a way, song bridges are very similar to literal bridges. Literal bridges carry us over an expanse from one landing area to another, just like song bridges may carry us from chorus to chorus. We leave the solid ground and return to it. How long is the journey in between? It could be long or very short. Bridges come in all shapes and sizes—they could be made of wood or steel, large or small, but either way, we're usually aware that the surface has changed beneath us. Maybe we love the view from the bridge because it offers a new angle to the world around us, and the new landing place we're headed to feels grander and more striking because we took the time to cross it.

Before building a physical bridge, its function needs to be determined. You can't build a bridge unless you know where you've come from and where you're going. In songwriting, this is mostly true, but we have a little more flexibility. The first section of a song you build could start turning into the bridge before you have the chorus, and that's okay. The main thing to remember is that bridges are transitional and feel *different* from the landing places. Bridges usually give a new or deeper perspective. For the most part, bridges don't feel like forever landing places.

Caveat: This may not be true for genres like corporate worship, where bridges sometimes function as *extended* landing places. Again, there are no rules.

What does bridge-building look like musically? If you're connecting a rhythmic, wordy chorus to another rhythmic, wordy chorus, you could build a bridge with sparser lyrics and stretchy rhythm. If you're connecting a floaty chorus to a quiet return of the verse, you could build a longer bridge with more active melodic rhythm and dramatic range. Musically *and* lyrically, we're being mindful of the song sections our bridge is "bridging." We're using the bridge to speak into that specific musical and emotional moment of the song.

We also need to consider what the bridge is trying to accomplish emotionally relative to the big idea of the song. Does the bridge provide new information that moves the story forward? Is it an emotional release? Is it a passageway to a new perspective for the singer? If you're not sure what your bridge is trying to accomplish, then you may very well be building a bridge to nowhere. Or worse, if you're building a bridge with too little contrast to your landing places, then your bridge might be purposeless. If we don't feel the texture change under our feet, we may become weary of the journey.

Bridges are primo playdough monster territory. Let's say you write a bridge for a new song, but then you try to write another bridge that's completely different from your first attempt. You're having fun, go for it! Have a long bridge? Try cutting it in half. Still playing? How about using your favorite two lines as the whole bridge? Bridge still not working? Re-envision part of it as a pre-chorus, or as an outro. Whatever you do, just don't build a bridge to nowhere. Much like a pre-chorus, you don't need a bridge unless you really need it.

Many beginning songwriters write excellent bridges, but often use them in the wrong song. They write the Golden Gate bridge, when what the song really needs is a rope bridge to cross a jungle ravine. Just because you create a killer bridge doesn't mean you should keep it if it's not working in between your landing spaces. But here's some good news: wise songwriters don't toss their brilliant pieces away. Sometimes, a fantastic bridge in the wrong song is an idea to save for a future song. We're looking to build bridges that fit perfectly and excite us along the way.

Here are a few songs that have epic and effective bridges. **Take a minute to study a few of them and see if you can observe how they create an interesting journey from one landing place to the next:**

"Since U Been Gone" Kelly Clarkson
"Before He Cheats" Carrie Underwood
"Driver's License" Olivia Rodrigo

To be honest with you, transitional bridges have fallen out of style in popular genres over the last 10-15 years. While they may always be a staple of roots and country music, other genres are moving away from them. Kristine Tran from LyricStudio argues this is due to the "increasing focus on hooks and the need for instant gratification in the age of streaming." Bridges are being traded in for another song form section that's all about hooks and more hooks. If a bridge isn't what your song needs, you might want to consider exploring a post-chorus.

Post-Chorus

A post-chorus is a feature of more modern song form that, strictly speaking, is a song section that:

- Directly follows the chorus
- Is directly *related* to the chorus (usually lyrically)
- But is distinct from the chorus in a noticeable way (usually melodically)

The post-chorus takes an element from the chorus, usually a notable lyric, and riffs on it. Melodically, there is the introduction of a new hooky earworm, setting the post-chorus apart from the chorus. Think of the post-chorus like the center of one of those candy-coated suckers. You have to work your way through the chorus to discover a bit of that bubble gum, but then once you reach the center, that's the part you really chew on. (I blame my dad for this inclination toward a horrible pun.)

Let's take a look at some examples of effective post-choruses. Notice how a significant lyric is reinvented on a new hooky melody, which emerges as a new song section. This comes from Ed Sheeran's "Shape of You":

Last Half of the Chorus

Last night you were in my room
And now my bedsheets smell like you
Every day discovering something brand new
I'm in love with your body

Post-Chorus

Oh-I-oh-I-oh-I-oh-I
I'm in love with your body
Oh-I-oh-I-oh-I-oh-I
I'm in love with your body

In this example, the lyric that has been plucked from the chorus is "I'm in love with your body." The new hooky melody introduced is *not* on this lyric line, but rather on the "Oh-I-Oh-I-Oh-I-Oh-I" that comes before it. These two elements—the chorus lyric and a new hooky melody—link together to build the post-chorus.

Some of you may argue that I'm creating a new song section category when this just appears to be a "tag." While it's true that most tags do repeat a significant, often final, line from a song section, what we are talking about here is the *function* of this song section. We'll dig into tags a little further down in this chapter, but the difference I'll note here is that a post-chorus can usually stand on its own as a song section. Furthermore, the post-chorus usually expands the meaning of the chorus to somewhere deeper, bigger, and hookier. In contrast, the functionality of a tag is usually to wind down momentum and put a bow on whatever section is being tagged.

Let's look at another example of a post-chorus that functions a bit differently. "Flowers" is a song recorded by Miley Cyrus that has a post-chorus emerging from its chorus, leading into a stickier, hookier bubblegum center.

Sidenote: I'm using the analogy of bubblegum, and yes, both of these examples are from pop music. Is the use of the post-chorus strictly limited to pop music? No. Does contemporary pop music often use this song section to its advantage? Yes.

Last Half of the Chorus
I can take myself dancing
And I can hold my own hand
Yeah, I can love me better than you can

Post-Chorus
Can love me better
I can love me better, baby
Can love me better
I can love me better, baby

The lyrics for this post-chorus come from the *first half of the last line* of the chorus. Once again, we see a new hooky melody that is combined, in some fashion, with lyrics we've heard before. Choosing a post-chorus is a way to expand the song, which is something a transitional bridge usually does. A post-chorus accomplishes this through more earworms and less storytelling. Often, songs with post-choruses don't have bridges because a song usually doesn't need both. If you're a songwriter who's open to play, I'd encourage you to try out post-choruses, especially when a bridge doesn't seem to be working for your song.

Auxiliary Sections

Let's briefly go over some other song form sections you may encounter. Most of these song sections serve auxiliary functions, meaning they provide additional but not essential support. Generally, they don't feature as many distinctive song elements. These sections may function as embellishments, segues, rock-out moments, or holding grounds for melodic hooks and repeats.

Intros

You might think of the intro as just the start of the track before the *real* song begins. But if you think that way, your intro will probably be boring. Astute songwriters don't just steal chord changes from another part of the song, slap them at the top, and call it finished. Instead, aim to fill this musical space with a melodic hook, distinctive texture, or an arrangement element that grabs the listener's attention from the beginning. In today's streaming era, a boring intro can make your song easy to skip. Don't waste space waiting for your song to get going.

Instrumentals

Instrumentals give instruments that are not voices an opportunity to speak into the emotion of a song. Sometimes there are no words left to say, but there are still feelings left to be felt. These moments are perfect for instrumentals. Writers often place them about three-quarters of the way through a song, before or after a bridge or chorus repeat, for a climactic, reflective moment. To determine the length, harmony, and dynamics of your instrumental, consider assessing the literal and emotional "weight" of your other song sections.

Interludes

Interludes are short instrumental moments that are not quite long enough to be labeled as full instrumentals. You usually find them between larger song sections. You can use interludes to give your song room to breathe so that quality lyrics and melodies don't crash right into the next section and get lost in the shuffle. They give a listener space to let ideas from one section really sink in before the next begins. Use interludes with discretion because too many can slow down the momentum.

Vamps

In the strictest musical terms, a vamp is a short chord progression that repeats with minimal variation. For our purposes, a vamp is a musical section that has enough vibe to justify repeating it over and over again. If the music or lyrics are not significant enough or fun enough to bear repeating, you probably don't have a justifiable vamp.

Tags

A tag is an addendum, a beautifully tied bow, at the end of a song section (usually the end of the entire song). It's best practice to only tag something if you're it's worth saying again. That said, tags don't always have to be exact repeats of the line they follow. You can fragment and only repeat a portion of the lyric, or you can slightly modify the melody or harmony when you repeat it. Just don't phone it in with a tag. Be sensitive and make sure your song is asking for a tag before you add one.

Outros

The choice of an outro should depend on the emotional weight of the song's ending. Should you "leave us hanging" and go with a hard out with little or no outro? Or do we need to hear some instrumental ear candy one more time? Or maybe we need a few bars of music to decompress or sink deeper into the ideas the song has left us with. Ask yourself what feels right for that moment, and be willing to try on lots of options. The ending of your song is important because it's the flavor that lingers.

Well, that's all there is to it, right? Every song piece you could ever need! Not so fast. Up to this point, we've discussed song form sections that are the basic building blocks of modern songs that utilize a chorus as a centerpiece. You can definitely mix and match all of the above pieces to come up with compelling combinations, but there are a few more song forms to consider that don't center around a chorus. Learning how to wield this next one is an essential step for the growing songwriter.

Verse-Refrain Song Form

I loved playing Tetris, but sometimes I felt like flipping the script. I was also a big fan of Dr. Mario, which was very similar to Tetris but kind of turned upside down. Sometimes you need a game that's just a little different to mix it up. The next song form we're going to discuss has many components similar to a verse-chorus-based song, but it's distinct in some key ways. If you've ever loved jazz standards or pop songs from the 1950s and 1960s, you might not have realized it, but you are very familiar with verse-refrain songs.

In its most basic iterations, verse-refrain songs feature two song sections: an A section that contains a crucial refrain line and a contrasting B section. Usually, the order of the song sections is presented as AABA. On paper, the lyrics for the song's sections will usually break down like this:

A section (verse with a refrain line)
A section (verse with a refrain line)
B section (that contrasts musically & lyrically)
A section (verse with a refrain line)

What's most notable about this song form is that there's no chorus to call "home." In the verse-refrain song form, the memorable melodic hook and lyrical big idea are contained in the single refrain line found in the A sections (anchoring the verses). Typically, this refrain line is the opening line of the A section or, more often, the very last line of the A section.

Here's an example of a verse-refrain song where the refrain line is the *first line* of the A-section:

Oh-oh, yes, I'm the great pretender
Pretending that I'm doing well
My need is such, I pretend too much
I'm lonely, but no one can tell
(from "The Great Pretender" by The Platters)

Here's an example of a verse-refrain song where the refrain line is the *last line* of the A-section:

I took my troubles down to Madame Ruth
You know that gypsy with the gold-capped tooth
She's got a pad down on Thirty-Fourth and Vine
Selling little bottles of Love Potion Number Nine
(from "Love Potion No. 9" by The Searchers)

The B section in a verse-refrain song is similar to a transitional bridge in that its function is to give us a break from the A section. The B section provides a contrasting melody, harmony, and perhaps a slightly different or deeper lyrical perspective. It is usually a section of decent length, but there's no feeling of *arrival.* The contrasting B section will *not* feel like a chorus. In this song form, the listener should be drawn back to the A section, craving a taste of the refrain line once again. In this way, the refrain line—the *one line*—attempts to achieve the same things accomplished by an entire chorus.

Some verse-refrain songs drop the contrasting B section altogether. This would take the song closer to "strophic" form, which is the repetition of multiple verses over the same music, like many hymns and folk songs. But for now, I'd like you to focus on understanding AABA verse-refrain form. Listen to the three following songs to notice how their song form flows. Observe how the lack of a chorus causes you to zero in on the refrain line that's acting as the centerpiece of the song:

- *"God Only Knows" The Beach Boys*
  Refrain line: "God only knows what I'd be without you"
- *"Can't Help Falling in Love" Elvis Presley*
  Refrain line: "I can't help falling in love with you"
- *"Still Crazy After All These Years" Paul Simon*
  Refrain line: "Still crazy after all these years"

You may notice that songs using the verse-refrain song form often use all or part of the refrain line as the title. If you're writing in verse-refrain form and are landing on a line that doesn't seem "title-worthy," then you may not have found your refrain yet.

We aren't exposed to verse-refrain form as often in our current popular music climate. However, don't let this stop you from engaging this song form. It can be a powerful way to deliver your ideas, especially if your big idea can be summed up into just one powerful lyric line and melodic hook. Some songs need a chorus, some need that one power punch of a refrain line, and some songs are just too unique for conventional song form altogether. There are times the shape of the song takes us on an unpredictable journey, and we'll call that form "through-composed."

Through-Composed

Even fans of Tetris and Dr. Mario sometimes need to throw caution to the wind and hurl some bombs. Every once in a while, I'd be tempted to try my hand at a more fast-paced and frenzied game. Unpredictable and a little chaotic. Like the Galaga to our Tetris, we're switching gears to look at a song form that plays fast and loose with listeners' expectations. These are songs that are through-composed.

I was recently browsing a list of the top 50 streamed songs of all time on Spotify. Currently, there's only *one song* on this list that was released before 2010. Any guesses as to what it is? You'd think that if this song is the only one in high demand cross-generationally on Spotify, then there must be something special about it. There must be something we can learn from its composition to create a song with staying power. What is this song that still feels relevant decades after its release?

"Bohemian Rhapsody."

We're gonna talk about it because it's a great example of a song that still works in a modern context, even though the song form itself is from another world. In the classical sense, "Bohemian Rhapsody" is actually a *rhapsody*, defined as "episodic, freely flowing, high in contrast, and with the narrative of an epic journey." But since we wouldn't consider it a classical piece, how do we label its song form? I got some help with the terminology on this one. A few experts break down its song form this way:

1. Acapella Vocal Section
2. Ballad
3. Guitar Solo
4. Opera
5. Hard Rock Shuffle
6. Return to Ballad

This is weird, and yet, it works. There is some repetition here, but nothing like the more conventional repetition found in the verse-chorus or verse-refrain song forms. Through-composed gives us the freedom to follow where a strong idea is taking us. However, keep in mind that even though we don't have traditional "verses" and "choruses" in the example above, there is still a definitive form. The listener is absolutely sure when one section has ended and the next has begun. Variation in the song sections is vital for the functioning of this song form, or else it might feel like a never-ending, pointless journey.

If you want to attempt a truly through-composed song, just make sure each of your song sections serves a unique purpose and brings music and lyrics that coordinate emotionally and build upon one another.

Playing with Song Form

Ultimately, song form should serve the heart of what your song is trying to communicate. Playing with song form is something I want to encourage you to be a student of, not a slave to.

Some song forms can be very simple, like "Rocket Man" by Elton John:

Verse, Chorus x2, Verse, Chorus x2, PostCh

Some song forms can be pretty elaborate, like "High Hopes" by Panic! At the Disco:

Chorus, Verse, Pre-Ch, Chorus, Verse, Bridge 1, Pre-Ch, Bridge 2, Chorus

And some break any semblance of modern song form altogether, like "Bohemian Rhapsody."

All of these songs demonstrate that different song forms can be suitable depending on the song. No one is better than the other. Whatever song form you choose, you should be picking your pieces intentionally to work together, complementing and balancing one another.

As you grow as a songwriter, you might be willing to let your song form sections change as you create them. This can feel like one of the more extreme playdough monster experiences. Rebranding the current pre-chorus of your song as the bridge can feel like plucking the arms right off your playdough monster and trying to envision them as legs. The weight and proportions of everything shift. This is not delicate play for the faint of heart; it's messy, outside-of-the-box songwriting. But this is where real compositional breakthroughs can take place. We must be willing to step back and acknowledge that what we intended that "piece" to be might be turning into something else.

Our willingness to let go of our original vision, especially where song form is concerned, is exactly how we create playfully, with joy and love. We are creating alongside our creation and allowing it to speak back to us. I can't count the number of developing songs I've edited where the songwriter's verse 1 is crying out to be verse 2 instead. We need a play-dough monster intervention so we can find the freedom to move things around and continue creating. Being willing to see our song sections as something else allows our songs to grow.

I had a teacher who never allowed us to label our song form when presenting a song lyric in class for this very reason. He knew that once we labeled a song section, it became much harder to see it as anything else. Remember red cabbages and onions? I want you to take everything you've learned from this chapter and use it as a guideline, not a strict rule book. Observe how the pieces of your song speak to you, and discern if a song section you've started and labeled as one thing is actually functioning as something else. Form and function should work together to create something of unique interest and beauty. And it feels pretty darn good when all those Tetris pieces line up just right.

PLAYTIME

Solo Activities:

The Un-labeler: Revisit a song you've already written, and take all the labels off the song sections. Identify your favorite song section and use it to write a new song. The only rule is that it can't serve as the same song section piece as in the original song.

If this activity feels overwhelming, pick a song idea you've started that has only one section so far. Then change your mind about what that song section is. For example, if you have a chorus sitting around with no other parts, reimagine the chorus as a verse instead. See if changing the label leads you to a new song idea for that song that feels "stuck."

Refrain Line Mix-Up: Choose a theme or emotion you want to convey in a song. Write down 3-5 potential refrain lines that capture the essence of this theme. (Remember this is just *one* line of lyric.) For example, if you picked the theme of "loss" you could create potential refrain lines such as "I'm at a loss for words" or "I've lost one time too many" or "It all keeps slipping through my fingers." Experiment with different rhythms and melodies for each line to see how they might sing, then pick your favorite refrain line and build a short A section verse around it with the refrain line being the first or last line. Extend the activity by then creating a contrasting B section.

Group Activities:

Song Analysis Guessing Game

Print out the lyrics to any popular song *without* the song form labeled (one for each participant). A well-known song like "Flowers" by Miley Cyrus will make this activity more accessible. Listen to the song as a group, then have group members try to label the song form, discussing why they chose each label. Continue this activity with songs that are less obvious to label, encouraging discussion about song form and its functions.

Collaborative Verse Refrain: Form groups of 3-4. Each group is given a pre-written refrain line provided by the leader. Using this refrain line, each member will write an A section of lyric that ends with the refrain line. Group members must decide on the number of lyric lines and rhyme scheme before writing their individual A sections so that they stay consistent. If one member is struggling, they can tackle a contrasting B section. Each small group then presents its lyrics to the larger group, explaining their choices and creative process.

Homework Challenge:

Post-Chorus Play: Write a chorus lyric, then identify a crucial line. Lift the selected lyric to create a post-chorus. The post-chorus should be memorable but also distinct melodically from the chorus. Now select a *different* lyric from the original chorus and try to create a completely different post-chorus option. Record both options (chorus with post-chorus 1, then chorus with post-chorus 2). Observe which post-chorus is the most compelling.

Analysis Frenzy: Listen to an unfamiliar song several times in a row. Look up lyrics that don't label the song sections. Try to label the song form, paying attention to how each section functions. Repeat this exercise at least three times with songs from different musical genres. Do you notice patterns? Are some genres more difficult to decipher than others?

Song Challenge:

1st Line Verse-Refrain: Write a song in AABA verse-refrain song form, where the refrain line is the first line of the A section. For an example, look up "The Great Pretender" by The Platters. Write the song about a nostalgic memory from your childhood, like playing your favorite game or watching a movie. Make sure the opening refrain line encapsulates the big idea and is easy to repeat at the top of each A section.

Through-Composed: Write a song that feels through-composed. Let the sections be as weird and wonderful as you wish. "Auxiliary sections" like solos and vamps might be helpful to utilize. You can use repetition, but try not to follow a conventional song form pattern. Let the music lead and make sure the song sections feel different from section to section. Let the lyrical content and emotion of this song be inspired by a poem or work of art made by someone else.

CHAPTER 13

The Roller Coaster

Beyond Clichés

"If there's one thing I've learned through my years of mistakes, it's that even the most perfect pattern becomes false when it goes unbroken too long. When a sequence becomes an inevitable march. We can break step. Magnificent living beings that we are, we humans are free to unravel our patterns." Louisa Hall

Do you remember those boring kiddie roller coasters they have at carnivals? A single pathetic bean-shaped loop with the slightest of turns. An "ascent" of mere degrees. Not a lot of drama or intrigue. You grudgingly hop on with your younger sibling because it's the only roller coaster they're tall enough to ride. Maybe it's fun once for a toddler, but that's all it's meant to be—a thrill only for someone incapable of envisioning the end. The kiddie coasters bore adults because we can see the ending from miles away.

Now, imagine yourself back in line, waiting to ride the scariest roller-coaster you've ever ridden. Mine's easy. The most torturous rollercoaster I ever experienced was called Runaway Mountain. I can vividly remember standing in line, an agonizing churning in my stomach. I already felt like I was about to drop, and I wasn't even strapped in yet. Minutes dragged by as I shuffled inch by inch on the hot concrete toward the front. First, the line snaked outside in the hot sun, then the wait continued inside.

The truly wild thing about Runaway Mountain was that it was a full-sized roller coaster completely enclosed inside a giant, unlit building. That's right. Not just twisted—*dark* and twisted. You couldn't see the beginning or the end, and you had no idea what horrible terror lay in between. I could hear the screams, the racing of metal wheels on a slick track, and the whooshing of artificial wind as coaster cars careened in the darkness, but I couldn't see any of it.

I want to encourage you to start thinking about your songs as roller coasters you are building for your listeners. What you are crafting has the potential to be an intriguing journey full of twists and turns, or it could be the bean-shaped kiddie ride that only goes in an endless flat loop. We don't want our listeners to see the end from the very beginning.

Most of this chapter focuses on avoiding clichés in lyric writing, but we will also look at some strategies to keep our melodies and harmony choices fresh. We're going to cover how to avoid clichés in rhyme schemes, metaphors, melodies, and song form. I'm sure there are other clichés to avoid, but this will be plenty to start with.

Cliché Rhyme Schemes

The words we choose to rhyme aren't the only moments when our rhyming can feel cliché. Sometimes, it's the *pattern* of our rhymes—the rhyme scheme—that makes our lyrics seem trite. Most writers are drawn to default patterns of rhyming. Beginning songwriters often write lyrics in couplets, which are two lines in a row that rhyme with each other. Let's look at an example of two sets of couplets in a row, which would be considered an AABB rhyme scheme.

We've spent so many nights apart (A)
I'm here alone with a broken heart (A)
While you're out embracing change (B)
The memory of you still remains (B)

There's nothing wrong with couplets, but it's easy for this rhyme scheme to feel cliché and too repetitive if we don't handle it with care. If we'd like to break away from couplets, the easiest thing to do is to put a little distance between the rhymes. Here is the same lyric with an ABAB rhyme scheme.

We've spent so many nights apart (A)
But the memory of you still remains (B)
I'm here alone with a broken heart (A)
While you're out embracing change (B)

Creating more distance between your rhymes allows them to breathe, which can make the rhyme payoff feel a little more rewarding and a little less singsong-y and predictable. If you'd still like it less rhyme-y, then you could take it a step further and work with an XAXA rhyme scheme. Remember, we use an "X" to indicate line endings that don't rhyme with any other line ending words.

We've spent so many nights apart (X)
But the memory of you remains (A)
I'm here alone, my bed is cold (X)
While you're out embracing change (A)

This rhyme scheme (XAXA) is usually the preferred setup for a four-line section with only one rhyming pair because it lands on the payoff rhyme in line four. Feel free to swap the order and play with AXAX as well, but you'll probably find it's typically not as effective.

Utilizing rhyme schemes gives your listeners a satisfying payoff, but it can also keep them on their toes. Don't stick to the same rhyme schemes over and over, and don't limit yourself to four-line song sections. There are lots of potential rhyme schemes to be found when you expand beyond the predictable four lines, and you're willing to play.

Powerful song sections can also feature three or six lines. Pairing an odd number of lines with an even number of bars can create interesting rhyme schemes, phrasing, and line length combinations. Let's revisit the pre-chorus of "Blinding Lights," which is a three-line song section stretched across eight rhythmic bars (downbeats of each bar in bold):

1 (2 3 4) | **2** (2 3 4) |
Sin city's cold and empty
3 (2 3 4) | **4** (2 3 4)|
No one's around to judge me
5 (2 3 4) | **6** (2 3 4) | **7** (2 3 4) | **8** (2 3 4)|
I can't see clearly when you're go - - ne   *(I said…)*

Notice how *clearly* in line 3 is a rhyme match with the ends of lines 1 and 2 (*empty* and *judge me*). The writer could have easily continued the pattern to have a song section with four short lyric lines that all rhymed with each other. However, the choice to extend line 3 through an internal rhyme gives us the rhyme we were hoping for, while also surprising us with a longer line length and an ending word that doesn't rhyme with anything. Both of these surprises create forward momentum into the next section. Additionally, because line 3 stretches to cover four bars, there is more rhythmic space created at the end of the pre-chorus, which allows for an early phrasing into the chorus on the pickup notes "I said."

No rhyme scheme is superior to the others, but we need to keep checking ourselves to make sure we're not just going through the motions. Don't forget that you can use rhyme schemes to surprise and delight your listener. The last thing we want is to make our listeners feel like they're watching grass grow or paint dry, or experiencing any other cliché metaphor for boredom.

Cliché Metaphors

Once during a long walk, I stopped in the middle of a bridge that was hovering over a small, man-made lake. I looked over and was immediately captivated by a group of turtles, watching them bounce against each other for about 10 solid minutes. Then, all at once, it came to me: "Turtles are the bumper cars of the sea." I went home and shared my revelation with my 12-year-old daughter, who thought it was the funniest thing I'd ever said. I'm pretty sure I have no future in stand-up comedy, but it was funny to her because I had created a somewhat comical metaphor.

We learned from Chapter 3 that metaphors find something in common between two things that usually don't go together. But sometimes, people make these uncommon connections so many times that they become cliché. Can someone's physical heart literally be broken into pieces? No. So a broken heart *is* a metaphor. However, have you heard the phrase *broken heart* a million times? Yes. And that is why it is a cliché metaphor.

The same intuition about cliché rhymes applies here. If it seems like an obvious choice, it's probably an overused metaphor everyone has heard before. A broken heart? Cliché. A broken fantasy? That's a little more interesting. Love is a battlefield? Yeah, we've already heard that song. Love is a trash can? Tell me more! Overused metaphors often combine basic emotions with easy-to-reach pairings. *Sadness* often connects with rain, storm clouds, the color blue, and verbs like drowning and wallowing. *Happy* easily connects to sunshine, rainbows, flowers, and verbs like burst, smile, or lift (me up).

However, if you connect predictable things with unpredictable counterparts, you can find metaphors that aren't cliché. I've heard *bursting with happiness* before. *Bursting with sadness* is definitely more interesting. If you want to find an original way to talk about going through something difficult, try steering clear of language about fighting a battle or weathering a storm. These metaphors no longer have much power because, in a sense, they seem literally true to us because we've encountered them so often.

Try a little cliché fighting right now. Write down the first five verbs and/or nouns that come to mind when thinking about anger. Now, refusing to use those, think of five verbs and/or nouns that you don't normally connect to anger. Try to connect one of your unpredictable words to anger in a lyric.

Examples: "She's got an angry grin," "My anger took a vacation," and "I'm as angry as a newborn babe seeing the light for the first time."

Strong metaphors give our listeners a new window into the world, so we need to do more than avoid cliché metaphors; we need to create new ones. This is where practices like a daily journaling habit, paying attention to nouns and verbs, and a commitment to living a life of noticing will start to pay off. We are able to build fresher metaphors when we experience more of life, soaking in the present and making time for reflection. If we only process our lives through the words and expressions of others, it's difficult to be in tune with how we uniquely experience the world. You must decide to pause on that bridge so that you can ponder the "bumper cars of the sea."

Cliché Melodies

Cliché things tend not to catch our attention or spark our imagination. They blend into the background because we've encountered them so many times. Can a melody be cliché? I'm not sure melodies can feel cliché the same way metaphors do, because if I write a melody I think I've "heard" before, I'll simply modify it to avoid directly copying another song.

Instead, let's explore what happens if a melody lacks the character needed to make it unique or memorable. How can we quantify a boring or predictable melody? A melody may lack distinct character if it only uses simple melodic rhythms, overuses rhythmic patterns, or doesn't take advantage of rest space. It could sound boring if the pitches primarily stay on chord tones, have little to no suspensions, or don't feature interval jumps. The problem could be one too many repetitions of a motif or specific pitches, or phrasing that becomes overused.

What makes a boring melody is pretty subjective, but for the sake of example, I'll briefly break down a melody I find too repetitive and uninteresting and explain why. The following pitches and rhythm make up the melody to the chorus of "Stereo Hearts" by Gym Class Heroes. I've simplified the repetitive syncopation and transposed the melody to the key of C for easier analysis.

Notice how the melody starts and ends on the 1, which is c. The melody features a great deal of scalar stepwise motion, with the beginning of almost every bar landing on scale degree 3, which is e. Bars 5-7 are essentially an exact repeat of bars 1-3. To my ears, the continued use of the rhythmic pattern and the little hill shape of the motif becomes excessive. This melody feels too repetitive, lacks "sparkle," and doesn't have enough unique character for me to want to hear it over and over again. Is this melody cliché? Hard to say. But it definitely feels uninspired. It hits me right in the "meh."

We want to build melodies that draw people in, not tempt them to tune out. Let's find some starting points to modify our melodies and give them a more unique character by taking a bland melody and making it more captivating. I've called this melody "cliché" because it doesn't have attention-grabbing shapes, rhythms, or pitches. I didn't put a lot of thought into the lyric, but that's the point. We're trying to bring interest primarily through the melodic choices. Our lyric is *"I'll give you all my love."*

Starting with quarter notes in the key of C, stepwise motion, and a melodic shape like a little hill, our sample cliché melody looks like this:

Ex 13.01:

Notice the following elements making this melody a little "cliché:"

- The melody lands on the c on the downbeat, which is the root note in our key of C.
- The melody notes landing on all the important beats (1 and 3) are chord tones (no suspensions).
- There is strictly stepwise motion, which is not necessarily a bad thing, but strict stepwise motion leaves us no interval jumps of interest.
- The melody is made from all diatonic pitches over a C Major chord, meaning that all notes remain within the key of C.
- The melodic rhythm is straight eighth notes, so all of the lyrics are getting equal rhythmic weight.

Let's try to make my bland example less cliché and boring. Play with these elements one at a time, or do it cumulatively if you like. Sing and play the melody as you make each adjustment to see how it sounds compared to the original:

1. Change the pitch on *give* so it's not scale degree 1 in our key.
2. Play with the melodic contour so the shape is something more interesting than a gentle hill.

3. Change a pitch or two to create an interesting interval jump somewhere in the melody. Make the interval jump at least a minor third (three half steps) or larger.
4. Change a melody note to add a non-diatonic note in your melody
5. Play with the rhythm. Add some rest space. Change rhythms to be faster, longer, or syncopated.
6. Change the chord or add a new chord over the word *love*.

Sometimes your melodies can become cliché simply because you keep copying yourself. I accidentally do this all the time—I call it "melody infatuation." It happens like this: You write a brilliant melody in a song, and then you keep finding it over and over again in the next three to five songs you write. This can also happen when we unintentionally copy melodies we hear in other people's songs. The solution to melody infatuation is exposing our own patterns so we can avoid ripping ourselves off. If you feel like you're copying yourself or stuck in a melody rut, ask yourself these questions as you analyze some of your melodies:

- What beat of the measure do your phrases typically start on?
- What is the overall *length* of most of your melodic phrases?
- What are your go-to melodic shapes?
- As far as your pitches are concerned, do you tend to gravitate more towards stepwise motion, interval jumping motion, or focus on rhythmic "flat" shapes?
- Do you have a go-to melodic rhythm pattern you use?
- What note in the scale do you tend to gravitate toward? Is this pitch usually at the beginning of phrases or featured frequently in your melodies?
- What is the overall range of your melodies? How much of the staff do you use?
- What register do you use for most of your melodies? What part of the staff do you stay in?
- How often do you use rest space? Only at the end of phrases?

On the other side of the coin, we've got to remember that melody can also be ineffective if it's trying to be everything all at once. These aren't generic, cliché melodies, but rather melodies in an identity crisis. Melodies in an identity crisis don't have enough intentional repetition and structure. I spent a whole chapter arguing that melodic motifs greatly benefit from repetition. However, you first have to craft something interesting enough that it bears repeating.

Cliché Chord Changes

If you think your chord progressions are starting to sound the same with every song you write, let's briefly recall some alternatives when the "predictable" chord might not be the one that suits the meaning of your song the best:

- Check for variety amongst song sections. Do all song sections have the same chord progression or begin with the same chord?
- Try on substitutions/suspensions or extensions (the "number" chords) on *some* of your chords.
- Try some diatonic substitutions like iii or vi for I, ii for IV.
- Try fewer chords or more chords. See which chords you can eliminate without really losing anything. Or try to add some passing chords between existing chords for more flavor.
- Try changing the harmonic rhythm. Instead of a new chord once every downbeat, try adding a chord mid-bar, or every two bars instead.
- Don't forget about neighbor keys and access to chords like the ♭VII and the iv.

Try on all these modifications and alternatives above before settling for your go-to harmony. Having more chord choices is like having more crayons in the coloring box, which helps us break out of cliché harmony. But it's not always a lack of chord knowledge that leads to cliché harmony—sometimes it's allowing the harmony to dictate your melody. I've said this before, but it bears repeating: Getting preemptively locked into a chord progression *before* you establish any sort of melodic idea will inevitably push you toward predictable melodic patterns that you've already explored. If you insist on writing harmony first, perhaps pick a new chord progression on purpose and see if you can create a melody that fits. Whatever you do, notice your go-to harmonic patterns and be intentional to mix them up.

Cliché Song Form

The last of the clichés that I want to wrestle with is being strapped to standard song form. We covered song form in the last chapter, but it's worth mentioning here that manipulating song form is a way to build roller-coasters instead of kiddie rides. There is nothing wrong with utilizing a standard song form, but breaking a predictable song form can be thrilling if you craft with care. It's setting up your listeners for a landing and then adding another loop to the ride.

Song forms can become cliché for you as a writer if you tend to only write in one. If your songs always have a chorus, try to play with verse-refrain song form. If you always add a bridge, perhaps try using a post-chorus instead. Do you always have three verses? Maybe try just two, or even one! Or try to write a song with two different bridges. You could also end a song with the pre-chorus. Stay open to new patterns of play.

We can keep zooming in to observe habits within our song sections. Do all your choruses from one song to the next have the same rhyme scheme? Have the same number of lines? Do you always use a tag at the end of your song? Do all your songs end with a chorus repeat? Taking a close look at your catalog can show you where you've started to lean into habits. Habits aren't necessarily a bad thing; they give each of us our own unique artistic voice. However, you're going to have a difficult time breaking the mold of your own making if you're not aware of what that mold is.

I want you to be the kind of songwriter who excites and engages your listeners. I want them to be slayed by your lyrics, not bored. If you're a performing songwriter, I aspire for you to be able to record a ten-song album where every song has its own unique identity. But I'm not asking you to continually reinvent the wheel. I want you to go looking for unique rocks and have fun polishing them. Push yourself to not settle for the first rhyme, first metaphor, first melody, or first chord progression that pops into your head. I want you to find something special that only you have, something that no other writer has. Clichés come from copies and overuse, but you are an original. No one else has your history and your story; no one else can see the world the way you do. Don't let someone else's words or melody take control of your mouth. Dig a little deeper. Build a rollercoaster. Write a song that excites and delights. Make them expect the unexpected.

PLAYTIME

Solo Activities:

Melody Roulette: Have your group decide on a sequence of six numbers, only pulling from the numbers 1–7. Numbers in the sequence can be repeated. *Examples: 1 - 3 - 6 - 4 - 4 - 1* or *2 - 6 - 7 - 1 - 1 – 3.*

Each number will correspond with a pitch on the C major scale. Using the first example above, the pitches would be c - e - a - f - f - c. Compose a melodic motif using these pitches in this exact order, but on any rhythm you choose. Try to continue creating additional melodic motifs based on this foundational motif.

Play with Melodic Rhythm: Create the blandest two-bar melodic rhythm you can think of, then add pitches (*not* lyrics). Begin to manipulate the rhythm and let the pitches inform your choices. Create five new melodic rhythms for your pitches that utilize faster rhythms, longer rhythms, syncopation, variety, or rest space. Take your favorite combination and try it on five different lyric ideas.

Group Activities:

Word Salad: Have each group member write down 10 nouns and 10 verbs on individual strips of paper. Then, ask everyone to place all 20 strips into a large bowl. After mixing, each person pulls out 10 strips at random. Now, members will use their strips to create interesting combinations. It's okay if the number of nouns and verbs is uneven. Explore how the pairs inspire metaphors that could generate an interesting lyric, title, or concept. You should have enough strips in the bowl to do the activity one more time (or throw the strips back into the bowl and repeat as many times as you want).

Rhyme Time: Have every group member create a random list of at least five verbs and five nouns. Going one at a time, have a group member select a word from either list and present it to the group. Then have every other member of the group suggest a non-cliché rhyming word for the original word. Encourage group members to stay away from perfect and cliché rhymes. After each group member suggests a rhyming word, have the first person select their favorite pairing and then write out a full lyric with the rhymed couplet. Continue this activity with the next person. For example:

- Group member 1 looks at her lists and selects the word *moon*.
- Other group members suggest non-cliché rhymes for the word. They suggest words like *cool*, *smooth*, *prove*, and *mood*.
- Group member 1 selects her favorite pairing (*moon* and *cool*) and writes a lyric couplet: *"Staring at the frosty moon, hoping one day I'll be cool."*

Homework Challenge:

Redefining the Melodic Hook: Write a short lyric (just one line) that has interesting rhythm when you speak it. Say it out loud many times until you settle on an exact rhythm. Then, choose four different melodic shapes to apply to your rhythmic lyric. Sing all the melody shapes on top of your rhythm and record each one in a voice memo. Listen back to the voice memos and decide which melody shape really brought the words to life.

Rap Analysis: Pick a quality rap song and circle all the rhyme connections, internal and line-ending. Then go back and note any recurring melodic rhythm patterns. Sketch them out if possible. Try to emulate some of these rhythmic patterns in a short spoken lyric. If you're not sure where to start, analyze "Lose Yourself" by Eminem.

Song Challenge:

Rap: Write a rap, like a *real* one, that utilizes internal rhyme and repeated melodic rhythm for momentum. You can create a musical refrain or chorus to break up the rapping sections. Make the song's big idea revolve around a specific conflict. If you'd like a more specific prompt, base your conflict on an impactful film or novel.

No Cliché Central Metaphor & Song Form:

Create a central metaphor out of two nouns that is not a cliché—something you've never heard anyone say before, like, *"Love is a trash can."* Explore the meaning of your non-cliché big idea through the lyrics of your song, and try to incorporate a song form or song form section that you don't often use. Make sure your choices are reinforcing the big idea of your lyric.

CHAPTER 14

Tug of War

On Balance

"Centering is crucial. When the clay is off-balance, the pot will collapse, or the clay will fly off the wheel." Dar Williams

A few years ago, I decided to redecorate my office. My desk, scratched, dented, and peeling, desperately needed to be replaced. I scoured the internet for hours looking for the ideal desk. My husband finally found one he thought was perfect for my office. It had tons of storage and room to write on, and we thought it was exactly what I wanted. My husband graciously spent an entire afternoon meticulously assembling it. But when it was finished, I realized it took up too much space. It blocked the view from my window, forcing me to look at a boring angle of the room, and there was no longer room for the armchair I loved. My piano was now in the "wrong" spot. We moved the desk into every conceivable angle of the room, but all of them felt off. I started calling it the "Big Dumb Desk."

Life lesson: It doesn't matter if a thing is a good thing if it's in the wrong place.

I needed a desk that was right for the room *and* right for me. The Big Dumb Desk threw off my sense of balance in my creative space, which was a big no-no. I couldn't think clearly or communicate as an artist in such an off-kilter environment. So I opted for a smaller, lighter desk. A desk that let me look out the windows and keep my keyboard facing the tree I love. I needed to write and sing out into the world, not toward a blank wall, because my sacred creative space matters.

Balance in aesthetic spaces, in the mind, and specifically in songwriting, is what this chapter is all about. We need balance in the songs we write. All the elements in a song should work together, with no single part making the song feel lopsided musically or lyrically. This balance is a form of tension. We're going to try to find that sweet spot suspended in the middle between two good but opposing forces in pursuit of balance. In a way, this is a game of tug of war you don't necessarily want to win. You want to imagine your song as stable, supported, and confidently suspended smack dab in the center of a rope being pulled with equal force from both ends. And what do we find at the end of each side of that rope?

REPETITION	----------------------------	VARIATION
UNIVERSAL	----------------------------	SPECIFIC
UNITY	----------------------------	DIVERSITY

Crafting a balanced song means keeping this rope stretched in both directions. Pull too hard on one side, and we lose the balance. I like the rope analogy for the visual of suspending these concepts in tension; however, we shouldn't write songs with the fear of losing balance and skinning our knees. For another thought picture, consider the balance in well-crafted foods. Balance is like pie à la mode—the perfect blend of warm and chilled. Or maybe balance is a chocolate-covered pretzel—both savory and sweet, creamy and crunchy. Balance is a delicious and worthy pursuit. Lean too much in one direction, and your creation might not appeal to the palate the way you hoped.

Repetition and Variation

A powerful song uses repetition to delight its listeners with ideas worth clinging to. A powerful song also delights its listeners with enough variation not to bore them to death. Just enough, but not too much. As we discuss the pull between repetition and variation, I want you to think of this dichotomy primarily in terms of melody.

Beginning songwriters often neglect the power of a strong melodic motif. The wise songwriter sees it for what it is—musical power—and uses it throughout the song, not just once. Remember, reusing a melodic motif isn't always about exact repetition, and that's where variation comes in! It's about extending the melodic idea, or shortening it, transposing it, inverting it, or exploring which iterations of the melody are connecting with the lyrics the best.

I'll use Coldplay's "Yellow" as a study of melodic motifs so you can see how a musical idea can be reused (repetition) without getting tired (variation). If you're unfamiliar with this song, please listen to it first. It would be even better if you look up a lead sheet so you can see the melody written out.

Line 1 of verse 1 gives us our melodic motif:
"Look at the stars"
Line 2 gives us an <u>extension</u> of that motif:
"Look how they shine for you"
Line 3 gives us a <u>transposition</u> of line 2:
"And all the things you do"
Line 4 gives us yet another <u>transposition</u> and slight <u>variation</u> at the end of the line:
"And it was all yellow"

Did you notice all that repetition and variation? And that was just the beginning of verse 1! The verses of "Yellow" are broken down into three subsections. Each subsection repeats this four-line motif pattern. So, the verse features repetition and variation…which are repeated.

There is even more melodic repetition in this song's chorus, which is pretty typical. I'm still only zeroing in on the melody, but it's important to note that the lyrics are also using a deft balance of repetition and variation. Let's take a look at what happens melodically as the song progresses.

The chorus opens with a new melodic motif for line 1:

"Your skin, oh yeah your skin and bones"

We get an exact repetition of that motif in line 2:

"Turn into something beautiful"

We get a near exact repetition with line 3, with just a slight variation at the end of the phrase:

"You know, you know I love you so"

Line 4 is an <u>exact repeat of the last half</u> of line 3:

"You know I love you so"

Line 4 is vital for the variation of this chorus. It gives the listener enough space to "breathe" in the moment of musical and lyrical rest, which helps the listener not get too tired of the melodic motif. This also illustrates the "rule of three" in action. The "rule of three" is a principle that suggests that listeners typically want to hear something three times in a row. By the fourth exact repetition, they begin to get bored. So, in the example above, we avoid boredom in line 4 thanks to the rest space. At the same time, we are musically comforted by the repeat of the end of line 3, which reinforces the newly introduced melodic variation. Brilliant.

Now, was Coldplay intentionally mapping out this masterful melodic motif plan when they were writing the song? I highly doubt it. But we take notice because we can learn that strong melodic motifs with critical repetition, and just enough variation, give a song power. There's even more melodic motif connection in the outro/post-chorus section of this song, but at the risk of fangirling, I'll stop talking about "Yellow" and instead ask you to start noticing melodic motif patterns for yourself. Observe how well-crafted songs have melodies that are repeated and then reinvented through variation. The pursuit of balancing repetition and variation is critical to melody crafting, but it is also a concept we can explore through lyrics.

Rule of Three

We're going to unpack the concept of the "rule of three" because I want you to consider it a magic bullet for crafting productive repetitions. Since we're not always writing lead sheets as we write songs, one of the easiest ways to see the rule of three manifested is through lyrical repetitions. In Taylor Swift's "Bad Blood," we can see the title appear in the chorus three times:

*'Cause baby, now we got **bad blood***
You know it used to be mad love
So take a look what you've done
*'Cause baby, now we got **bad blood** (hey!)*
Now we got problems
And I don't think we can solve 'em
You made a really deep cut
*And baby, now we got **bad blood** (hey!)*

Repeating your title in a chorus or another song section is usually a good way to reinforce it and solidify your big idea. Sometimes, the lyrical repetitions can be even tighter together. Look at the first chorus line of this song by the Grey Havens, titled "Anywhere":

*"So take me **anywhere, anywhere, anywhere**, but here"*

Not only is the title of this song prominently featured in the first line of the chorus, but we also see the rule of three in action (three uses of *anywhere* clustered together), which creates interest in that word within one line of lyric.

The rule of three can appear in melodic motifs, lyrics, and even in melodic rhythm patterns. Clay Mills and Bill O'Hanlon, in their book *Mastering Melody Writing*, present a thesis about the rule of three manifesting at the opening and closing moments of a line. Their theory "Line +3" suggests that rhythm patterns in the melody, featured at the beginning or end of lyric lines, are key elements in making a melody more hooky. Often, these clustered rhythmic patterns come in groups of three, but the *repetition* of a pattern is ultimately more important than the exact number of hits.

So what's so special about hearing something three times? Some believe that things that come in threes help our brains process and remember them more easily. Three is also the smallest number needed to establish a pattern. Basically, things that come in threes are catchier. And that's what we want as songwriters. With an abundance of simple patterns, we have enough repetition to keep our listeners hooked, but enough variation to keep them interested.

Why not set the rule of four as the standard? Sometimes four repetitions of the same thing can start to feel redundant. That's why children's nursery rhyme songs can get on your nerves as an adult. You don't need that many repetitions to understand what's going on, but a toddler might really enjoy it because their brain is still trying to figure out what patterns are in the first place. When in doubt, opt for three repetitions and then change it—unless you're writing children's music!

Our simple takeaway? Find a short melody or lyric idea you like, then find a way to repeat it three times total (but don't forget to mess with it a little bit.) There's a lot of magic in the rule of three. Now that we've covered the importance of balancing repetition and variation, let's move on to the next power couple: universal and specific.

Universal and Specific

My friend Wendell once said that songs are like a Rorschach test. If you can give people a general outline of the emotion, then they start to hear whatever they want to based on their own stories and experiences. A powerful song is one that creates an emotional connection with the listener through grounded, *specific* content that leads to a *universal* emotional experience. As we discuss the pull between universal and specific, I want you to think of this dichotomy primarily in terms of lyrics.

We covered the importance of vivid specificity in Chapter 3, so let's discuss how to balance the use of specificity with a universal experience. Many songs attempt to do this by grounding the verses in detail and combining them with a chorus containing the song's universal emotion. Some choruses attempt to do this with just one significant line of lyric.

Songs like "Don't You Worry 'Bout a Thing" by Stevie Wonder, "You're Beautiful" by James Blunt, or "Someone Saved My Life Tonight" by Elton John are good examples of this specific versus universal balance. These songs connect through a compelling emotional lyric line, often the title, that is universally applicable to a variety of situations for the listener. These title-bearing lyric lines can usually survive on their own, even when removed from the rest of the song. Many of these songs contain wildly specific verse content that might not relate to most people's lives, but the universal title line or emotional chorus content helps the song connect.

The first time I heard "Someone Saved My Life Tonight," it felt like a spiritual experience. It was late at night, and I was driving alone through a heavily wooded area, praying no deer would cross my path. Although I had been a lover of 60s and 70s music since I was young, somehow, this song had fallen through the cracks, and I'd never heard it before. I could immediately tell it was Elton John singing, so I was hooked from the beginning. The words, however, only grabbed me when the chorus arrived:

"You almost had your hooks in me, didn't you dear?"

I immediately thought of a complicated breakup I had recently gone through. It was a time in my life when I almost lost touch with who I was. It felt like this was a song about me and my story. Then, a few lines later, I was hit with another lyric:

"Sweet freedom whispered in my ear: you're a butterfly"

This song felt true to me in the moment—I really had flown away from the destructive relationship. It helped that the melody of the chorus masterfully aligned with the sensation of breaking free. I understood the story without really understanding the meaning of the verse lyrics. Honestly, I didn't know what the verses were about, and that didn't matter. I saw myself in the story of the chorus. I'm sure you can think of many songs that have spoken to you the same way.

However, the specific content of the verses is still important even if I didn't quite understand it. If I wasn't given sights to see, things to touch, and sounds to hear, I probably wouldn't have believed this song was grounded in reality. The specific lyric content of the verses grounds us in the context of a story, which allows the more universal lines to emotionally connect. So don't be afraid to be specific. People need the details to know you're being real. We're looking to create a collection of words with a suitable melody that allows almost any listener to say, "Yes, someone saved my life tonight, too."

Many songs achieve the connection to the universal through a strong central metaphor. Songs like "Firework" sung by Katy Perry, "Fire and Rain" by James Taylor, and "Red Dirt Road" by Brooks & Dunn come to mind. Songs like these take an object that almost everyone has seen or experienced and attach a deeper meaning to it. The listener can say, "I've seen fireworks, but now I see how they could represent my life." Object writing and journaling can help us if we want to dig into creating central metaphors.

Of course, when using strong metaphors, we need to watch out for clichés. We've talked about how choosing a storm as your central metaphor in a song that centers on sadness might be a bit too predictable. But cliché phrases aren't always a no-no for song titles and concepts. Doja Cat recently proved this with her 2023 release "Paint the Town Red," which stayed on the Billboard charts for months. This phrase, dating back to 1837, is so old that it felt fresh in a hip-hop context. So, if you use clichés, make sure to add a fresh angle. It's about finding something people are familiar with but presenting it in a new way.

Although we're mainly focusing on lyrics with this dichotomy, let's consider another way we can attempt to balance the universal and specific: through eliminating lyrics altogether. Using "nonsense words" can allow a singable melody to truly be king. These are songs that let the melody do all the work of universality because they're easy to put on people's lips. They are the earworms of their generations, regardless of what the rest of the song is really about. If you'd like to study some of these songs for inspiration, listen to the choruses of "Land of 1000 Dances," by Wilson Pickett, "Do Wah Diddy Diddy," by Manfred Mann, or "Oogum Boogum Song," by Brenton Wood. For more recent examples, check out "Umbrella" by Rihanna or "I Love Your Smile" by Shanice.

Songs like these remind us that if you can find a melody with that singable magic, you might even be able to skip the lyrics altogether. This isn't a great writing device for *most* of your songs, but maybe once in a while, try to let the melody make the universal connection all by itself. Just remember to consider your melody *and* lyrics when balancing universal and specific.

So far, we've gone over the balance between repetition and variation, as well as universal and specific. Lastly, I want to consider the pair of unity and diversity.

Unity and Diversity

As we discuss the pull between unity and diversity, I want you to think of this dichotomy primarily in terms of the macro experience of the song as a whole: the combination of melody, lyrics, and harmony. Repetition/variation and universal/specific are concepts we wrestle with on a more micro level, going line by line or motif by motif. Unity/diversity is more of a macro consideration within a song, even across our catalog or genres. A powerful song is one that maintains unity in its elements: melody, lyrics, and harmony, all working together around a big idea. It also creates diversity among those elements so they aren't doing the same thing at the same time. In this balancing act, there are two potential problems that can pull in opposite directions: a lack of a well-defined big idea, which indicates a lack of unity, or the "same/same/same" problem, which suggests a lack of diversity.

We talked about the same/same/same problem in Chapter 5. However, you may ask the question, "How could having complete unity be a problem?" It's easier to explain when you see same/same/same plodding along in action. Imagine you've opted for a chorus that has a lyric and melody that repeats exactly four times in a row. And this might absolutely be working—"Born in the U.S.A," anyone? But what if your verse also has the same structure on all of its lines. And your verse also has the same four chords. And your verse tells the same things lyrically as your chorus. And they have the same phrasing and the same rhyme scheme. Same same same.

This is a comically extreme example, but I hope you get my point. The unity we are after is not overuse but rather an *alignment* of all our song elements to bring our big idea to life. There should be diversity in what each one of these elements is trying to accomplish in each song section. Not all elements should attempt to accomplish the same thing in pursuit of unity. We need a diversity of line lengths, chord changes, rhyme schemes, melodic rhythms, and melody shapes in each section so our song can become its best possible self.

There Are Always Exceptions

I was listening to the song "We Found Love," made popular by Rihanna, and realized I had found a hit song that seemed to harness the same/same/same problem as a strength instead of a weakness. The verse and chorus melody in "We Found Love" are *exactly the same*. I couldn't believe it. I had always assumed that this could never work because of too much "unity" or sameness. The lyrics of the song and the arrangement/production variation are the primary things that differentiate the song sections. The genre expectations for this song might also give it more leeway for melodic repetition. Listen to the song now. Does it feel too same/same/same to you? Would you have noticed that the verse and chorus melodies are identical if I hadn't pointed it out? Let's continue to keep in mind that no matter what songwriting technique we are discussing, there will always be exceptions and guideline breakers.

Fall too far into unity, and our elements feel same/same/same. But what about the flipside? Too much diversity in a song can cause it to feel unfocused. We often fall into too much diversity if we refuse to sufficiently edit. This issue may begin with a big idea that isn't well defined, harmony that lacks a clear enough pattern, or melodic motifs that don't repeat. You could also have two different song ideas fighting each other, crying out to be separated.

A lack of a pattern is chaos. We don't want to bash our listeners over the head with redundant patterns, but we've got to give them some baseline patterns to hold onto. It's always unsettling to have no resolution; it's like a plane that doesn't know how to land. If you think you may have a "too much diversity" problem, be intentional in adding more patterns in your melody, lyric, and harmony. Melodic motifs may be the best place to start because if you have strong melody patterns, you will have a much easier time establishing patterns in lyric.

Remember that your harmony is the environment, and it shouldn't be complicated just for the sake of being complicated. Beginning songwriters can be tempted to use any chord that kind of fits at the moment, but they may not realize the importance of establishing a pattern. Simplicity is better at first. Once you establish a basic harmonic pattern using diatonic chords, you can always go back and add variety. One of my students submitted a verse with the following chord changes for a song in the key of C:

| Dm | Em | G | Am |
| F | G | Dm | Em |

This progression was paired with lyrics and a melody that were pretty straightforward. This presented a "too much diversity" problem because it failed to establish a cohesive pattern or consider the melody it supported. If you find you have a similar problem, the simplest solution is to choose a four-chord pattern and stick to it. It might not line up with the melody exactly how you want, but you can adjust as you go. I suggested she simplify her verse chord changes by sticking to the first pattern.

| Dm | Em | G | Am |
| Dm | Em | G | Am |

This might not be the final harmony she settles on, but it's a more solid place to start. There's diversity in the four chords, but there is still unity in the established harmonic pattern.

Diagnosing a lack of balance in the pull between unity and diversity usually requires some honest feedback from a trusted listener. As writers, we tend to stay interested in our own songs even if there's too much or too little going on. If you have a listener who's willing to honestly tell you, "I'm bored" or "the song feels long," it may reveal that the song has too much unity. If, instead, the feedback is that "the song is kind of random," "I'm lost," or "I can't remember how it goes," then perhaps you have too much diversity.

A Case Study on Lack of Balance

I'd like to use modern contemporary worship music as a case study for what can happen when you don't consider balance. As individual songs and as an overall genre, I find popular corporate worship songs to consistently have balance problems. It is my primary critique of the bulk of these songs as a songwriter, or at least the ones that get the most radio airplay. Let me be clear that what follows is *not* a criticism of:

1. Individual songwriters of the songs
2. The people who love these songs

3. And, most importantly, the genuine worship experiences this music helps facilitate

This is not a critique of the heart and intention of modern worship music, but rather an analysis of its most widely consumed songwriting. What follows is a brief consideration of what a lack of balance can do from a compositional standpoint. It could also provide evidence for why many music lovers don't enjoy this genre of music. But this problem is not exclusive to modern worship music. Compositional balance problems can arise in any genre that focuses more on function than form.

Remember that balance is achieved by holding together the following dichotomies: repetition/variation, universal/specific, and unity/diversity. We will consider the pull of all these things simultaneously. In both music and lyrics, modern corporate worship songs tend to lean primarily toward the repetition, universal, and unity sides of the spectrum. Songwriters in this genre often aim to find words and music that can appeal to most people in the room at any evangelical megachurch on any given Sunday. The lyrics should address struggles and pain, but not be so specific that they exclude anyone's story. The music must be engaging enough to hold everyone's attention, but it can't provide any level of difficulty that would make it inaccessible for anyone to sing after just one listen. The result is a song that feels good the first time you hear it. But by the 10th listen? That's another story.

When we are out of balance and ignore variation, specificity, and diversity, we are left with lyrics that may feel cliché, generic, and lacking in the emotional depth of someone's real story. My church does a song called "Raise a Hallelujah." Considering the song on its technical songwriting merits, I find it lyrically boring. There is no depth to the words I am supposed to connect to. Who are "my enemies" and what is "the storm" I'm supposed to be singing in the midst of? I've heard these metaphors before, and they don't mean much to me now. Defenders of the genre will argue that this ambiguity is effective and intentional, but I'll push back and say that's exactly my point. It's a means to an end, not a balanced work of art. Well-crafted songs are universal *and* specific. You tell me part of your story, then I can understand how it relates to mine. There's no specificity in this lyric, making it mostly *tell* and little *show*.

And let me just say I mean no offense to anyone who is profoundly touched by this song. Songs speak to listeners differently! And if you like it and it's meaningful to you, I'm glad it made a connection.

I did a little research and discovered the specifics of the inspiration behind "Raise A Hallelujah." It was written as a "cry for a miracle" for a young child who was sick and dying. Suddenly, this song made sense to me. Once I knew this crucial detail, I was able to emotionally connect to the song. As a songwriter, I was deeply frustrated that the writers had kept this important detail from me. This was the *show* I needed in order to emotionally connect!

Looking at the bridge of "Raise A Hallelujah," a listener encounters a great deal of melodic and lyrical repetition. (The bridge is the portion that begins with "sing a little louder.") How do you know when too much repetition is, well, too much? Criticizing the repetitiveness of the lyrics in modern worship music has become a favorite punchline for those who don't connect with it. But a repetitive chorus or bridge isn't the core of the problem for me with this song.

In the Book of Revelation, we learn that the four living creatures in the presence of God say "holy, holy, holy" day and night without ceasing. So there's nothing wrong with repetition—*as long as it's something that bears repeating*. In the case of the four living creatures, repeatedly asserting truths about God in his presence makes sense. But considering the bridge of "Raise a Hallelujah," I'm struck with the question: How many times can you compel someone to sing a little louder before there are no new decibels to reach? Maybe there could have been a better, truer line to repeat. Perhaps it would have been better to acknowledge that we cannot win the battle through our own dynamics. To me, the excessive repetition of this lyric misses the nuance that it's okay to be quiet and let God sing on when we cannot.

The issue of repetition/universal/unity lopsidedness can also impact the musical aspect of this genre. Melodies that are crafted to be so universally accessible that everyone can sing them after just one listen often lack a distinctive character. Interval jumps? Minimized. Interesting melodic rhythms? Squashed flat. These melodies become so generic that they start to blur together. Harmony can suffer in the same way. These chord progressions are so predictable that AI could easily compose them, and no one would notice. While this approach to songwriting is highly practical, it sacrifices the beauty of unique form.

Case Study Continued: Song Swap

One Sunday morning, my worship leader, Brandon, accidentally started singing the lyrics to "The Lion and the Lamb" as the band began to play the opening song of the set, which was *supposed* to be Phil Wickham's "This is Amazing Grace." No one noticed that Brandon was singing one song while the band played another. The arrangements, tempo, harmony, and overall feel of the songs are so similar that it didn't matter. This suggests that we have a collection of music that is too similar to itself in its effort to be too functionally universal.

When we limit our songwriting palette to primary colors, we only allow ourselves to paint basic pictures. My heart for faith-based songwriters is that they would refuse to be hamstrung by limiting their chord choices, melodic ranges, and a small pool of metaphors and themes to pull from. Intricate melodies can be engaging and memorable. They're worth writing. It's okay if they're a little hard to learn because beautiful things often take time. If you think your congregation doesn't have the skill to sing a compelling melody, ask yourself, can these people sing "Don't Stop Believing" on karaoke night? Absolutely, they can. They took the time to learn and to fall in love with a melody worth singing.

Matt Redman proved this point 10,000 times over with his song "10,000 Reasons"—a song that truly achieves songwriting balance. This song has quite literally reached "universal" status, traveling around the world to almost every tribe, tongue, and nation. It has been embraced by believers around the globe, regardless of their musical skill. And yet, it has an intentionally crafted melody that is difficult in its variation and specificity. It has interesting interval jumps, a wide range, and varied melodic shapes and rhythms that you can't learn in one listen. It has a soaring chorus melody that is contrasted by a verse whose lyrical and melodic content is aligned with the big idea. People are not musical dummies. They are willing to learn beautiful things.

No Formula

I know all this talk about balance might seem too philosophical and not practical. But you, my friend, are an artist, and I want you to believe that there is no formula. Consider submitting yourself to the pursuit of quality *art*. In a commercial music space driven by worldly success, you might find the so-called "rules" to follow to be a hit songwriter. But our culture will always change the "rules" on a whim, and you'll never see it coming. Songwriter, may I step onto my soapbox to encourage you toward purer, even holier, goals?

Only you can write the way you write, and you can write with function *and* form. Don't let fame, songwriting contests, publishing deals, and the like be your ultimate goal—these things should not define your success. Consider the hometown crowd at your coffee shop before all the scrollers on TikTok. And if you write worship music, perhaps consider your home congregation before you consider CCLI. Let success be writing quality songs that only you can write. Let success be writing better this year than you did last year. Let success be bringing something good, true, and beautiful into this world. Success is *in* the making. It is taking your specific perspective and connecting it to universal emotions. It is finding unique variation in the comforting repetitions of daily life. It is your diverse voice that can bring people together in unity through the songs that you write. Good songs have balance, and good writers do too.

PLAYTIME

Solo Activities:

Rule of Three: Keep the rule of three in mind when building your melodic motif, and write a verse and chorus. In each song section, try to feature a specific melodic motif three times. Remember, these don't have to be exact repeats—manipulating the motif through techniques like extension or transposition is encouraged. And remember, the melodic motif in the verse should be different from the one in the chorus. Feel free to add lyrics and chords, but focus primarily on developing the melody.

Same Chords/Different Melody: Create a verse and chorus with harmonic unity by committing to a simple chord progression (four chords max) that is exactly the same in both song sections. Work toward diversity by creating a melody and lyric that feels very different from the verse to the chorus. In the end, the verse and chorus should sound like distinctly different song sections even though the chord changes are identical. Reference "Fly" by Sugar Ray for an example.

Group Activities:

Repetition/Variation Melody: Divide into groups of two or three. Provide each group with the same tempo and meter to work from (such as 80 bpm in 4/4). Have one person in each group construct a two-bar melodic motif. Other members can then take the motif and modify it through tools like transposition, shortening, or extension. Each group will take their motif and its variations to build the melody for a complete song section with at least four lines or eight bars. Afterward, bring all the groups together and assign each group's song section to different song form sections. For example, try using group 1's completed melody as the verse and group 2's melody as the chorus.

Object Metaphor for Emotion: Have the group create a list of at least 20 interesting objects or places, like "wrecking ball," "fireworks," or "red dirt road." Go back through the list and assign at least three distinct emotional ideas that could be represented by each object or place.

Example: wrecking ball = sudden loss, or overcoming outdated traditions, or trying to withstand a powerful attack.

Notice how the different objects/places evoke differing emotional ideas in the group members.

Homework Challenge:

One-Line Lyrics: Create a list of at least 10 one-line lyrics that could function as a song title and feel universal in their content (in that most listeners could find a way to work this lyric into their life). Select one of your favorite ideas from the list and write a *specific* story (not lyrics) that would lead up to this line. Who are the characters, where are they, what are they seeing, hearing, and doing? If you're on a roll, try to develop your story into verses and use the one-line lyric as the anchor lyric for your chorus.

A Melody to Remember: Create a melody that is intricate, beautiful, and a little "difficult." Think of the chorus to "10,000 Reasons" by Matt Redman or "The Joke" by Brandi Carlile. This melody shouldn't feel like an "instant hook" or be easy to learn on the first listen. You can be mindful of motifs, but beauty and contour should be of utmost importance in this exercise. Look to hymns, cherished folk songs, or classical music for inspiration. Once you settle on a beautiful melody, ask yourself: "What part of a song does this melody feel like?" Then try adding lyrics.

Song Challenge:

Title Three Times: Write a song where the title is featured in the chorus lyric three strategic times. If you'd like more specifications for the prompt, use a central metaphor that focuses on something associated with the number three. For example, poison ivy has three leaves, water has three forms, atoms are made of protons, neutrons, and electrons.

Cliché Rebirth: Write a song by finding a dated cliché like "paint the town red" and try to look at it differently. Make it your own by avoiding using the cliché in the way listeners will expect you to. If you need some ideas to get started, you can pull from this list:

- plenty of fish in the sea
- falling head over heels
- only time will tell
- don't judge a book by its cover
- a knight in shining armor (or on a white horse)
- the girl next door
- it was a dark and stormy night
- a chip off the old block
- add insult to injury
- an axe to the grind
- another day, another dollar

CHAPTER 15

Playing Dress-Up & Pretend

Genres, Emotional Justice, Co-writing, and Identity

"As a songwriter, there is an emotional honesty that I must adhere to, because while I don't have to have lived the things I sing about, I do have to believe them." Mary Gauthier

When I attended Berklee College of Music, everyone around me was trying to figure out who they were as artists. One student would ask another, "What does your music sound like?"

"Oh, it's like pop/rock with a little bit of soul that dabbles in jazz fusion," or some sort of nonsensical answer like that.

Young creatives are not about fitting into boxes; they're about playing with all the toys. They struggle to answer this question because they love so many different genres of music, and they're trying to explore them all.

Let me be the first to say I actually hate genres. They're not for artists; they're for business and consumers. And they creatively hold us back. Genres try to tell us what is and isn't "the style." Says who? The people trying to turn your art into a commodity, that's who. Things are changing, and even consumers don't seem to care much about genres anymore.

Don't just take my word for it—BBC said: "As the lines between traditional music genres have blurred, they no longer define a listener's taste quite like they did pre-streaming era."[3]

But I'm not trying to hate on whatever kind of music style you love. Are you a country writer who doesn't just write and listen, but also eats, sleeps, and breathes country music? More power to you, cowboy. I love that you found a musical space you love to live in. The problem is that a lot of us want to dip all 10 of our toes into different pools. When I've told industry pros that my serious influences range from Elton John to Darlene Zschech to Gwen Stefani to Kimbra, their response is something like, "Yeah, yeah, everyone says that. We know you *like* a lot of music, but what kind of music do you make that's a recognizably marketable genre?" I want to rage at this. Marketability is not the point of creativity.

Okay, so I *try* not to rage, but instead come to peace with what I believe about songwriting. With every year that I get older, I care less and less about fitting into a category that people can easily understand in one bite. I am a complex delicacy. I have many "notes." I once released an EP that had legitimate elements of folk, jazz, electronic music, and country all wrapped up into four songs. And yet somehow it was cohesive and very much "me." Miraculous. Was it everyone's cup of tea? Honestly, not my problem. It would be dishonest of me to censor myself for the sake of being an easily accessible commodity.

I remember watching a YouTube video that attempted to explain musical genres in eight minutes or less. At first, I was intrigued. I'm always eager to learn something new about music. But unfortunately, this video was aimed at songwriters who prefer to craft their music to fit a genre. It was for those who would let Judge Genre set the rules and hand down the edicts. The video suggested that songwriters attempt to find their genre by defining their music first by its similarity to other popular artists. Then, it went further and encouraged songwriters to just go ahead and commit to a genre before they've even conceived of a melody or lyric. It is not my

---

3 Brooks, By Christian. 2023. "Spotify Wrapped 2023: 'Music Genres Are Now Irrelevant to Fans.'" November 29, 2023. https://www.bbc.com/news/entertainment-arts-67111517.

intent here to disparage another teacher and students who prefer to work this way. But for me, letting your creativity and creations be pre-conformed to categories and labels before even starting is not writing with love.

Perhaps I'm being too impractical. I know there are people out there who dream of writing for other people, and I think dreaming of collaborating with artists you respect is a noble aspiration. So let me meet you somewhere in the middle between "Judge Genre" and "let's throw all genres away." Let's play dress-up.

Genres: Playing Dress-Up

Instead of viewing genres as tight-fitting suits we're squeezing into for the gaze of others, let's place all of our genres—and all that's attached to them—into a giant "costume bin." You know the one: it's in the attic or closet somewhere collecting dust. It's that unruly bin or chest where you hide old Halloween costumes, wigs, cowboy hats, Mardi Gras beads, and everything in between. Let's crack open the bin and play.

Growing up, my brother and I loved playing dress-up. It was a playground for the imagination; we could be the mermaid, the cowboy, or the gymnast. But the real fun was breaking the "rules" and becoming the cowboy mermaid, the doctor gymnast, or the alien chef. Similar to this childhood game, I want you to open your mind to the possibility of envisioning your songs in many different musical contexts. We start here because, most of the time, all you need to have a song are two things: melody and lyrics. A strong melody and lyrics should be able to waltz right past Judge Genre and be free to play in lots of different musical environments.

You can try on some wild outfits by taking a song and manipulating the following things: tempo, groove, harmony, song form, lyrical idiosyncrasies, and arrangement. What's important in this process is the bones, which are the song that is wearing all those different outfits. A song with good bones can stand the test of a change in groove, harmony, or song form and still *feel* like the same song. Sometimes, the melody itself is enough.

If we think back to our tree analogy, genres are most closely related to the environment. They are like different soils our trees can be grounded in. On a technical level, genres are usually defined by harmonic choices, groove, and sometimes by song form and the instruments most widely used. For example, jazz is recognized for its chord complexities and song form, while reggae features a prominent backbeat. EDM uses electronic instruments and has a danceable tempo. Still, these elements do not define the song itself because melody and lyrics live on the top tier. If you straightjacket yourself to the genre as your first priority, then I'd argue your priorities aren't well-ordered. You're putting the cart before the horse. A good song should be able to weather many soils and many different genre interpretations.

Genre classifications *could* be functional if they were entirely based on musical choices and tendencies. However, we have major genres that are defined by how audiences interact with them. For instance, pop isn't a genre based on anything musical or lyrical at all. Pop, at its core, is an abbreviation for *popular*, which is subject to cultural fads. The label "alternative" arose simply as a counterpart to pop, and Christian music is a genre defined completely by lyrical content. Don't even get me started on what "world" music is. How are we supposed to find ourselves as artists when genre keeps changing the parameters?

Musical genres are impossible to definitively define as they are always changing, influencing each other, and being newly created. There are countless subcategories and crossovers. But how can you play with different genre outfits if I don't give you some basic characteristics? At the end of this chapter, there is a very unscientific list I've pulled together encompassing the biggest genre categories and a few attributes that usually support a song being placed in that category. This is by no means an exhaustive list, but you can visit it to pull from different genre norms just to play around.

I hope you won't exclusively chase creativity within a genre—I hope you will chase a great song. Even if your career goals include being a full-time writer making a living pitching songs in a marketable genre, the demands and preferences of that genre are always going to change. There is a higher calling found in discovering *who you are* as a songwriter and artist. Be a cowboy astronaut. Be a writer who can tackle Americana and jazz. Allowing those unique tendencies to emerge, regardless of what market it may drive you toward, is good work.

Emotional Justice: Playing Pretend

If playing dress-up is trying on musical and stylistic ideas in new combinations for discovery, then playing pretend is trying on other lives and lived experiences. We can pretend to be an astronaut, a Renaissance painter, or a saber-toothed tiger. But this pursuit of embodying other people's lived experiences can get a little messy when we're talking about real lives and stories. How can we "play pretend" by trying on other lives without committing emotional appropriation? Isn't it dishonest to try on other people's stories? Aren't we only supposed to "write what we know"? Or is there truth that's worth seeking out, even if it's outside our own lived experiences?

In my late 20s, I entered a performing songwriter competition that was a part of a three-day workshop for indie artists. I made it to the finals held on the last night of the event, playing my song "Moses," written from the perspective of Moses from the Old Testament. I hadn't performed as much as I'd liked since my children had been born, and I was legitimately nervous as I sat down at the keys. I had to belt out a high note at the end of the song that was at the very top of my range—on a good day. I felt like I had everything to prove. Despite the tension, I opened my mouth to sing:

Sometimes my feet won't move because it hurts too bad
I face another day of a dry and weary land
And every mile I move is filled with longing for a home
But every step is taking me to places more unknown
I'm in the wilderness and I am wandering
But leaning desperately on your plans

And I will follow you through wind and water
To see your promise and your promised land

I did it. I played my best, hit the high note, and ended up winning the competition. Shortly afterward, I found myself celebrating alone, eating a cheeseburger in my car in a McDonald's parking lot at 10 PM. Winning by yourself is an unglamorous letdown. But before we get too caught up in my sad cheeseburger, I want to rewind to the moment right *before* I left the competition venue that evening.

Still standing on the stage after the trophies had been awarded, I was approached by a man who would eventually become my manager for a brief time. He wanted to compliment me on the emotional honesty of my lyrics. He said something like, "The way you relate to Moses through your writing, I can really tell you've been through some hard stuff and wilderness moments in your life." I simply responded, "Thank you," but inside I was saying, "Nope, not even close to correct."

Now, I want to be clear that I know my future manager was genuinely trying to be kind. I was thankful to receive his kindness, but the truth was that I'd never really wandered or suffered like Moses. At that time in my life, I had never experienced a true "wilderness" season. I hadn't been thinking about myself at all when I wrote those lyrics.

Were my lyrics a lie? Was my forging of an emotional connection with my listeners through someone else's story dishonest? I don't think so. I believe truth was able to shine through in spite of myself because I was willing to do emotional justice to a part of Moses's story. I was willing to put myself in his sandals and ask, "If this were my context, what would I feel? What would I say? What are the questions I would wrestle with?"

It's good, fruitful work to write from our own experiences. Writing from our own experiences helps us to avoid "conjuring." But sometimes, as a writer, you want to learn from someone else's story. I'm encouraged by novelist Madeleine L'Engle, who said in *Walking on Water*, "In the creative act, we can experience the same freedom we know in dreams. This happens as I write the story. I am bound by neither time nor space." Maybe you want to write the words someone else so desperately needs to say, but they don't know how. Maybe you want to explore an experience you hope to live one day. Maybe you want to process your own experience through someone else's lens.

I recently heard a beautifully honest song about a man trying to learn to forgive his wife, who had cheated on him. This song was *not* written by the man with the unfaithful wife, but by John, a gifted songwriter and close friend of the man. John wanted to give his friend some words to help him process his grief—a song of comfort and healing. Was it dishonest of John to write about infidelity when he had not personally experienced it? No, I don't think so. His expression of art was effective because it aimed to heal through acknowledging grief. It was vulnerable in its emotions, and it wasn't preachy. It didn't offer advice or quick fixes; it sat with the emotions of the experience and called them valid. In her book *How to Write a Song that Matters*, Dar Williams makes an important point about approaching songs like this with utmost care when she says, "We must be very careful not to recommend anything to someone who is suffering, as if we know what to prescribe to heal despair."

John was able to speak into this situation because he was willing to approach the song with "emotional justice." He took the time to sit with the experience. So, how do you do this? If it's a historical experience you are far removed from in time and space, then you need to do your research. Read about the experience. Interview people who lived through it. Immerse yourself in the art and culture of the time and place. Work with a co-writer who is closer to the experience.

If it's a situation that someone you know has experienced, try to ground the big emotions in their real tactile details. Ask them to talk about it if they're in a place where they feel comfortable sharing, but don't push. Don't be a preacher and don't spin propaganda. Doing emotional justice in songwriting is about listening before you write, while you write, and as you edit. Dar Williams said, "If [the] writer recognizes, in the metaphoric space of her own construction, what really happened, how it really felt, and what its unique qualities were, then she will be writing what she knows." So, in the end, we can do emotional justice to someone else's story *if* we are willing to take the time to truly *know* the story.

Playing Nice with Others: Co-Writing

I never really enjoyed playing pretend with my youngest daughter when she was a preschooler. She would beg me to play dolls with her, but then she proceeded to dictate my every choice. "Put these clothes on your doll and take it to this room in the dollhouse. Now make your doll say this!" She was making all the decisions, and it's pretty boring playing with someone who doesn't let you decide anything.

As songwriters, we play dress-up, we play pretend, and we often are required to play with others. I have a lot of things I could say about co-writing, but for this chapter, I want to leave you with one takeaway: The key to good co-writing is being a generous "playmate." A quality co-writer will acknowledge the other co-writers' voices, inclinations, preferences, and style. You might fear that deferring to other writers' preferences is risky and frustrating, but let me assure you, it is usually a safe and worthwhile endeavor. You sacrifice some autonomy by sharing your toys, but this is a good practice for creative people who tend to prefer to play alone.

Co-writing can be scary because you have to be willing to subject your ideas to being poked, prodded, and reimagined by someone else. We are tempted to think of our ideas as precious babies all over again. You might wonder, "What if my co-writer messes up my song?" or "What if they change it in a way I don't like?" My warning is that if your song idea is too precious to you, then don't bring that idea into a co-write. Maybe that's a song you really need to work out on your own. Remember: It's no fun to play with someone if you don't let them play too.

Co-writing is valuable to the life of a songwriter because playing with others prevents us from cycling through the same old choices that have become our crutch. We have to expose our creativity to new people and ideas to grow. This requires courage, vulnerability, humility, and honesty. Sometimes, you discover that the other writer is as much or more in tune with the big idea of your song than you are. Selfish co-writers sulk and withdraw. Generous co-writers allow the song to evolve, and sometimes that means taking your hands off even more.

I recently scheduled a three-person co-write. The other two guys in the room were both phenomenal writers. David is a melodic genius and Graham is a brilliant wordsmith. I brought five song ideas and let them choose the one that excited them most. We picked one and started running with it. By the end of our three-hour co-write, I probably contributed the *least* to the final version of the song. However, I was the one who brought the title and chorus hook, and I was the driving force behind sticking to a specific "big idea" throughout the write.

On the drive home right after the session, my ego tried to cry out, "You only got two lyrics in the whole song! They ran away with all the chord changes without you, and you had no input in this verse melody whatsoever." This is the wrong way to think about co-writing and songs that are co-written. Even though many of the choices we landed on weren't "mine," in a sense, they were still all mine. As a part of the group, I signed off on every idea that we collectively decided was the strongest. Furthermore, the song would never have been created without me. I brought the people together. I brought the initial song "rock" from my collection. I kept the song focused on the big idea that was important to me throughout the entire write. And that's the point. Every co-writer in a session affects the room, impacts the song, and adjusts the temperature of the creative process. Every co-writer matters regardless of who said what when.

When you enter a co-writing session, it should not be a battle of egos. At its best, the co-writing group, for a brief time, becomes like a body—one unit, all coming together, with different parts contributing different things. Depending on how the song develops, more influence may be needed from some writers and less from others. Let the eye be the eye and the foot be the foot, so to speak. A song is a unique creation, and different skills are called upon depending on the nature of the work. If you always *have* to be in charge, you won't be a generous playmate, and people might not want to write with you again.

If you haven't tried it yet, I hope you'll consider co-writing. I mostly wrote alone for the first 10 years. When I turned a corner and began to trust other writers to speak into my songs, my productivity, community, and creativity exploded in the best way. The most recent album I released had 12 songs, and 11 of them had co-writers. Trusting other people's creativity will help you become a better writer, artist, and champion of other artists.

Identity: Finding Who You Are

During a lesson, my student Ava reflected back on the first song she ever wrote. In her words, she was surprised by how "sappy" the lyrics were. They felt honest and compelling when she wrote them, and she was proud to be able to capture her thoughts and feelings in a song. So why did they feel so cringeworthy years later? Should she be embarrassed about her past as a writer?

Absolutely not. In fact, this is a good indication that she's growing as a songwriter. I still go through this growth process myself. I recently listened to a song I wrote and recorded a couple of years ago. When I released it, I felt like it was the most honest and emotionally raw thing I'd ever created. I was proud that I found a way to translate my big feelings into art that was authentic and might connect with others. However, on my latest listen, the song felt overly dramatic. It didn't hit me in quite the same way anymore. It almost felt a little cringe. Why? Because I was kind of over it. I've processed those big feelings, grown, and moved on.

Did it make the song any less valid or diminish its inherent quality? I don't think so. I believe that song of mine can still reach people and speak to something tender and real. But personally, I've moved on from that moment as a writer. And that's okay! In fact, I'd say that's great. As writers who build new things, we should grow and evolve toward new artistic themes and expressions. And we can do so without regretting where we've been or the things we've learned along the way.

I often remind my students that their measure of growth shouldn't have anything to do with another artist or writer. Taylor Swift won a

Grammy when she was 20 years old. Cool. That doesn't have anything to do with you. Your goals as an artist will be more life-giving if you work toward the *next* thing being better than the *last* thing. Will you always succeed? No. But at least the pace of your creative journey won't be defined by someone else's shrines on the road map of what it means to be an artist.

Do you like the songs you're writing now more than the ones when you first started? This is a much better indicator of growth than comparison. You can only glory in your past creations for so long before you grow stale as an artist. Are you challenging yourself? Are you changing, learning, and moving on to the next adventure? I hope so. Even if it makes your older material feel a little cringe.

When I was first starting out, I struggled for years to find something deep, interesting, and true to say. I often missed the mark, but I kept writing anyway. Sometimes there were glimmers of brilliance, but more often than not, I was simply putting in the work to become a more skillful writer. For me, it took time and more life experience before I discovered themes and ideas that felt like my authentic voice as an artist and writer. I look back on those songs and treasure them as a slow and precious start to a grand adventure.

In his book *Originals,* Adam Grant discusses "geniuses." He says, "The more experiments you run, the less constrained you become by your ideas from the past." Furthermore, if you find that you are not a young genius, then "slow and steady experimentation can light the way to a longer stretch of originality." Finding who you are as an artist will probably take some time. Some of us—well, most of us—are just late bloomers. Enjoy the journey. Don't put the expectations of super stardom on your tender writer self. Give yourself some sunshine, steady nourishment, daily gentle attention, and time to grow.

What Do You Want?

In a famous scene from the movie *The Notebook*, Ryan Gosling's character asks Rachel McAdams' character a pivotal question:

"What do you want?"
"It's not that simple!"
"What do you want!"

In the quest to find your identity as a writer, you need to ask yourself this question often, as it applies to your creative output. You will constantly feel the pressure to write about what you *ought* to write about, or write about what the genre says you *should* write about, or what your culture says you *have* to write about. But what do you *want* to write about?

"It's not that simple!" you might be tempted to say, along with Rachel McAdams. "I'm a Christian, so I have to write Christian music. I'm a mom, so I can't write hard rock. I'm a jazz musician; no one will let me write country." Or maybe you're tempted not to write about anything at all because you think you need to be doing so many other things. But it's not about what you need to write, or feel like you have to write. It's about what you want to write.

Being sensitive to what we want is important as songwriters because much of what we do is driven by our own pace and the projects we create and manage. "Want" has the spark of passion, the creative drive. However, being sensitive to our desires does not give us free rein to reject everything we need to do. Some short-term need-to-dos are ultimately long-term wants. Things like a daily writing habit, a regular exercise routine, and cleaning that maintains the sacredness of your creative space can be thought of as burdensome needs—or reframed as the pursuit of long-term wants. I choose the long-term want and let that override the short-term thinking that these things are needs that I am slave to.

But it's not just about recoloring your duties. Again, it's about being sensitive to your creative passion in the moment, even if it flies in the face of the to-do list. If you want to color outside the lines of musical genres, do it. If you want to write about new topics, then go explore. If you want to grow as a writer, focus on the long-term goal of writing a little every day. If you want to be a braver writer, send that text to a friend and set up a co-write. If you want to discover who you are, start listening. Play dress-up, play pretend, and play with others.

Genres (for Songwriting)

Alternative	Foundationally, this is rock music, tied to punk origins, but it can be anything felt as the harder or stranger *alternative* to what's "popular."
Blues	Uses blues scales and chord progressions, with a 12-bar progression being most common, and distinct rhythms from a walking bass or shuffle. There are call and response lyrical patterns and often themes of lament.
Children's	Highly repetitive and simple melodies and lyrics used for sing-along, movement, lullabies, and more. Themes suited for children include family life, animals, food, imagination, and daily life routines.
Classical	In a modern context, any non-folk style Western music released before the year 1950 often gets thrown into this category, which can span from Gregorian chant to Serialism. This covers like 1500 years. Attempt to learn about and draw inspiration from a period you connect with, like the Baroque, Classical, or Romantic period.
Comedy	Novelty and parody songs aim to entertain with their silliness, exaggeration, or a witty spin on an existing work.
Commercial	Jingles, theme songs, and background "canned" music. Practical in their length and dynamics, these songs are usually composed for their functional quality in a specific setting.
Country	At its core, it is a hybrid of American folk music and blues traditions. Musically, it is usually more accessible (diatonic) than other genres and defined by the use of folk instruments like the acoustic guitar, fiddle, and banjo. Its lyrics also tend to be more applicable to the "everyman" in working-class spaces.
Electronic	Electronic music is made primarily with synthesized instruments, beats (drum machines), and samples with a wide variety of tempos. EDM (electronic dance music) is intended for movement. At the core, electronic music is made primarily with computers, and there are more subgenres than you can count.
Folk / Singer - Songwriter	In a modern context, this style of music includes songs written by the performing artist, features personal storytelling in the lyrics, and leans more on acoustic instruments (but not always). Its roots are in oral traditions of songs and stories passed down generationally.

Gospel	Music with its roots in the African American church. Features musical influences from jazz, blues and soul. Often features call and response, strong harmonies, or choral vocals and deal with themes of the good news and fervent spiritual expression.
Hip-hop/Rap	Hip-hop emerged in the 1970s, primarily as a cultural movement. Compositionally, the foundation is rhythmic spoken wordplay over looped music or beats.
Holiday	A catch-all term for songs from many musical genres with holiday lyrical themes (or famous melodies), most of which revolve around Christmas.
Inspirational	(or Christian) is another catch-all category that hosts many musical styles and is primarily defined by its lyrical content. There are HUGE melodic, harmonic, and even lyrical differences between southern gospel and christian metal, but here we are. This is a genre classification made for consumers, not creators.
Jazz	Finding its roots in ragtime and blues, jazz originated in New Orleans in the late 1800s. In a modern context, craft elements that connate jazz include improvisation, intricate harmonies, mode mixture, AABA song form, and the rhythmic technique of swing.
Latin	Latin music hosts a plethora of subgenres. It is a blend of African-based rhythms, European song forms, indigenous cultural influences, and rhythmic complexity. Some of these genres are based on groove (like salsa and samba), and many feature characteristic instruments such as maracas, conga, or bongo.
Metal	With origins in rock music, metal is usually defined by loudness, electric guitar distortion and extended solos, aggressive and often screaming vocals, and lyrical themes of darkness or rebellion. Metal songs often feature extended song forms and highly skilled instrumentalists because of the musical complexity.
Pop	Defining pop is impossible because it simply stands for "popular." It is the music that is currently in demand. Pop has been Elvis, The Beatles, Michael Jackson, Britney Spears, and Billie Eilish. Stylistically, pop lives in cycles of creative expansion toward an accepted current sound and then oversaturation that begets new creative periods.
R&B	R&B (rhythm & blues) is a genre classification that has shifted many times since it's origination in African American communities in the 1940s. Originally a marketing term to describe jazz music with heavier beats intended for African American audiences, it has been used as a blanket term for blues, electric blues, and even funk over the years. In the 1980s "contemporary R&B" emerged as a term combining R&B with other genre influences including pop, soul and funk. You basically need a music history degree to accurately define this genre.

Reggae	Originating in African and Caribbean music, reggae is always in 4/4 time or swing and is usually harmonically simplistic (in that there are usually no more than one to two chords). Strong bass lines and lyrics about spiritual and social awareness are also key elements.
Rock	Historians argue about where rock & roll really started, but we're pretty sure it came from some combination of blues, folk, country, jazz, and gospel music. In our modern context, rock tends to be defined by a band comprised of electric guitar, bass, and drums, specifically with a snare drum providing an accentuated backbeat. The use of power chords allows for harmonic exploration outside of the diatonic key. Choose your subgenre based on preferred timbre, lyrical themes, and popularity.
Soul	Originating in African American communities in the south in the 1950s, soul has a musical foundation in R&B and gospel music. Soul specifically features heavy back beats and horns. Powerful vocalists usually deliver raw lyrical themes about love or social injustice.
World	Our genre classifications are so Western-centric that often anything outside gets thrown into the very ridiculous category of world music, which comprises songs from African, Asian, Celtic, Indian, and many more traditions and cultures.

PLAYTIME

Solo Activities:

Bask in the Cringe: Find an old song of yours and first bask in the cringe. Now, really consider it. Are there any interesting melodic ideas you could reuse? If you were to rewrite the lyrics, would you say things differently now? Use your old song as a starting point for inspiration for creating something new. If you don't have a song that feels "cringe" yet, analyze a popular song you find cringy and try to rewrite the lyrics.

Playing Dress-Up with Genre: Take one of your songs (or someone else's) and try to reimagine it in a completely different genre. Change the lyrics, the melody, the chords, the groove, the tempo, the song form—anything you like. Whatever you do, just make a definitive change.

Group Activities:

A Mini Co-Write: Break into groups of two or three drawn out of a hat and try to write a song section together based on one of the following subjects: an astronaut, Napoleon, or an endangered antelope. Or use one of your own ideas if there's something your group really wants to write about. Work your song section until you feel really good about it, but try to keep the mini-write to 30 minutes or less.

One Line at a Time: Break into pairs and try to write a song section one line at a time. Play Rock Paper Scissors to see who gets to create the first line. Compose one line of lyric and melody at a time and trade off responding to the line that was just created. Remember, staying on theme lyrically and utilizing productive repetition melodically will help this activity go smoother!

Person 1: Creates an opening line of melody with lyrics.
Person 2: Responds by singing line 1 and then creating line 2 (melody and lyric) in response to line 1.

Person 1: Sings lines 1 and 2 and then creates line 3 in response.
Person 2: Sings lines 1-3 and responds by creating line 4.
(continue for longer song section, or move on to next song section)

Homework Challenge:

What Do You Want? Every morning for five days in a row, spend five to ten minutes journaling about what you really want. Don't think of it as goal setting. Sit in silence. Listen. Dream. What do you *really* want? On day six, write a reflection on what you learned from your five-day "want quest." On day seven, rest.

Biographical Song Map: Choose a historical figure and create a song map based on their story. The song can tell as little or as much of this person's story as you choose. The song map should have three verses and a title contained in the chorus or refrain line that resonates with the big idea. Also, identify a central emotion. For example:

Song Map: Song about Judas Iscariot
Verse 1: He was called and had the opportunity to know the son of God
Verse 2: He cared more about the money than the sacrifice when the perfume was poured out
Verse 3: He threw his life away for 30 pieces of silver
Chorus/Refrain: He had everything but chose the lesser things
Title: "Lesser Things"
Central Emotion: Regret

Song Challenge:

Emotional Justice: Write a song about something you've never personally experienced, but do it emotional justice. Do the research, conduct interviews, and take the time to find the emotional connection. Make sure you define your big idea and central emotion before you get in too deep. Don't be preachy.

Co-Writing: Take a song idea that's been sitting on the shelf for a long time and ask someone to finish it with you in a co-write. WARNING: Don't present the idea unless you're truly ready to work with someone who might change it. Choose your co-writer carefully. Before you reach out to a potential co-writer, think about what the song is about and which of your songwriter friends could really speak into the emotional center of the song.

CHAPTER 16

Solitaire

Self-Editing

"Creative criticism is the Spirit's continual response to its own creation." Dorothy L. Sayers

WARNING: Do not consult this chapter *before* you begin writing a new song.

Writing this book was like learning to write all over again. Writing a song, that's one thing. But writing a book? I would repeatedly type a paragraph, delete it, write another paragraph, and rewrite it. Constantly rewording and undoing only to end up right back where I started. It took me a while to learn that writing a book is like writing a song. Your writer and your editor can't be present at the same time, or everything you put down on the page feels overworked and uninspired, and it's hard to make progress. Seasoned songwriters will tell you that you must first "write fearlessly" before you can "edit mercilessly." We are not trying to edit while we write.

My student Ava once said, "My creative flow stops when I have to think about it," and she's absolutely right. When we first begin a song, we are writing with love. We start by tapping into the emotion, the spark of creativity, and the joy of impulsivity, making sure not to overthink. At some point, we must turn the corner and take the next step toward polishing our rock once it's been removed from the tumbler. But how do we go forward into editing and still approach songwriting with a sense of play, joy, and love?

My firstborn is a natural artist. I could tell from the time she was very small that she saw the world in a unique way. She was passionate about expressing that insight through visual art. The first time she was old enough to truly appreciate a Christmas tree for what it was, she was so overcome with emotion that she ran to her room to finger paint one on paper. She felt compelled to capture and process her emotions through the creative act. I wanted to foster her passion for visual art early on, but she was too young for private lessons or formal training. So I found a book on art fundamentals for children, and we started an "art club" with her little brother and two neighbor girls. We bought a whole lot of fancy markers and drawing paper, and I did the best I could while teaching from the book. I have very little talent as a visual artist, but it was fun to give it a try.

The book I used to guide our homemade art class had many helpful principles, but there's one in particular that stuck with me forever. It's an important principle because it applies not only to how we interact with visual art but also to anything we might create. The lesson was this: When evaluating something we've created, even if it's still a work in progress, we should avoid making value judgments like "it is good" or "it is bad." Instead, our language, our framing thoughts, should be "I like it" or "I don't like it." This shift has monumental consequences for how we continue to interact with our work.

We touched on this in Chapter 1, but I want to revisit it. If you label something as bad, you might be tempted to crumple it up, throw it away, and never touch it again. Instead, as we edit, we will work on identifying parts of our songs we don't like and make changes accordingly. If you have a tendency to label your first drafts as good, you might quit the work too soon because you've reached a point that's good *enough*. It's more helpful to identify the parts of your song you like and try to elevate all other parts to that same level of enthusiasm. "Give up" or "settle" become our default options when we use words like *bad* or *good* as we edit. I don't like those options.

If we shift to saying "I like it" or "I don't like it," we give the work the space it needs to grow. We also acknowledge that imposing a moral absolute, such as good or bad, on a developing piece of art puts a lot of pressure on it, and it's probably not ready for that. "I like it" shows that we've stumbled upon something that resonates and helps us see where our ideas are starting to connect. "I don't like it" allows us to keep engaging with the work in a healthy way. We can shift our expectations of what we thought the work should be, and help it become something else. We can even phone a friend for a fresh perspective.

I want to help you adjust your mindset of what quality editing is all about. What we aren't doing is just looking for what's "wrong" with a song. When you approach editing as a means to elevate, you are not being unloving to the writer who wrote the first draft of the song (that's you). You commend your former self and say, "Excellent first attempt, a lot of great stuff to work with here!" And then you decide to wrestle and play with the material to take it to the next level.

You Are the Writer

You are the writer of your songs. You are the artist. You are the creator. You are the vessel bringing something out of nothing. Since this song is your creation, no one is forcing you to change anything. (Unless you have a publishing deal, and if so, you must deal with that particular blessing and curse!) I want to assert that ultimately, no one can tell you there's something "wrong" with your song, but my friend and tenured philosophy professor Dr. John R. Gilhooly suggests there is a moral axis to address before we move on.

So let this be the line in the sand: When thinking about "right" and "wrong" in your songs, you can only be wrong if you are asserting lies, encouraging despair or hate, or advocating for chaos. I believe these things are wrong in life *and* in art, and I try to call them out if I see them. A deeper discussion of what makes something right or wrong, good or bad in art is, again, beyond the scope of this book. So, unless you're creating with evil intentions, there's nothing inherently wrong with the first draft of a song.

There isn't any objective standard by which we measure songs. We know it's wrong to assert that 2+3=6, so we would need to fix that equation because the rules were broken. But if we choose to use a consonance rhyme instead of a family rhyme in our verse? No one can say that's the wrong choice. However, there are choices that might not work as well as others. Listeners can also assert what they like and don't like, and we would be foolish not to acknowledge it. We can find help in the best practices of the songwriters who have gone before us to discover the things listeners tend to resonate with. There may not be anything *wrong* with your song, but there could be subjectively better choices. You'll never know until you try them out.

Since we don't have rules, we can sometimes feel lost when refining and elevating our first draft. Maybe you're a songwriter who doesn't have a community of other writers to give you quality feedback. This chapter is called Solitaire because I want you to see it as a tool for self-editing. Once you've taken a step back from your initial burst of creation and let the dust settle on draft one, think of these as your go-to pages when revisiting the content we've covered in this book. When I work with students and colleagues to help them with their songs, what follows is my mental checklist of editing topics.

I have broken them down into two categories: micro and macro issues. Micro issues involve simpler edits that take just a little bit of wrestling to refine. Macro issues might compel the songwriter to rewrite big portions of the song by reworking entire sections of melody, lyrics, or harmony. This list is by no means exhaustive, but it will give you a good place to start if you're editing alone. It's also a helpful reference if you're trying to give a friend specific and quality feedback. Let's start with the micro list.

Micro Issues

1. **Playdough Monstering:** One of the first things I try to do when editing is "playdough monster" existing pieces. This can range from reordering the lines of the verses to rearranging entire song sections. When reordering individual lyric lines within a song section, it usually works best to place lines with tactile details at the top and move down toward lyrics with more emotionally charged ideas. The "weightiest" content line should be the last.

   If you're considering moving entire sections around, sometimes the edit can be simple (for example, your bridge should be your chorus, so swap them), but other times it can be more complex (like verse one really needs to be verse two, so now you have to write an entirely new verse one). Playdough monstering in editing can also mean shortening or lengthening lines or sections. Try not to see things as set in stone and be open to what *could* be there.

2. **Lyrics Outside of the Big Idea:** Check your lyrics line by line to make sure everything is reinforcing the big idea. This is a micro issue if it's just one song section, a line or two, or a few words that are off-theme. It can become a macro issue if many of the lyrics are off-topic.

3. **Rhyme Scheme Inconsistency:** Listeners find comfort in a consistent rhyme scheme and will expect it to stay the same within song sections, whether they realize it or not. For example, if verse 1 has an ABAB rhyme scheme, listeners will anticipate ABAB in subsequent verses. However, this *doesn't* mean you have to adhere to ABAB throughout all song sections. There are exceptions to this guideline. If you don't follow this guideline, just do it intentionally, not out of neglect.

4. **Cliché Rhymes and Phrases:** Did you hear any of your rhyming words coming from a mile away? If any of your rhymes or phrases feel predictable, cheesy, or too easy, go back and try to say the same thing in a more original way. Dig deeper and don't settle for a line that's just "good enough."

5. **Mis-set Lyrics:** Sing or speak through your lyric with a metronome to check if any unimportant words or unstressed syllables land on strong beats (1 & 3 in 4/4 time; 1 & 4 in 6/8). If you find an issue, move words around or play with phrasing so that the most important words fall on the most important beats.

6. **Phrasing:** Conduct a phrasing inventory of your entire song. Label each line as "early," "on time," or "late" based on where the melody begins in relation to the downbeat. If all of your song sections have the same phrasing, consider modifying the phrasing of a few lines or entire sections for more variety. Think about the emotion of the lyric and choose phrasing that complements that emotion.

7. **Lyrical "Trimming":** Evaluate your lyrics and identify where you can trim lines down to the heart of what you want to say. Don't say something with seven syllables when five would suffice. Try to cut out unnecessary words clogging up your lyric. When in doubt, say less. Example:

   "I went out on the Golden Gate Bridge" could be trimmed to *"Went out on the Golden Gate Bridge."* Trim more to get *"Out on the Golden Gate Bridge"* or even *"On the Golden Gate Bridge."*

   Feeling extreme? You could even trim it to *"On the Golden Gate."*
   All of these lines essentially mean the same thing. Choose the syllable count that best serves the melodic rhythm, and if that's open-ended, usually a shorter line is better.

8. **Point of View Problems:** Confirm your lyrics have a consistent point of view. Then try on the other POVs you didn't use to see if a different one works better. To recap, our primary points of view are direct address (you and I), first person (I no you), second person (you no I), and third person (no I, no you, just he/she/they).

9. **Title and Title Placement:** Is your title serving the song? Is it distinct and featured in a prominent or memorable place in your lyric? Could someone easily guess the title of your song? If not, consider choosing a different title, placing it in a more obvious spot in your lyric, or how you could repeat the title more times. You could try reinforcing it at the end of a verse, or putting it at the top *and* bottom of the chorus. Or perhaps you could add a post-chorus section. Make sure the title is doing its job of being easy to find and properly representing the big idea.

10. **"Spotlight" Line Check:** How powerful is the opening line of your song? Does it grab your listener's attention and make them want to keep listening? What about the opening and closing lines of your chorus? And the last line of your bridge? Make sure you're not wasting any words in what Pat Pattison would call the "spotlight" lyrical spots. These are typically important emotional moments.

11. **Melody Lacking "Sparkle":** If there are places in your melody that seem forgettable or bland, try adding a "sparkle" note on an important word to add interest. Sometimes all it takes is an unexpected interval jump or an accidental to give a dull melody new life.

12. **Melodic Rhythm Is a Bit "Basic":** Try speaking your lyrics in time to see if they're fun to say, not just sing. If the rhythm of your words feels basic, try modifying it so that the words begin to dance. Find a rhythm that helps you feel them in your body. Regardless of the content of the lyric, you should be able to find some delight or interest in the way your lyrics feel when you speak them.

13. **Melodic Contour Burnout:** Take inventory of your melodic shapes in each song section. Draw them out section by section on a piece of paper (not staff paper, just squiggly lines on a blank piece of paper will do). If you're overusing one melody shape and totally neglecting others, take note. Try changing some of the melodic shapes to increase variety and help differentiate your song sections.

14. **Landing the Plane:** Check your melody to see if there are any spots where you struggle to "land the plane." For many, this usually happens at the end of the chorus. Remember when my friend Jonathan told me to ask the question "WWTD" for "What would Taylor (Swift) do"? We had a good laugh, but it was actually helpful advice. Look to other writers with songs that have similar melodic sensibilities and observe how they "landed the plane." What was the contour and rhythm that helped them round out that section? Try on lots of "landing" options.

15. **Chord Changes:** Strive for balance to use chord changes effectively. If the chord changes start to feel too repetitive, try some basic diatonic substitutions in key spots. Sometimes, instead of changing the chords, the easier solution is to eliminate some chords altogether. In this case, we can allow some chords to stretch two bars instead of one, or allow some harmonic resolutions to happen less frequently.

    On the flip side, some measure of repetition of chords within song sections is necessary. Remember that your listeners like patterns. If too much chordal variation is the problem, find a progression that works with your melody and repeat it until you feel like you've heard it too much.

16. **Additional Environmental Issues:** Consider spots where the harmony is not aligning with the melody. Listen to check if all the harmony you have chosen supports your melody line and the mood of your lyric. Be aware of when harmonic choices seem to be a mismatch for other parts of the "tree." For example, if your melody and lyrics are intentionally leaning toward a specific genre, there might be some implications for your harmonic choices. A song that you're trying to craft for a country space might not benefit from jazz chord voicings. Lastly, remember that your chord choices should not be the driving force behind your song. Don't sacrifice a beautiful melody by refusing to adjust your harmony.

17. **Kick the Tires:** Don't forget to go to the foundation of your song and question if you've made the best choices for your key, time signature, and tempo. Shifting key and tempo can be micro edits that make a huge difference in how your song feels. Changing the time signature is a more dramatic shift, but I've seen it done a few times where it really paid off.

That Audience Engagement Scale Again

Let's take a brief break from issues to remind ourselves why we do this. Often, the difference between audience engagement going from "interested" to "obsessed" is found in the compositional details. It could be ensuring all song form elements work together for peak momentum. It could be adjusting that one note in the melody that prevents it from being truly memorable. Sometimes, it's about choosing the best word for a lyric line.

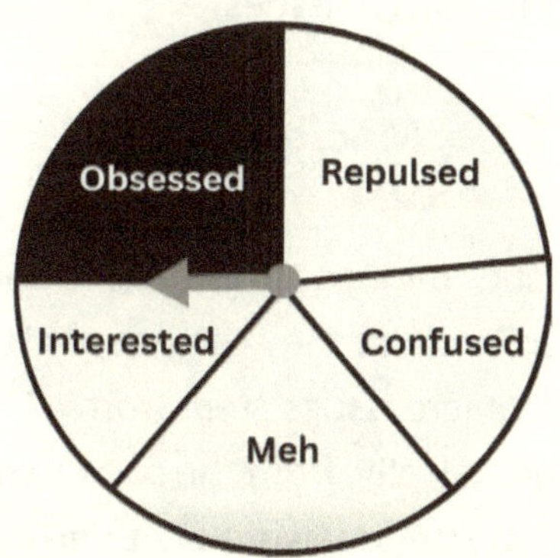

Can one word really make a difference? In verse 2 of the Miley Cyrus song "Flowers," it matters that the singer painted her nails *cherry* red. The writer could have chosen bloody red or firetruck red, but cherries are bright, fun, and happy. Bloody colors suggest revenge. Fire trucks scream emergency. The big idea of this song is about finding joy in loving yourself, not about taking bitter revenge or averting a crisis. The point is that every word matters because words are tied up with emotions and meanings.

We often carefully consider compositional details when recording and producing a song. We edit the breaths out of every vocal take and endlessly adjust the EQ on the guitar. We listen to mix after mix, modifying the sonic landscape because we're secretly hoping for an obsessed listener who will pore over the details. But we often forget this attention to detail in our songwriting after completing our first draft.

The details are where beauty and mastery are found. Commit to having the same mindset when revising your songs as you do when you're analyzing a recording or a mix. Take the time to consider what could be better. Are you giving your listeners a lyric and a melody to be obsessed with? Or are you settling for sufficient? Remember, sufficient is not delicious, and we want a flavor that lingers. So we commit to editing the "micro" issues and take the time to tweak individual words, notes, lines, and chords. But sometimes the editing is more holistic and comprehensive. Becoming an effective editor is also summoning the commitment and bravery to deal with "macro" issues.

Macro Issues

The following macro issues might seem similar to some of the micro issues we've already discussed because they can be small things that compound on one another. Often, macro issues stem from a lack of clarity in the big idea, both musically and lyrically, from the song's conception. Sometimes these issues arise when we are unaware of our go-to writing habits. Other times, we have several strong ideas fighting one another instead of working together. Check in with this list if you feel like your song has larger problems that may need a complete "overhaul."

1. **Playdough Monstering Aftermath:** Sometimes, playdough monstering forces us to consider that we might be missing a song section that still needs to be written. You might realize you're missing something even without playdough monstering. Writing new song sections from scratch can feel daunting, but it's one of the more

enjoyable macro issues to resolve. It's always better to write more than you may need.

2. **More than One Rock:** Sometimes you've got two big ideas trying to take control of one song. It might be two great melodic ideas that just aren't working together, but it's often two great song sections that don't belong in the same song. Whatever you do, just don't delete great ideas and lose them forever. Untangle them and separate them into two (or more) different songs.

3. **Lack of Clarity on the "Big Idea":** One of the most significant macro issues is the lack of clarity in the big idea. I often ask students to define what the song is about before we begin editing. The problematic big idea might not be original or well-defined enough, or it might need more support through musical and lyrical choices. If you can't sum up your song's big idea in one definitive phrase or short sentence, you've got major work to do. Redefining or clarifying your big idea may require extensive lyric rewrites. This also applies to melodic big ideas. If you don't have any memorable melodic motifs, you may be doing a lot of melody rewriting.

4. **Too Much Telling**: This is especially true for lyrics. Scan your lyrics to see if there are any places you can show instead of tell. Achieve more showing through vivid specificity, engaging your senses, and using strong nouns and verbs. More showing typically leads to greater emotional impact.

5. **Drab Harmony:** Usually, harmony issues are micro issues, but if you really dislike all your chords, it's time to strip them back to the most basic ones you hear in your head, then rebuild. Try substitutions. Try borrowing from neighbor keys. Or you can phone a friend. If you ask for collaborative help with your chord changes, present your co-writer with the melody and lyrics, but don't tell them the original chords.

6. **Out-of-Time:** Out-of-time edits are needed when things don't seem to be lining up right between the music and the lyrics. You might find

you've changed time signatures or added or dropped bars along the way. If something feels off, sit down with your worktape and a metronome, and just count. Identify where the downbeats are and how long each chord is held. If something feels off, then adjust to reach more predictable song section lengths, such as four, eight, or sixteen bars. Irregularities in timing are not necessarily bad, so only tackle this edit if something truly *feels* off. If you're new to playing instruments, you may have a hard time catching out-of-time issues. There's nothing wrong with asking for help from a more experienced player. Just don't give up.

7. **Melodic Hook Lacking Memorability**: Lack of hookiness or memorability should probably be the number one macro issue if you're being serious about the "priority tiers." If melody is king, its reign will be short-lived if your melody is bland, forgettable, or uninspired. Remember, this isn't just about pitches; it's hugely important to consider your melodic rhythm. Sometimes our melodies lack a musical hook because we've been composing them as an afterthought, focusing primarily on the words on paper rather than the sung lyrics. What do you do? Leave your song for a day or two. Can you remember the melody? Sing the hookiest part of your song to someone a few times. Can they sing it back to you? Keep working on the melody until you love it, because if you don't, then other people might not care to remember it.

8. **When Is the Now:** If you don't have a clearly defined "now" in your song, it can lead to macro issues of narrative confusion. Sometimes this can be resolved easily by bringing the song into a consistent past, present, or future tense. However, it's often a more complicated problem to untangle. Don't forget to be sure when now is (physically, mentally, and emotionally) for the singer. There should only be one now.

9. **Song Form Overhaul:** Sometimes, the song form we've chosen just isn't working. You might lack the momentum you want, or feel like the song isn't highlighting the important things. A song form overhaul can be a micro issue if we're playdough monstering by swapping song

sections or making cuts to emphasize the best parts. But sometimes it can be a macro issue if we're questioning our form altogether. Do we really have a refrain line instead of a chorus? Maybe we should try an AABA verse-refrain form instead of a verse-chorus structure. A song form overhaul can be an interesting exercise, even if you don't make the jump to a new form in the end. Anything that opens your mind to more possibilities will expand your versatility as a songwriter.

10. **Same/Same/Same**: Pushing back against the same/same/same problem means being aware of the musical/lyrical choices you are making from one song section to the next. Songs tend to drag when the line length, number of lines, rhyme scheme, melodic rhythm, melodic contour, phrasing, and/or chord patterns stay consistent throughout the entire song. More variety among these elements from one song section to the next will help. Consider: Is it clear by ear where the verse ends and the chorus begins? Think of your song as a listening experience *without* looking at it on paper.

11. **Nothing Else Is as Good as THAT:** You have one song section that's killer and all the other sections are "meh." You need to keep writing. Don't settle for good enough. Continue to elevate the other sections that you don't like as much as the section you do like. Or rewrite the "meh" sections from scratch.

Abstract Macro Issues

As we journey forward into more macro editing topics, we're getting increasingly abstract and subjective. The lines between "what's working" and "what's not working" are highly dependent on your listeners and you. Nevertheless, these are important questions to ask as you evaluate your song during the editing process.

12. **Balance:** Have you achieved a balance in the middle of the rope between universal and specific, repetition and variation, as well as unity and diversity? Too much of one side can make the song feel bland, boring, and

inauthentic. Too much of the other side might make it seem unrelatable, confusing, or unmemorable. If any of these words come to mind when you think about your song, you might have a balance problem.

13. **Originality**: Originality is in the *ear* of the beholder because everyone has been exposed to different music and experiences. What seems original to me may seem overdone or derivative to you. Ask yourself if you've approached a universal theme from a unique or original angle. For example, Billie Eilish's song "Ocean Eyes" has a title that offers a unique metaphor. The title, apart from her unique vocal delivery, is the most original element in the song. Sometimes, that's all it takes—just one original idea.

    But originality isn't just about lyrics. My student Clay decided to write a song inspired by Mary's Magnificat from Luke Chapter 1. Plenty of songs have been written from this text, but his version was a funk arrangement. A funk Magnificat was an original idea. Every song you write shouldn't aim to reinvent the wheel, but it *should* try to offer us an approach to a word, sound, or story from your unique viewpoint.

14. **Emotional Impact:** Does your song make you feel something? Identify the core emotion you're after and assess if you've captured it. Emotional impact can be hard to judge when you're editing on your own. At the end of this chapter, I'll give you some more tips on how to gauge emotional impact.

15. **Emotional Justice:** Does your song feel authentic? Is it art or is it a means to an end? Consider if you are sharing yourself or who you think other people want you to be. Perhaps you are only sharing partial truths because the real truth feels too scary. If your song is inspired by events outside of your own life, make sure you have done the topic emotional justice by doing the research and attending to the story with depth and care without being preachy.

16. Synergy/Prosody: When I was studying at Berklee College of Music, we were taught the term *prosody* to represent moments when the music and lyrics of a song are working together. We were not using it in its formal poetic definition. Prosody, for us, was about the alignment of song pieces, making the song's meaning stronger. Since using the term *prosody* seems to confuse people who are also students of language and poetry, I'm going to opt for the term *synergy* instead. *Synergy* is defined as "the interaction or cooperation of two or more organizations, substances, or other agents to produce a combined effect greater than the sum of their separate effects." When Josh Groban sings the words "you raise me up" as the melodic shape of the line ascends—this is synergy. When Aretha Franklin repeats "chain chain chain, chain of fools," we see the links of the chain being built as she sings them with productive repetition—this is synergy. But this isn't just about how melody and lyrics align. It is every part of your song working together to reinforce the big idea. Are you making intentional, synergetic choices?

When Is It Done?

You might wonder, "If I keep editing and trying to improve it, how will I ever know when a song is finished?" I learned this helpful tip from songwriter Michael Farren. He says he usually finds peace about a song being "done" when he realizes that he has crossed the line from making the song better to just making it different. This is a difficult concept to quantify. How can we tell if we're actually improving the song or just making it different?

There are a few tools you can use to help you gauge your progress. The first and easiest method is capturing your progress consistently. When I create edits of songs, I keep a record of each version, especially if the song is a cowrite. I create a digital document, like a Google Doc, and a voice memo worktape for every version of the song when it reaches a stopping point. Saving the original version along with the updated edits will help you make the most of one of your most important songwriting tools: time.

We don't want to fall out of love with our songs by editing them so much that they no longer resemble what initially drew us in. Sometimes, we just need time. Try making an edit, record it, and then let it sit for a few days. When enough time has passed, try to remember. Do you recall the edits or the original version? What melody do you keep coming back to? What words are still stuck in your head? What piece of the song feels most important? Re-listening to worktapes after giving them time can bring incredible clarity about what works and what doesn't. But time might not always be on your side if you have a tight production deadline, a pitch, or an assignment. So where can you turn if you don't have the luxury of time? Other listeners.

I encourage you not to start with professional editors. Turning to songwriting contests, publishers, or pro producers isn't the best way to get initial quality feedback. The most helpful feedback comes from peers. Try to find other songwriters who have roughly the same amount of experience. Share songs with each other and give honest, constructive criticism. In his book *Originals*, Adam Grant points out that when it comes to judging creative work, "There is one group of forecasters that comes close to attaining mastery: fellow creators evaluating one another's ideas." Where can you find fellow creators? Attend open mic nights, join online groups, or start your own group. You need peers to grow in this craft.

If you don't have a song circle or peer songwriters yet, you still have music listeners all around you. You have your roommate, your coworker, your boyfriend, your best friend, or your barista (okay, probably not your barista unless you have a really great relationship with them). Sharing a song in process with one of these casual listeners means you need to ask them the right questions. Most supportive people in your life will be happy to listen, but you'll need to ask them more than "what do you think?" They probably won't know how to tell you why they feel the way they feel about your song. Equip yourself with the following list of questions for the casual listener to gather helpful critique:

- *What part of the song do you remember the most?*
- *Did any lyric really grab your attention?*
- *Can you sing your favorite part of the song back to me?*
- *Was there a moment in the song where you lost interest and it felt too long?*
- *Was there a part of the lyric that lost or confused you?*
- *What do you think was the message or emotion that I was trying to communicate?*
- *Did you know which part was the chorus/refrain?*
- *Can you guess what the title is?*

Asking your listener to be specific about what was memorable, distracting, exciting, or boring will give you a good clue where your song excels and where it needs improvement. Asking them about the central message and emotion will help you to discover whether they are emotionally connecting with your song. If they didn't understand your message, but it still made them feel something, ask them to describe that feeling. Is it the one you were going for? This kind of feedback may help you realize that the song is actually going somewhere else emotionally, and you might choose to follow that new direction.

Throw It in the Crockpot

My friend Bonnie once said that if she's wrestling with a song for a while and it still doesn't feel right, she "throws it in the crockpot." Some songs are "frying pan" songs. They cook up quickly, and just like that, they're done. But some songs take time. They need a slow simmer in the back of our minds for a while before they can become what they're supposed to be. If a song keeps fighting you during the writing or editing, just throw it in the crockpot and let it cook for a while. Calling it done too early might just make you sick!

When you decide to pull a crockpot song back out to play with, make sure you're genuinely having fun with it. If you're still fighting it after a few minutes, it might need to go back into the crockpot. Usually, I don't take a song out until it calls to me—the timer in my mind starts ringing while I'm in the shower or on a drive. All of a sudden, the missing ingredient that's been holding the song back will reveal itself. My heart and mind needed the space to realize that the pre-chorus is really the bridge, or the tempo is too fast, or the chorus melody needs more repetition. Ding ding ding! Be sure to answer when the crockpot calls.

You are the only one who has the power to allow your songs to grow and change. It requires maturity and humility as a songwriter to acknowledge that most of our songs aren't finished after the first draft. It's natural to feel excitement, even love, for the first draft of a song. We should always be a little obsessed with a new creation! But it's an even greater act of love to let our songs be tested, refined, and improved. Those who never submit to informed feedback and critique cannot grow in a healthy way.

Proverbs 15:31–32 tells us that "If you listen to constructive criticism, you will be at home among the wise. If you reject discipline, you only harm yourself..." (NLT). Again, you don't have to implement all the edits you try or the feedback you receive. You simply have to be mature enough to genuinely consider constructive criticism. Be brave enough to push yourself to find new paths and not settle—you may be surprised that your song could be even better than you first imagined.

PLAYTIME

Solo Activities:

A New Song Form: Select one of your completed or in-process songs that uses the verse-chorus song form. Then, try to reimagine a new version of this song that is in AABA verse-refrain song form. In this form, you will have three verses that either end or begin with an identical refrain line with a contrasting B section. The refrain line should attempt to accomplish what your previous chorus was doing functionally. This activity may be difficult, and it may not work, but it will stretch you if you try.

Nothing Else Is as Good as THAT: Look through your catalog of completed songs. Find one that is overall "meh" but has one brilliant section. Preserve the brilliant section and either elevate the other sections or rewrite them from scratch. Once you've completed a new version, ask yourself: "Do I like the new version of the song better?"

Group Activities:

Partner Feedback: Break up into pairs, and have each pair do a song swap. After partner one presents their song, partner two will give detailed, constructive feedback. Use the lists in this chapter as a guide for feedback. Then partner two will present their song, and partner one will give detailed feedback. After this round, swap partners so that everyone in the group has a new partner and repeat the song swap.

Group Discussion: Have a group discussion about the micro and macro editing lists. Do any of the topics stand out as the most important to the writers in the group? Which ones do they personally think they will reference and struggle with the most? Are there any topics they don't understand? For the most abstract macro topics, ask the group members to come up with examples of songs that they feel achieve the pursuit of balance, originality, emotional impact, emotional justice, and synergy. Ask them to defend their position on how each song meets one of these ideals.

Homework Challenge:

Feedback Part 1: Write a complete first draft of a new song. Reach out to a peer songwriter or other careful listeners for honest, constructive feedback. Make sure to record the feedback you receive so you can work with it later. Before you start editing, take a moment to reflect in your journal. Explore how you emotionally responded to the feedback. Affirm your willingness to make changes in specific areas and identify the elements you are open to editing. This affirmation not only solidifies your artistic intentions but also provides clarity for the reworking process.

Feedback Part 2: After evaluating the feedback and confirming your creative choices, take a leap of faith. Dive into the process of editing your song, applying the insights gained through feedback. Embrace this challenge as an opportunity to grow, allowing your songwriting to evolve and flourish based on the collaborative exchange of ideas. Once you've completed your edits, compare both versions of the song side by side and write another brief reflection. Was there wisdom in receiving the feedback and trying it out? Do you like your song better now that you've edited with listener feedback? Do you think further feedback from another listener would benefit the song?

Song Challenge:

Crockpot Song: Search through your old songs to find something that's been simmering in the crockpot for a while. Before you begin your edit, make sure the big idea has been clearly defined. If you can remember, play through it as it was originally written two to three times in a row. Are any melodies no longer working for you? Do any of the lyrics feel off topic? Can you feel where the song lacks momentum? If you now understand what to edit, take the song out of the crockpot and get to work. Still feeling stuck? Back in the crockpot it goes.

Bowl an Emotional Split: Write a song about a time or experience in your life when you had to hold two conflicting emotions at the same time. Balancing two foundational emotions in one song is difficult, so make sure you ground the experience in vivid details. If you need more direction, think of a time when you were excited about a new season of life, but conflicted to leave old things behind. The challenge of this song will be to convey the big idea clearly and to determine what you want your listeners to take away. For an example, check out "Anyone Who Had a Heart" by Dionne Warwick, where the singer holds the emotions of devoted love, sadness, and hopelessness all at the same time.

EPILOGUE

Growing Up

On Writing with Love

"Love, not answers." Madeleine L'Engle

At the time of this writing, my firstborn child is almost 14 years old. She came into this world nearly three weeks early, and she's been keeping us on our toes ever since. In the summer, she sleeps past noon and makes rice for brunch. She uses the word *genuinely* a little too much. She is passionate about art, music, volleyball, her friends, and everything she loves. Often, she is brilliant, but sometimes her train of thought wanders. Occasionally, she is in a MOOD all of a sudden. She is growing and changing, and while we can't control her, we *can* help her grow up in love.

There are times I think of my songs like passionate teenagers. I know, I know, at the very beginning of this book I wrote that songs are playdough monsters, not precious babies. What changed? How can I now say that they can be passionate teenagers? Why in the world would a playdough monster need to be treated with love? Aren't we supposed to smash it and bash it? Slice it and dice it? Twist and dismember all in the name of healthy songwriting play?

In the beginning, I do think we should treat our creations and the creative process with fun, delight, and jumbled wonder. But at some point, we do turn a corner. This doesn't mean that our playdough monster of a song becomes a precious baby. Nor does it become an extension of ourselves. Instead, somewhere in the creative sandbox, our playdough monster starts to grow up. The song begins to develop a unique identity that holds value. It has moved beyond the point where we should smash it and start over. It's like a passionate teenager, one we must help to grow with love. We should start to have a little more tenderness when we have real art in our hands.

I get it. This is quite a metaphoric jump from modeling clay to middle schooler. Just trust me and I'll help you get there.

Passionate Teenagers

Thinking of your creations as passionate teenagers is the best metaphor I've come up with for raising songs with love. Some of you reading this may not be parents, but you've probably experienced a teenager in the wild, so I think you can follow. My real-life teenager is fully mine in the sense that her very DNA was pieced together from my own and my husband's, but she is still a completely separate creation. Her body, her being, literally came from my body, yet she has a life and identity all of her own.

It is my job to steward her as a creation I have been entrusted to help grow. We tried violin lessons. I took her to volleyball practice. She tried out the debate club. She once said she wanted to be an electrical engineer. Recently, she's been into musicals. I have hopes and dreams for her, but my greatest ambition for her is that she would discover her gifting and walk in it, no matter what it may be.

In *Walking in this World*, Julia Cameron says, "If you overplot a piece of work first, trying to dictate its shape, you can run into the same problem a parent might have deciding at a child's birth that he should be a mathematician, doctor, lawyer or opera singer—the child may not agree." So the first step in writing with love is being open to possibilities. It's beginning the work of writing a song with wonder, delight, and play. Give it some options. Try on lots of different things. And when your song begins to stand on its own two feet and talk back, treat it with tenderness and take it seriously. It takes practice, patience, and wisdom to help it grow.

What does this look like in practice? My daughter needs me to provide her basic needs, and my songs have basic needs of strong melody, thoughtful lyrics, and suitable harmony. If either my daughter or my songs feels overwhelmed, I need to recognize when to let them rest for a while. Sometimes my daughter needs space; so do my songs. Both need time, and they also need correction. Often, my daughter needs other people to speak into her life. Daughters need mentors, and some songs may need a co-writer, an editor, or an arranger.

In the end, my daughter has to decide who she's going to be. Let your songs do the same. Don't approach them with an endgame agenda. See where they go. You have to take your hands off if the chorus melody starts to soar into something else. Your song's big idea may become clearer, and you have to sacrifice to rework all the verses. Your song might be a dance pop song and not the folksy ballad you'd hoped for. It's not easy to let go of something you love, but it's worth it to let your teenager and your song thrive. Real love is hard work.

My philosopher in residence, Dr. John R. Gilhooly, pushed back on this metaphor of "songs as teenagers" because of free will. He rightly pointed out that songs, unlike teenagers, do not have souls, and so they cannot possess free will. He struggles to understand artists when we talk about the creation "speaking back" to us. Instead of trying to explain a mystery that is far too deep for me to fully comprehend, I'll simply say that I *have* felt songs "speak back" to me. (Perhaps it is the creative spirit within me that is speaking, but I hear it, nonetheless.) I have even observed songs take on a "free will" of sorts to become things beyond what their writers could have ever planned or dreamed.

I think of the song "Good Riddance (Time of Your Life)" written by Billie Joe Armstrong of Green Day. Armstrong wrote this song about a girlfriend who moved away, but the song seemed to have its own agenda. It wasn't a breakup song. The song became a cultural phenomenon and a staple of high school proms, eventually being named by Billboard as one of the "20 Best Graduation Songs of the Past 20 Years (1995-2015)." Some songs have the power to assert a will and go beyond the writer to become something more. It takes love to accept what your song wants to be because it might run away from you, whether you like it or not!

Writing with Love

As someone who creates, I want to make those things in and through love. I'm not talking about squishy feelings and cartoon flowers. I'm talking about *real* love—love that is active yet patient, tender yet enduring. Much like a relationship, writing songs this way isn't always going to be happy, cheerful, and easy. But it's not real love if you aren't willing to risk getting hurt and work through it.

I got the phrase "writing with love" from Dorothy L. Sayers. Sayers was an English novelist and playwright who wrote *The Mind of the Maker,* a book that dramatically impacted how I think about art. She believes that "the business of the creator is not to escape from his material medium or to bully it, but to serve it; but to serve it, he must love it. If he does so, he will realize that its service is perfect freedom."

When we neglect to write with love, we risk being lured into the traps of the ego, which may lead to writing with fear. When fear leads our creativity, we overthink. We censor. We begin to worry about how the song will be perceived by others, so we put on false selves that we hope will better please a crowd. We get sidetracked by how others will respond to our art before it is even completed. We try to control things too much when we are afraid. Fear dominates, but love serves. Sayers goes on to say, "...the only way of 'mastering' one's material is to abandon the whole conception of mastery and to cooperate with it in love: whosoever will be a lord of life, let him be its servant. If he tries to wrest life out of its true nature, it will revenge itself in judgment, as the work revenges itself upon the domineering artist."

We don't want to write out of fear, dominating our creations into shallow songs that are pretenders, shadow puppets, or cheap hits. They might retaliate and exact their revenge on us. They won't have staying power, fulfill us as creators, or lead to freedom. But fear isn't the only nemesis to writing with love. We could also be writing out of self-indulgence or indifference.

If we are writing from a place of inwardness and apathy to the outside world, our songs may reveal a lack of character. Songs written this way may be tempted to spiral toward untruths, nihilism, selfishness, obsession, or chaos. If we are *posturing* in our songwriting, we are asking people to fall in love with a charlatan. If we are *hopeless* in our songwriting, we shouldn't be surprised that no one wants a ticket to the pity party. And as much as Hollywood would try to make you believe it, people really don't want anti-heroes. There is no comfort in chaos. There is no intimacy and connection in hardened hearts. It may be *easier* to write songs that offer no vulnerability or redemption, but it's not worth it.

The more challenging but more meaningful pursuit is to write with love. To observe the world, share what you've seen and experienced, and try to make a connection by writing it down in song. You can ask difficult questions. Love is not always a warm glow; it can be a refining fire. Sayers says, "This is perhaps what we should expect when we consider that a work of creation is a work of love, and that love is the most ruthless of all the passions, sparing neither itself, nor its object, nor the obstacles that stand in its way." I hope you will choose to write with love as you grow your songs up and continue to grow yourself as an artist.

Growing Up

They say that "breaking up is hard to do," but I think growing up is even more difficult. It's about confronting the realities of life that seep in like an unrelenting rain, but also hit us monsoon-style from time to time. Writing with love isn't always just about sandcastles and finger painting; it can be painful. I have students bring in rough drafts of songs about complicated relationships with parents, lovers, or even strangers. At some point, it becomes necessary to ask hard questions during the editing process. "What is this song *really* about? Describe where you were and what the context was when you encountered these emotions. What does the metaphor in the song actually represent?"

Less than a year after her father suddenly passed away, Hallie brought a song for us to edit that was very painful for her to write. She had a good but complicated relationship with her dad. I could tell that the first draft of her song was tiptoeing around the wounds of the past, as she was not quite ready to face the reality of her feelings. So I asked Hallie some of those hard questions above and then let her decide if, when, and how she would move forward.

I never probe a fellow songwriter in an attempt to unlock trauma, but if they are unwilling to get at the heart of these kinds of songs, they may not uncover the truth. Writing with love means being vulnerable and honest. Are you willing to keep going if it gets real? Are you willing to dig in, reflect, journal, and immerse yourself in whatever tender spot your song is trying to touch? You may not be ready to go there yet, depending on the song's center. Again, it's okay to put a song away for a while and give it space and time. I'd never force a student to work on a song they're not emotionally ready to tackle.

The more you create, the more willing you will be to trust the process. In standing independent and outside of you, your song can help you process and heal. In *Writing Down the Bones,* Natalie Goldberg says, "Writing is deeper than therapy. You write through your pain, and even your suffering must be written out and let go of." Whatever you do, don't try to cover up a painful song with a shallower version of itself and call it done. Facing your pain and fears, when the time comes, is part of growing up.

Rapper to Flutist

André 3000, best known for his work in the visionary hip-hop duo Outkast, released an album in 2023 called "New Blue Sun." People had been waiting 17 years for one of the greatest rappers of his generation to release new music. But what he released was *not* what people expected. It was entirely instrumental music featuring André 3000 on flute. The first track is titled "I swear, I Really Wanted to Make a 'Rap' Album but This Is Literally The Way The Wind Blew Me This Time." The rest of the world had put André 3000 on pause, yet he continued to have an artist's journey. In an interview for NPR, he said, "I never knew that rapping would even take me to producing, and producing would take me to playing instruments, and instruments would get me here…I see this as just [being] further down the road."[4]

Discussing his writing process, he went on to say, "I'm a writer, and not necessarily a pen and pad writer, but I construct and architect verses in a way. That's what I've been doing all my life. So I look at it in that way, and if I'm not satisfied with what it is, I just don't put it out."

This is an artist letting "I like it" or "I don't like it" guide his creative output, not only for individual songs but also for who he is continually becoming as an artist. As artists, we may reach some mountaintops on our journey, but we can't stay there forever. We fall in and out of favor with the crowds and popular styles, but we never truly "arrive." An artist who has "arrived" isn't going anywhere anymore. They are not learning or growing.

A major turning point in my life as a songwriter happened through some significant conversations I had with my dad in my mid-20s. I was still trying to find my footing and establish an "artist identity." I had spent a few

4 Npr. 2023. "From Rap to Experimental Flute, How and Why Musicians Reinvent Their Sound." *NPR*, December 2, 2023. https://www.npr.org/2023/12/02/1216797522/from-rap-to-experimental-flute-how-and-why-musicians-reinvent-their-sound.

years hustling to become the artist I wanted to be—the coolest version of myself I could imagine. I wanted a loud band performing in legit venues, and I wanted to be wearing big boots and black jewelry. I wanted God to use me, but I had already created a vision of what that was supposed to look like. The problem was I never stopped to consider who I was uniquely made to be.

When I took the time to consider my history, my strengths, and my values, a lot changed. I finally understood why my songs struggled to connect emotionally with my audience. I was an artist who was hitting her head against the wall. I hadn't questioned if I was on the right path to begin with, and you have to know where you're starting before you can begin the journey to somewhere else. I read this passage from *Images & Idols* by Thomas J. Terry and J. Ryan Lister to my songwriting majors regularly:

[A] lack of an origin story for your creativity shapes you more than you can imagine. Creativity actually needs direction, which means creativity needs a starting line…Without a beginning point for our creativity, we end up lost in a wilderness of our own design. We are susceptible to every mirage the culture offers us…This haphazard itinerary often has the intersection of exhaustion and superficiality as its final destination.

If you're just now catching a vision for who you're meant to be, let me remind you that you are uniquely gifted. Creativity takes time, space, and play. Ultimately, it's living with love that lets go of a predetermined agenda. I hope that through the joyful art of songwriting, you discover both yourself *and* the world.

Play, Shape, Create

I have an unusual personality for a musician. I am more rational and less emotional. I am more practical than impulsive. I often have to force myself to slow down and listen because these things don't come naturally to me. Yet, I believe in the power of the unseen world—the magic of weaving words and melodies together. I hear things that are gifts from the air. I know that the combination of these unseen things can mean more than the sum of their parts. I am drawn to certain songs, and I have enough belief in the mystery not to need to know why they speak to me on a subconscious level.

In 2003, the band The Mars Volta released a song called "Televators," which I love. But the funny thing is, I don't know why I love it. I never did the research. I have no idea what the significance of the band's name is, nor do I understand why "Televators" is the title of the song, as this word never appears anywhere in the lyrics. It's over six minutes long, and I usually despise long songs. Every rational part of me and my preferences should have disliked this song. But I listened to the song, and I loved it. The melodies, the harmonies, the weird lyrics, the arrangement. Yearning, sad, but in a deep, dramatic way. It touched a part of me emotionally that felt significant at the time. I didn't need rational songwriting craft to convince me that it was a song that was meaningful for me.

Bathed in the blue light of my computer screen saver, I'd play it over and over late at night while I lay on my pop-up trundle in my college dorm apartment. It was the end of senior year, and "real life" was at my doorstep. Maybe this song felt like the ache of growing up and moving on? I was staring straight at the fears that came with diving into the real world. I still don't know why I loved this song, but I did, and I still do. The songwriter probably didn't have me in mind as his ideal audience when he wrote this song, but it still spoke to me on a deeper level than surface understanding.

I share this with you as evidence that you can't outthink songwriting. Use your brain, use your skill, use your tips and tricks, and be a ruthless editor, but *lead* with your heart and write with love. Sometimes love is so powerful that you can't understand how it works or why it works. Sometimes you will write a song that doesn't follow the guidelines, yet there's still love and sacred magic. There is no checklist for true songwriting greatness. There is only love and the bravery to create and grow.

If you want to write songs to be rich and famous, please find another hobby. If you want to write songs because you want to, because that desire to know yourself and the world more by making songs feels right, then you can. Just play on. Play, and then take your play and shape it. Then take what you've shaped and create art with love that means something more than yourself.

Play.
Shape.
Create.

"Our creator gives us a mandate, despite our brokenness: to create in, through, and for love." Makoto Fujimura, *Art and Faith*

Recommended Reading

Braheny, John. *The Craft and Business of Songwriting.* New York: Billboard Books, 2000.

Cameron, Julia. *The Artist's Way: A Spiritual Path to Higher Creativity.* New York: Jeremy P. Tarcher/Putnam, 1992.

Cameron, Julia. *Walking in this World: The Practical Art of Creativity.* New York: Jeremy P. Tarcher/Penguin, 2002.

Davis, Sheila. *The Craft of Lyric Writing.* Cincinnati, OH: Writer's Digest Books, 2003.

Forsyth, Mark. *The Elements of Eloquence: Secrets of the Perfect Turn of Phrase.* New York: Penguin Group, 2013.

Fujimura, Makoto. *Art & Faith: A Theology of Making.* Downers Grove, IL: InterVarsity Press, 2015.

Gauthier, Mary. *Saved by a Song: The Art and Healing Power of Songwriting.* New York: Flatiron Books, 2022.

Goldberg, Natalie. *Writing Down the Bones: Freeing the Writer Within.* Boston: Shambhala, 2000.

Grant, Adam. *Originals: How Non-Conformists Move the World.* New York: Viking, 2016.

Jordan, Barbara L. *Songwriter's Playground: How to Write Songs with Meaning and Power.* Los Angeles: Rowman & Littlefield, 2009.

Kostka, Stefan, and Dorothy Payne. *Tonal Harmony. 8th ed. New York: McGraw-Hill, 2012.*

L'Engle, Madeleine. *Walking on Water: Reflections on Faith and Art. New York: Penguin Books, 1980.*

Mills, Clay, and Bill O'Hanlon. *Mastering Melody Writing: A Guide to Writing Successful Melodies. Milwaukee, WI: Hal Leonard, 2012.*

Orrico, Mike. *Music, Lyrics, and Life: A Field Guide for the Advancing Songwriter. New York: Schirmer Trade Books, 2009.*

Pattison, Pat. *Writing Better Lyrics: The Essential Guide to Powerful Songwriting. 2nd ed. New York: Watson-Guptill, 2009.*

Perricone, Jack. *Great Songwriting Techniques. New York: Random House, 2004.*

Perricone, Jack. *Melody in Songwriting: Tools and Techniques for Writing Hit Songs. New York: Routledge, 2007.*

Rogers, Dr. Susan, and Ogi Ogas. *This is What It Sounds Like: What the Music You Love Says About You. New York: W.W. Norton & Company, 2022.*

Rubin, Rick. *The Creative Act: A Way of Being. New York: Penguin Press, 2023.*

Sayers, Dorothy L. *The Mind of the Maker. London: Methuen, 1941.*

Seabrook, John. *The Song Machine: Inside the Hit Factory. New York: W.W. Norton & Company, 2015.*

Seidman, Billy. *The Elements of Song Craft. Nashville: Writers Digest Books, 2008.*

Stolpe, Andrea. *Beginning Songwriting: Writing Your Own Lyrics, Melodies and Chords. New York: Backbeat Books, 2007.*

Terry, Thomas J., and J. Ryan Lister. *Images and Idols: Songwriting in the Modern World. Nashville: Crossway, 2014.*

Turner, Steve. *Imagine: A Vision for Christians in the Arts. Downers Grove, IL: InterVarsity Press, 2001.*

Tweedy, Jeff. *How to Write One Song: Loving the Things We Create and How They Love Us Back. New York: Dutton, 2020.*

Walker, Rob. *The Art of Noticing: 131 Ways to Spark Creativity, Find Inspiration, and Discover Joy in the Everyday. New York: Knopf, 2019.*

Williams, Dar. *How to Write a Song That Matters. New York: St. Martin's Press, 2014.*

Wright, Vinita Hampton. *The Soul Tells a Story: Engaging Creativity with Spirituality in the Writing Life. Downers Grove, IL: InterVarsity Press, 2005.*

Recommended Articles and Resources

BBC News. "How Queen's 'Bohemian Rhapsody' Became a Classic." *BBC*, October 8, 2023. https://www.bbc.com/news/entertainment-arts-67111517.amp.

Be a Better Writer. "Clichés in Writing." Accessed January 9, 2025. https://www.be-a-better-writer.com/cliches.html.

Bennett, David. "David Bennett Piano." *YouTube*. Accessed January 9, 2025. https://www.youtube.com/@DavidBennettPiano.

Classic FM. "The Structure of Queen's 'Bohemian Rhapsody.'" *Classic FM*, October 2, 2023. https://www.classicfm.com/discover-music/music-theory/queen-bohemian-rhapsody-structure/.

Cross, Alan. "Give Up on Music Genres." *Global News*, December 3, 2023. https://globalnews.ca/news/10141225/alan-cross-give-up-on-music-genres/amp/.

Hidden Brain. "The Mystery of Beauty." *Hidden Brain Podcast*. Accessed January 9, 2025. https://www.hiddenbrain.org/podcast

Lyric Studio Blog. "Why Modern Songs Don't Have Bridges Anymore." March 16, 2023. https://blog.lyricstudio.net/2023/03/16/why-modern-songs-dont-have-bridges-anymore/.

May, Brian. "Brian May Interview." *YouTube*. Accessed January 9, 2025. https://www.youtube.com/watch?v=3Ym7X_wCsPQ.

Musicgenrelist.com Musicgenrelist.com

Native Instruments. "Pop Chord Progressions." *Native Instruments Blog*. Accessed January 9, 2025. https://blog.native-instruments.com/pop-chord-progressions/.

Secrets of Songwriting. "7 Chord Progressions That Work All the Time." February 21, 2011. https://www.secretsofsongwriting.com/2011/02/21/7-chord-progressions-that-work-all-the-time/.

Skoove. "What Are Musical Modes?" *Skoove Blog.* Accessed January 9, 2025. https://www.skoove.com/blog/musical-modes/.

Songwriter Theory Podcast. "Level Up Your Melodies." November 7, 2022. Accessed January 9, 2025.

Thanks & Acknowledgements

To my family always: Clint, Jovie, Dallas, Cohen, and Juno Calhoun.

To even more of my family who have always believed in me (literally so many of you), but special thanks to my dad, mom, and brother, who have been there since my first song: Jerry, Aundrea & Cole Campbell.

To my students found here in the pages and always in my prayers: Hallie Mares Jewett (who named this book!), Leah Butcher, Clayton James Camfield, Simón Jiménez, Grace Fisher, Ava Kellner Pence, Anna Grace Stuart, Brandon Williams, Jennifer Thurston, Maggie Keepers, Rachel Arant, and many more.

To my songwriting teachers who are always in my head: Pat Pattison, Mark Simos, Scarlet Keys, Jack Perricone, and the Berklee College of Music.

To my encouraging and skillful editor, quite literally a Godsend: Katie Rios.

To my friends and colleagues just one call away: Hallie Mares Jewett, Jonathan Camacho, Shannon Camacho, Steven VanHorn, Jenny Ayers, Paul Demer, Graham Jones, David Belt, John Heinrich, Emma Fox, Anne-Claire Luna, Caroline Cobb Smith, Clayton Luckie, Todd Agnew and all the Art House Dallas crew, Meg Ammons and the Mercy Tribe crew, Steph Andrews, Ginger Gilhooly, and Dr. John R. Gilhooly.

To my school that digs a deeper place in my heart with every year: Visible Music College.

About the Author

Aryn Michelle Calhoun is a Dallas-based songwriter, recording artist, music professor, and mother of four. A graduate of Southwestern University (classical voice) and Berklee College of Music (songwriting), she records and performs original music under the name Aryn Michelle, with a catalog of acclaimed singles and albums. You can discover more on her artist website at arynmichelle.com.

Aryn also serves as the Songwriting Division Head at Visible Music College, where she teaches and mentors emerging songwriters. She also offers online songwriting resources and editing services through her independent platform, thesonguru.com. *Play, Shape, Create* is her first textbook, written to inspire and equip her students.

www.ingramcontent.com/pod-product-compliance
Lightning Source LLC
LaVergne TN
LVHW050927080826
845145LV00001B/232

* 9 7 8 1 9 6 7 2 6 2 2 2 9 *